Encyclopedia
— *of* —
LIFE SCIENCES

Second Edition

5

Ecology and ecosystems – Fertilizers

Marshall Cavendish
New York • London • Toronto • Sydney

Marshall Cavendish
99 White Plains Road
Tarrytown, New York 10591-9001

www.marshallcavendish.com

© 1996, 2004 Marshall Cavendish Corporation

Created by **The Brown Reference Group plc**

Library of Congress Cataloging-in-Publication Data

Encyclopedia of life sciences / [edited by] Anne O'Daly.—2nd ed.
     p.   cm.
Summary: An illustrated encyclopedia with articles on
agriculture, anatomy, biochemistry, biology, genetics,
medicine, and molecular biology.
Includes bibliographical references (p.   ).
     ISBN 0-7614-7442-0 (set)
     ISBN 0-7614-7447-1 (vol. 5)
     1. Life sciences—Encyclopedias. 2. Biology—Encyclopedias. [1.
Biology—Encyclopedias. 2. Life sciences—Encyclopedias.] I. O'Daly,
Anne, 1966–
     QH302.5 .E53   2003
     570'.3—dc21

                                    2002031157

Printed in Malaysia
Bound in the United States of America

07 06 05 04 03 6 5 4 3 2 1

Artworks by:
Darren Awuah, Bill Botten, Jennie Dooge, Dax Fullbrook,
and Mark Walker.

For The Brown Reference Group:
Project Editors: Caroline Beattie and Lesley Campbell-Wright
Editors: Richard Beatty, Robert Cave, Simon Hall, Rob Houston,
Jim Martin, and Ben Morgan
Designer: Joan Curtis
Picture Researcher: Rebecca Cox
Managing Editor: Bridget Giles
Design Manager: Lynne Ross
Indexer: Kay Ollerenshaw

For Marshall Cavendish:
Project Editor: Joyce Tavolacci
Editorial Director: Paul Bernabeo
Production Manager: Michael Esposito

Title page: fertilized egg of a garfish (Frank Lane Picture
Agency)

PICTURE CREDITS
Biophoto Associates: *584, 597, 627, 628, 651, 673, 687, 695, 698, 699, 700, 704, 707b, 711;* **Bill Botten:** *586, 588, 590, 598, 599, 601, 610, 611, 617, 631, 632t, 664, 666, 667, 668, 669, 672, 674, 676 ,686, 688, 697,691b , 705, 714, 716;* **Corbis:** Lester V. Bergman *592,* Gallo Images *661,* Richard T. Nowitz *636,* Gianni Dagli Orti *637, 638,* Roger Ressmeyer *639,* Joseph Sohm/ChromoSohm Inc. *684;* **Jennie Dooge:** *679, 689, 690, 703t, 707t;* **Frank Lane Picture Agency:** *581, 582, 583, 585, 587, 589, 593, 594, 595, 596, 600, 603, 604, 605, 606, 607, 608, 609, 615, 616, 619, 620, 626, 632b, 642, 643, 647, 648, 649, 650, 655, 656, 657, 658, 659, 665, 670, 675, 680, 685, 691t, 692, 693, 694, 696, 709, 712, 715, 718;* **Getty Images:** *Ross Whitaker 660;* **Imagingbody.com:** *662;* **Marshall Cavendish, London, U.K.:** *652;* **Mary Evans Picture Library:** *602, 621, 629, 633, 644, 653, 671, 678;* **NASA:** *681, 682,* Jet Propulsion Laboratory *683;* **Photodisc:** Geostock *663;* **Science and Society:** Science Musuem *591;* **Science Photo Library:** *613, 614, 618, 622, 623, 624, 625, 635, 645, 702, 703b, 708, 710, 713, 717;* **Telegraph Colour Library:** *640;* **TRH Pictures:** *634.*

CONTENTS

USEFUL INFORMATION

Use this table to convert the English system (or the imperial system), the system of units common in the United States (e.g., inches, miles, quarts), to the metric system (e.g., meters, kilometers, liters) or to convert the metric system to the English system. You can convert one measurement into another by multiplying. For example, to convert centimeters into inches, multiply the number of centimeters by 0.3937. To convert inches into centimeters, multiply the number of inches by 2.54.

To convert	into	multiply by
Acres	Square feet	43,560
	Square yards	4840
	Square miles	0.00156
	Square meters	4046.856
	Hectares	0.40468
Celsius	Fahrenheit	First multiply by 1.8 then add 32
Centimeters	Inches	0.3937
	Feet	0.0328
Cubic cm	Cubic inches	0.06102
Cubic feet	Cubic inches	1728
	Cubic yards	0.037037
	Gallons	7.48
	Cubic meters	0.028317
	Liters	28.32
Cubic inches	Fluid ounces	0.554113
	Cups	0.069264
	Quarts	0.017316
	Gallons	0.004329
	Liters	0.016387
	Milliliters	16.387064
Cubic meters	Cubic feet	35.3145
	Cubic yards	1.30795
Cubic yards	Cubic feet	27
	Cubic meters	0.76456
Cups, fluid	Quarts	0.25
	Pints	0.5
	Ounces	8
	Milliliters	237
	Tablespoons	16
	Teaspoons	48
Fahrenheit	Celsius	First subtract 32 then divide by 1.8
Feet	Centimeters	30.48
	Meters	0.3048
	Kilometers	0.0003
	Inches	12
	Yards	0.3333
	Miles	0.00019
Gallons	Quarts	4
	Pints	8
	Cups	16
	Ounces	128
	Liters	3.785
	Milliliters	3785
	Cubic inches	231
	Cubic feet	0.1337
	Cubic yards	0.00495
	Cubic meters	0.00379
	British gallons	0.8327
Grams	Ounces	0.03527
	Pounds	0.0022
Hectares	Square meters	10,000
	Acres	2.471
Horsepower	Foot-pounds per minute	33,000
	British thermal units (Btu) per minute	42.42
	British thermal units (Btu) per hour	2546
	Kilowatts	0.7457
	Metric horsepower	1.014
Inches	Feet	0.08333

To convert	into	multiply by
Inches (continued)	Yards	0.02778
	Centimeters	2.54
	Meters	0.0254
Kilograms	Grams	1000
	Ounces	35.274
	Pounds	2.2046
	Short tons	0.0011
	Long tons	0.00098
	Metric tons (tonnes)	0.001
Kilometers	Meters	1000
	Miles	0.62137
	Yards	1093.6
	Feet	3280.8
Kilowatts	British thermal units (Btu) per minute	56.9
	Horsepower	1.341
	Metric horsepower	1.397
Kilowatt-hours	British thermal units (Btu)	3413
Knots	Statute miles per hour	1.1508
Leagues	Miles	3
Liters	Milliliters	1000
	Fluid ounces	33.814
	Quarts	1.05669
	British gallons	0.21998
	Cubic inches	61.02374
	Cubic feet	0.13531
Meters	Inches	39.37
	Feet	3.28083
	Yards	1.09361
	Miles	0.000621
	Kilometers	0.001
	Centimeters	100
	Millimeters	1000
Miles	Inches	63,360
	Feet	5280
	Yards	1760
	Meters	1609.34
	Kilometers	1.60934
	Nautical miles	0.8684
Miles nautical, U.S. and International	Statute miles	1.1508
	Feet	6076.115
	Meters	1852
Miles per minute	Feet per second	88
	Knots	52.104
Milliliters	Fluid ounces	0.0338
	Cubic inches	0.061
	Liters	0.001
Millimeters	Centimeters	0.1
	Meters	0.001
	Inches	0.03937
Ounces, avoirdupois	Pounds	0.0625
	Grams	28.34952
	Kilograms	0.0283495
Ounces, fluid	Pints	0.0625
	Quarts	0.03125
	Cubic inches	1.80469
	Cubic feet	0.00104
	Milliliters	29.57353
	Liters	0.02957
Pints, fluid	Ounces, fluid	16
	Quarts, fluid	0.5

To convert	into	multiply by
Pints, fluid (continued)	Cubic inches	28.8745
	Cubic feet	0.01671
	Milliliters	473.17647
	Liters	0.473176
Pounds	Ounces	16
	Grams	453.59237
	Kilograms	0.45359
	Tons	0.0005
	Tons, long	0.000446
	Metric tons (tonnes)	0.0004536
Quarts, fluid	Ounces, fluid	32
	Pints, fluid	2
	Gallons	0.25
	Cubic inches	57.749
	Cubic feet	0.033421
	Liters	0.946358
	Milliliters	946.358
Square centimeters	Square inches	0.155
Square feet	Square inches	144
	Square meters	0.093
	Square yards	0.111
Square inches	Square centimeters	6.452
	Square feet	0.0069
Square kilometers	Hectares	100
	Square meters	1,000,000
	Square miles	0.3861
Square meters	Square feet	10.758
	Square yards	1.196
Square miles	Acres	640
	Square kilometers	2.59
Square yards	Square feet	9
	Square inches	1296
	Square meters	0.836
Tablespoons	Ounces, fluid	0.5
	Teaspoons	3
	Milliliters	14.7868
Teaspoons	Ounces, fluid	0.16667
	Tablespoons	0.3333
	Milliliters	4.9289
Tons, long	Pounds	2240
	Kilograms	1016.047
	Short tons	1.12
	Metric tons (tonnes)	1.016
Tons, short	Pounds	2000
	Kilograms	907.185
	Long tons	0.89286
	Metric tonnes	0.907
Tons, metric (tonnes)	Pounds	2204.62
	Kilograms	1000
	Long tons	0.984206
	Short tons	1.10231
Watts	British thermal units (Btu) per hour	3.415
	Horsepower	0.00134
Yards	Inches	36
	Feet	3
	Miles	0.0005681
	Centimeters	91.44
	Meters	0.9144

ECOLOGY AND ECOSYSTEMS

Ecology is the study of the interrelationships of organisms and their environment

E cology is the study of relationships of organisms —or groups of organisms—with each other and with their environment. The word *ecology* comes from the Greek *oikos*, which means "house" or "place to live." People have always taken an interest in their environment: ancient Chinese and Native American cultures have described the relationships between living organisms for thousands of years. There was no accepted scientific word to describe the study of organisms interacting with their environment until 1869, when German zoologist Ernst Haeckel coined the term *ecology*. Influenced by Charles Darwin's book *On the Origin of Species*, he hoped to further develop a science-based worldview within biology.

Looking at the biosphere
Ecologists study the interaction of the biotic (living) and the abiotic (nonliving) elements of the biosphere (Earth's land, water, and atmosphere in which organisms and people live) that support life. Ecologists aim to understand the various factors that influence the distribution of living organisms. The life-support system of the biosphere comprises a vast network of separate but interlinked systems whose history can be traced back to the first microorganisms on Earth.

An aerial view of tropical rain forest and open land in Brazil. The rain forest contains the largest number of organisms and the greatest variety of species on land. The complex interactions between these organisms provide a rich area of study for the ecologist.

CONNECTIONS

- Restoration ecology, which aims to restore damaged ecosystems to their original state, is an important area of **CONSERVATION**.

- The complex interactions within an ecosystem are often represented in **FOOD WEBS**.

- Organisms within an ecosystem may be in **COMPETITION** for resources or they may live in a relationship called **SYMBIOSIS**.

CORE FACTS

- The study of the interrelationships of organisms and their environment is called ecology.
- Earth's landmass may be classified into three types of habitats: developed, cultivated, and natural sites.
- An ecosystem is a complex system made up of both organisms and their nonliving environment, linked by a variety of ecological relationships.
- Energy flow through an ecosystem is always one way and is eventually dissipated as heat.
- Nutrients, such as carbon, nitrogen, and phosphorus, cycle through ecosystems.
- In all ecosystems microorganisms are as essential as any animal or plant.
- Biotic pyramids show the interdependence of all life-forms and demonstrate the upward flow of energy through the levels of the ecosystem.

ALDO LEOPOLD

Best known as the author of *Sand County Almanac*, U.S. ecologist Aldo Leopold (1886–1948) brought together in that book the three themes that directed his work: preservation of natural resources, promotion of the beauty of the environment, and moral standards governing the use of the environment. The book is based on a lifetime's work devoted to wildlife management, conservation economics, and wilderness preservation.

Leopold's ideas about wildlife management were based on balance and long-term stability in the environment. From 1909 to 1928, he worked for the U.S. Forest Service and was one of the leaders in the new profession of forestry. In 1931 he made one of the first studies of game population in the United States, and in 1933 he was appointed professor of wildlife management at the University of Wisconsin. Leopold was always interested in the ethical, economic, and philosophical aspects of his work, and he published a series of articles on environmental ethics during the 1930s.

DISCOVERERS

A population is a group of organisms of the same species living in a given area. The population of bees (shown below) from a single hive constitutes a population.

Earth's earliest atmosphere had no oxygen and was subjected to lethal ultraviolet radiation, poisonous gases, and extreme temperature variations. Over millions of years, the earliest microorganisms (archebacteria) interacted with Earth's atmosphere to change it into one containing oxygen. Eventually green plants spread across Earth. These plants could make their own food through photosynthesis, could produce oxygen as a by-product, and were themselves food for a variety of living organisms.

A view from the air shows how ecological systems join together, like the pieces of a giant jigsaw puzzle. Most noticeable are bodies of water, which

cover more than 70 percent of Earth's surface. Bodies of water purify the air, moderate the temperature, and assimilate waste. Broad categories of environments include developed sites, cultivated sites, and natural sites. Developed sites include cities, industries, transportation corridors (roads, railways, and airports), and derelict sites. Cultivated sites comprise croplands, managed woods and forests, and artificial lakes and ponds. Natural sites cover wilderness areas, unregimented woodlands and forests, prairies, mountains, natural streams, lakes, rivers, and oceans.

Some ecologists examine the types and quantities of energy used by each type of environment. People in developed areas, called fuel-powered sites, use mostly fossil fuels (coal, oil, natural gas), which took millions of years to accumulate. Although developed sites take up only a small proportion of Earth's landscape, the energy consumed in them and the waste heat and pollution created there adversely affect the other two types of environments. An urban-industrial area uses up to one thousand times more energy per year than the same area of forest.

Cultivated areas called subsidized solar-powered sites rely primarily on the Sun for energy. Solar power is supplemented by human labor, machines, fertilizers, and pesticides. Fossil fuels, used for machines and to make fertilizers and pesticides, affect the other two environments by producing further waste heat and pollution. Moreover, wind and runoff water carry dust and residues of fertilizers and pesticides to the other environments.

Agricultural sites and natural sites are critical life-support systems for people, animals, plants, and microorganisms. Agricultural sites provide food. Natural sites recycle water, assimilate waste, and purify the air. Developed sites where people live also provide habitat for a variety of species, such as peregrine falcons, raccoons, and squirrels.

Varied ecological perspectives

Ecology is concerned with living organisms, and in their study of the complex relationships involved, ecologists cross boundaries into other areas of study. For example, Arthur Tansley (1871–1955), a British botanist who founded the world's first ecological society, encouraged the study of geology and psychology.

Several areas of research that contribute significantly to ecologists' understanding are subspecialities of biology: genetics, physiology, botany, microbiology, and zoology. Genetics is the study of how the information needed to make an individual is stored and transmitted. Physiology looks at the vital processes of living organisms. Botany deals with the structure of plants, the function of their parts, their places of growth, and their classification. Microbiology is the study of microorganisms. Zoology looks at animal life and the classification of animals.

Ecologists categorize systems in terms of organizational arrangements. A population is a group of organisms of the same interbreeding species living

*The restoration ecologists who restored a segment of the tallgrass prairie in Wisconsin were able to reintroduce the American buffalo (*Bison bison*).*

within a single environment. A biotic community includes all the different populations living in a particular area. An ecological system (or ecosystem) encompasses a biotic community and its associated nonliving environment, functioning together.

Ecosystems are part of larger regional units called biomes, such as an ocean or a grassland region. Biogeographic regions are the major continents and oceans, each with its own particular living organisms. The biosphere includes all of Earth's ecosystems functioning together (see BIOSPHERE).

For example, moving from the smallest to the largest, an ecologist might examine an organism, a population, an ecosystem, a biome, a biogeographic region, or the biosphere (see BIOGEOGRAPHY).

While some ecologists broaden their area of study to cross the boundaries of other disciplines, some narrow their attention to subspecialties of ecology. Population ecologists, for example, are interested in numerical data about such characteristics as density, birthrate, death rate, age distribution, and rate of growth of the population as a whole. Researchers are also interested in a population's genetic characteristics in relationship to its ecological system, including adaptability, fitness to reproduce, and persistence (the likelihood of leaving descendants, considered over a long period of time).

A community ecologist might look at relationships between different organisms. Attention might be directed toward a minor community, which more or less depends on neighboring groups, or a major community, which is of sufficient size and organizational completeness to be independent, needing only to receive its energy from the Sun.

The more complex the system under study, the more complex the equipment and procedures needed. For example, a simple sweep net might be all that is needed for an insect study of a salt marsh,

but researchers examining marine communities in a coastal bay, perhaps to determine the effects of toxic substances, might need sophisticated equipment to sample the different levels in a given depth of water.

Restoration ecology

Restoration ecologists try to return ecosystems to their former states. For example, in 1935 a group of American Conservation Corps workers replanted tallgrass prairie plants in an abandoned area of agricultural land in Wisconsin. Their work resulted in 60 acres (24 hectares) of restored prairie land and was one of the first efforts in habitat restoration.

Habitat restoration is one of the most controversial areas of applied ecology. As more land is lost to agriculture and development, there is increasing pressure to return some areas to their natural state. The efforts to protect endangered plants and animals by preserving their habitats has helped emphasize the importance of habitat restoration.

Restoration can be divided into two types, depending on the level of restoration achieved and the ecological factors considered. In many cases restoration simply refers to the revegetation of a site. Plants are introduced to an area to stabilize soil or to create an economic resource, such as timber. The greater ecological challenge lies in true restoration, in which ecologists try to reconstruct a habitat for plant and animal communities. It might involve preparing the soil, removing nonnative species, and assessing the reinvasion of animal species over time. The success of these efforts varies but continues to improve as ecologists learn more about natural ecosystems.

Ecosystems

An ecosystem is a complex, self-sustaining system of organisms living in communities that interact with

RACHEL CARSON

When Rachel Carson's book *Silent Spring* was published in 1962, the chemical industry's representatives characterized her as a crank and a "health nut." However, she was the first to draw attention to the ecological disaster wrought by DDT (dichlorodiphenyltrichloroethane; see CARSON, RACHEL LOUISE; DDT).

DDT was one of a range of pesticides developed during World War II that was designed to kill insects, unwanted plants, and fungus blights such as mold. DDT worked extremely well on its targets. However, it also killed birds, fish, and small animals. Unaffected by Sun, rain, bacteria, or acids in soil, DDT remained poisonous for years. After being eaten, it was stored in body tissues and passed through the food chain. When a friend complained that several birds died in her yard following a pesticide spraying by a mosquito-control plane, Carson became intensely interested in the effect DDT had on ecological systems.

A quiet, determined woman, Carson stood up to her critics on behalf of the environment. As a small child, she had written stories and drawn pictures of wildlife and flowers she discovered near the family farm in Springdale, Pennsylvania. Her plans to become a writer changed after she took a biology class in her second year of college—at Pennsylvania College for Women (now Chatham College). Although science was virtually closed to women in the 1930s and few women were admitted to graduate school, Carson won a full scholarship to obtain a master's degree in marine zoology at Johns Hopkins University in Baltimore, Maryland. Her degree helped her find temporary work, writing radio scripts for the U.S. Bureau of Fisheries (later renamed the U.S. Fish and Wildlife Service). In 1938 she became the editor in chief for the agency's publications. *Silent Spring* inspired many readers to become involved in the battles to protect specific ecological systems and the overall environment. The book eventually had an impact on government policy, but Rachel Carson died of cancer in 1964, nine years before the U.S. government banned the use of DDT in the United States.

DISCOVERERS

metabolize inorganic compounds such as hydrogen, ammonia, and hydrogen sulfide. The other component is heterotrophic (other nourishing) and has the capacity to rearrange and decompose materials synthesized by the autotrophs. The network of energy transfers linking autotrophs and heterotrophs is called a food web (see FOOD WEBS).

Two abiotic (nonliving) functions make ecosystems operational: energy flow and biogeochemical cycles (see below). Energy flows from the Sun into a biotic community, where the combination of energy, water, and carbon dioxide in the presence of chlorophyll creates carbohydrates and oxygen. Carbohydrates are broken down by cellular respiration to provide energy for the cells' activities (see CARBOHYDRATES; CELL BIOLOGY).

Energy may be stored and used later, but energy flow is a one-way path. Once used, energy cannot become sunlight again to make food. If food production is to continue, sunlight must continue to flow into the system.

Because some energy in a closed system is always unavailable as entropy (disordered energy: see ENERGY), no transformation, such as from light to food, can be 100 percent efficient. To survive and prosper, ecosystems, whether natural or human-made, need high-quality energy, storage capacity for periods when input is insufficient, and the means to dispose of heat. If energy flow through a city or a forest is reduced or the dispersal of heat is insufficient, the ecosystem of the city or the forest itself becomes disorderly.

Although energy cannot be reused, matter (the material from which living organisms are made) can. Biogeochemical cycles are the paths chemical substances follow in passing between organisms and the environment—water, for example, cycles by evaporating and falling back to Earth as rain or snow. About 24 nutrients vital to organisms (such as carbon, nitrogen, phosphorus, calcium, potassium, and others) are distributed throughout an ecosystem. They exist in large, not-easily-available pools and in small, active, available pools and generally cycle slowly from unavailable to available amounts (see CARBON CYCLE; NITROGEN CYCLE).

Ecological models

To cope with the complexities of ecosystems, ecologists create simplified models. To study a large ecosystem, such as a lake, an ecologist might use one of two simplified approaches. The holological (from the Greek *holos*, "whole") method examines the inputs and outputs of a large ecosystem by treating it as a "black box," a unit whose function is considered without specifying its internal contents. The merological (from *meros*, "part") method examines parts of the system and then tries to construct a whole from them.

Another approach to producing a simplified model is for ecologists to build a micro-ecosystem. This type of system ranges from

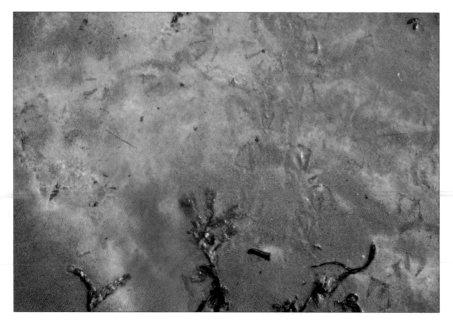

Bacterial growth (bloom) on a sandy beach. By breaking down organic material to provide energy, bacteria play a vital ecological role.

each other and with the nonliving components of their environment. Ecological systems have two major biotic (living) parts. One part is autotrophic (self-nourishing): it has the ability to manufacture food from simple inorganic substances such as carbon dioxide and water. Photoautotrophs—plants and some algae—make food using energy from the Sun (see PHOTOSYNTHESIS); chemoautotrophs closed systems that require only energy from solar radiation (such as a bottle garden) to complex arrangements regulating the inflow and outflow of nutrients and organisms.

Small worlds

A good example of a microecosystem is the balanced aquarium, which is set up to achieve an approximate balance of food and gases. Amateur attempts to set up balanced aquariums usually fail because the fish are overcrowded. To succeed, the ratio of fish to water and plants must be kept low. Snails must also be in the tank to convert some wastes into nourishment for the plants, otherwise they would become poisonous.

The search for a balanced ecosystem has important implications for the development of space travel. Using a variation of the balanced aquarium and with the long-range goal of developing complex ecosystems to support human colonies in space, Joe Hanson, a scientist with NASA's Jet Propulsion Laboratory at the California Institute of Technology, set up a series of closed micro-ecosystems in 1980.

In each of several sealed glass flasks, Hanson enclosed about ⅕ gallon (750 ml) of artificially pre-pared sea water, 16 small tropical red shrimps, assorted algae, and many varieties of bacteria, viruses, and microscopic animals.

Inside the flasks, the algae produced oxygen and food to sustain the shrimps and other animal life. The animal waste provided carbon dioxide and fer-tilizer for the algae. The cycle was driven by energy entering the flasks during 12 hours of artificial sunlight provided by lamps.

The closed aquatic communities sustained them-selves for more than 15 months. All flasks began with similar amounts of water and similar mixtures of algae. In a few flasks the shrimps died, but in most they thrived. The algae survived in all the flasks, even in those in which the shrimps had died.

A typical home aquarium. In theory, a sealed aquarium containing a balance of plants, fish, and microorganisms can exist indefinitely.

THE HIDDEN WORLD OF MICROORGANISMS

Ecosystems include the hidden world of microorganisms. That world was the subject of *Microcosmus* (1986), a book by Lynn Margulis, professor of biology at Boston University, and science writer Dorion Sagan. They pointed out that microbes—including microorganisms, germs, bugs, protozoans, and bacteria—are the building blocks of life (the symbiotic theory), occupying and being indispensable to every known living structure on Earth (see CELL BIOLOGY).

During the first two billion years of their existence, bacteria transformed Earth. They created all of life's essential chemical systems: fermentation, photosynthesis, respiration, and the "fixation" of nitrogen gas from the air.

Twentieth-century discoveries emphasize the importance of microorganisms. Discovering the structure of DNA in 1953 made it possible to understand how a living cell can make a copy of itself. Cells can also mutate, which increases their chance to survive environmental change. For more than a half century, scientists have observed that bacteria routinely and rapidly transfer bits of genetic material to other individuals. At any given time, each bacterium can use visiting genes from very different strains to perform functions not possible with its own DNA. Some visiting genetic bits can be moved easily into the genetic apparatus of people and other animals.

Within a few years, bacteria, composed of cells with no nucleus, can adjust to change on a worldwide scale that would take cells with a nucleus a million years. The rapid adjustment of the world of microorganisms ultimately affects every living organism.

Mutation and bacterial genetic transfer alone do not account for the evolution of all life-forms present on Earth. A third discovery completes the picture. Scientists have observed mitochondria—tiny membrane-bound organelles—in the cells of animals, plants, fungi, and protists (a variety of organisms including amoebas). Without mitochondria, most cells with a nucleus cannot use oxygen. Scientists suspect that ancient bacteria took up residence inside other microorganisms, where they provided waste disposal and food in return for food and shelter. Such merged organisms evolved into more complex oxygen-breathing forms of life (see CELL BIOLOGY). Symbiosis, the way different organisms adapt to living together, is a major power for change on Earth (see SYMBIOSIS AND COMMENSALISM).

A century before scientists learned about DNA, genetic transfer, and symbiosis, English naturalist Charles Darwin (1809–1882) wrote, "Each living creature must be looked upon as a host of self-propagating organisms, inconceivably minute and as numerous as the stars in the heaven."

A CLOSER LOOK

The biotic pyramid

A well-known model, the biotic pyramid, intended to help the public understand why they should care about the wellbeing of the biosphere, was presented by ecologist Aldo Leopold in a landmark address to a joint meeting of the American Foresters and the Ecological Society in 1939. If the public understood the model, Leopold said, "the layman might be less insistent on utility as a prerequisite for conservation, more hospitable to the 'useless' cohabitants of the Earth, more tolerant of values over and above profit, food, sport, or tourist bait."

The biotic pyramid (below) shows how ecosystems work. It looks like a series of blocks piled one on top of another, each representing an organism (or group of organisms) dependent on the one below for nourishment. Each level in the pyramid is called a trophic level. In the upward energy flow from one level to the next, up to 90 percent of energy may be lost as heat, and so each block is smaller than the one below. For example, 22,000 pounds (10,000 kg) of grass should support around 2,200 pounds (1000 kg) of crickets, which in turn should support 220 pounds (100 kg) of frogs, which support one heron weighing 22 pounds (10 kg). This type of pyramid, which includes weights of organisms, is called a pyramid of biomass (an estimate of the total amount of living material.)

Sometimes a pyramid of biomass appears to be upside down, with more primary consumers than primary producers (see the diagram below left). At first sight, this pyramid appears to be impossible. However, the inverted pyramid is found in situations in which the producers reproduce very rapidly, despite being eaten by the consumers. The trophic levels represent the rate at which biomass is being produced. Even though there may be few producers at a given time, the rate at which they are reproducing is much greater than the rate of biomass reproduction for the primary consumers.

A similar biotic pyramid can be constructed for the numbers of organisms at each level, called a pyramid of numbers, in which the number of organisms in each trophic level gets smaller as the pyramid is ascended. Another type of pyramid can be constructed for the rate of energy flow from one level to the next. The rate of energy flow is usually expressed in Calories (see CALORIE). This pyramid shows how rapidly energy is lost at each level and makes it clear why the number of links in a food chain is usually less than six. Unlike pyramids of biomass, a pyramid of energy is always larger at the bottom than at the top.

These are simplified ideas. The pyramid of the whole living world is a complex tangle of food chains dependent on cooperation and competition among the links. If there is a change in any one part, many other parts must adjust accordingly.

M. DICANIO

A pyramid of biomass showing the trophic levels of a food chain in an area of grassland (top), and an inverted pyramid of biomass showing what happens when the lowest trophic level has a high reproductive rate (bottom).

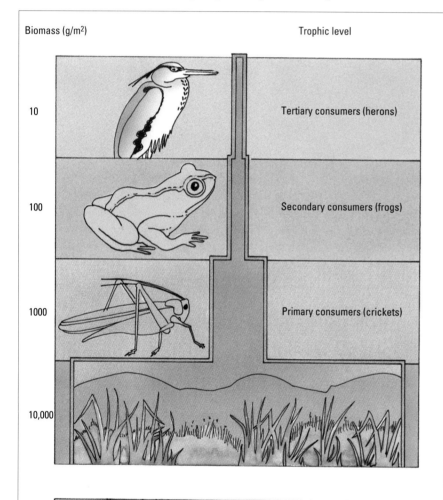

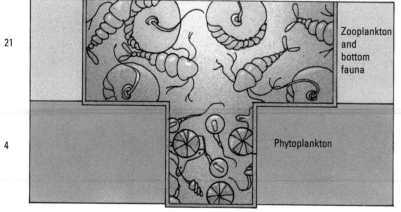

See also: ADAPTATION; BACTERIA; BIOGEOGRAPHY; BIOMES AND HABITATS; BIOSPHERE; CALORIE; CARBOHYDRATES; CARBON CYCLE; CARSON, RACHEL LOUISE; CELL BIOLOGY; CHAOS, ORDER, AND COMPLEXITY; DDT; ENERGY; GAIA HYPOTHESIS; NITROGEN CYCLE; PHOTOSYNTHESIS; POLLUTION; SOIL ECOLOGY.

Further reading:

Carson, R. L., 1994. *Silent Spring*. Boston: Houghton Mifflin.
Flader, S. L., and J. B. Callicott, eds. 1991. *The River of the Mother of God and Other Essays by Aldo Leopold*. Madison: University of Wisconsin Press.
Morin, P. J. 1999. *Community Ecology*. Boston: Blackwell Science.
Vogt, K. A., J. C. Gordon, J. P. Wargo, and D. Vogt, 1997. *Ecosytems: Balancing Science with Managment*. Berlin: Springer Verlag.

EGGS

Eggs are the mature, unfertilized
female reproductive cells of plants
and animals

The fertilized egg of a garfish, shortly before hatching (magnification x10). The egg has 60 to 80 sticky filaments, which help to attach it to seaweed and rocks.

The egg, or ovum (plural, ova), is a specialized reproductive cell that does two things: it transmits genetic information from the female to the next generation, and it constructs an embryo once the mature egg is fertilized.

Eggs, which tend to be relatively large compared with nonreproductive cells, have some unique characteristics that help them carry out these tasks. The mature egg contains storage material to nourish the developing embryo, structures that enable it to manufacture proteins rapidly, a protective outer coating, and granules that prevent more than the desired number of sperm cells from penetrating the egg. Mature eggs, in contrast with mature sperm, cannot move under their own power.

EGG CELLS IN ANIMALS

Even before a female animal is born, during her development as an embryo, she begins to store egg cells. The earliest precursors of eggs are called primordial germ cells. These cells are diploid, that is, they contain two sets of each chromosome: one set from the mother and one from the father. In people the diploid number of chromosomes is 46.

The primordial germ cells migrate to the ovary during the development of the embryo. Once in the ovary, they begin the process, called oogenesis, of becoming mature egg cells. The germ cells begin to multiply rapidly through a process called mitosis (see CELL BIOLOGY). Before mitosis starts, the cell makes a duplicate copy of each chromosome and then splits to form two identical daughter cells. The daughter cells are now called oogonia. These germ

cell descendents give rise to oocytes (immature eggs), which produce gametes (in this case, mature eggs). While the primordial germ cells are small and irregularly shaped, oogonia are large and spherical. The oogonium nucleus is very large, leaving little room for the cytoplasm and organelles.

The beginning of meiosis

Meiosis is a form of nuclear division that takes place in eukaryotic cells to produce reproductive cells (gametes: eggs and sperm) that have half the amount of genetic material (deoxyribonucleic acid, or DNA) of the original cell. Meiosis involves two divisions of the germ cell nucleus, meiosis I and meiosis II, which give rise to four gametes (sex cells).

An oogonium entering meiosis is called a primary oocyte. The primary oocyte enters an early period of the first stage of meiosis, called prophase I. The oocyte can remain suspended in this phase for days or years, according to species. In human females, for example, the primary oocytes remain in this state of readiness until just before ovulation begins (from the age of about 12 years, when a girl enters puberty) to about 50 years (when a woman reaches menopause).

During this time the oocyte prepares itself for the very early development of the fertilized egg. The eggs of amphibians and other vertebrates that develop outside the mother's body, in a sometimes hostile environment, need to accumulate and store large amounts of materials that will enable the fertilized egg to develop rapidly before being eaten by predators or falling victim to any number of other mishaps. The most obvious result is a tremendous increase in the size of the oocyte: the oocyte of one species of frog, for example, increases 25,000-fold in volume. However, whatever its size, an egg remains a single cell.

Amphibians and fish, which produce hundreds, thousands, or millions of eggs at a time, maintain a pool of oogonia throughout their lifetimes. They generate a new batch of oocytes from this pool each year. In species that produce fewer eggs, including humans, the oogonia divide at some point in

CONNECTIONS

● Egg cells are produced by both animals and plants. Eggs that have matured are ready for **FERTILIZATION**, after which the **EMBRYO** begins to develop.

● An egg contains all the **GENETIC** information needed from the mother to help make a new individual.

CORE FACTS

■ No matter how large, an egg is a single cell.
■ The human female is born with between 700,000 and 2 million oocytes (immature eggs). Of these, about 40,000 survive to puberty, but only about 400 mature into ova.
■ Yolk can make up as much as 95 percent of bird, reptile, and amphibian eggs, but in mammalian ova it is less than 5 percent.
■ Plants exist in alternating generations, gametophyte and sporophyte; eggs are produced by the gametophyte.

MEIOSIS

In meiosis two distinct cell divisions take place (see CELL BIOLOGY). Each chromosome in the oocyte entering the first stage of meiosis consists of a joined pair of duplicate chromatids. In the first meiotic division, the homologous chromosome pairs (one from the mother, one from the father) come together and exchange genetic material in a process called crossing over. The homologous pairs separate into two daughter cells that have only one copy of each chromosome. Each chromosome still consists of two identical sister chromatids, so the second meiotic division separates these sister chromatids into different cells. The result is four haploid cells, each having a single copy of each chromosome. At fertilization the haploid sex cells produce a diploid embryo.

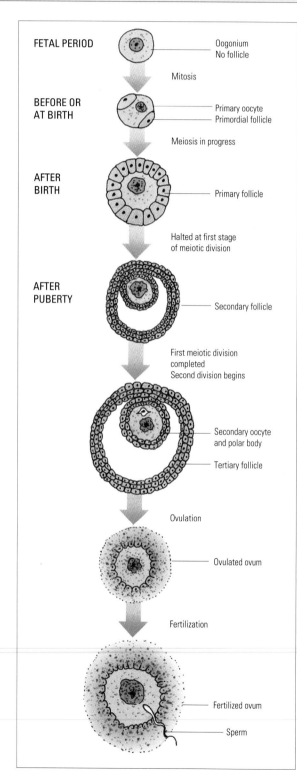

The principal stages in human oogenesis: the development of the cell from a diploid oogonium through the formation of the follicle and ovulation to the moment of fertilization.

development, to form a pool of oocytes. During human oogenesis, which takes place between the second and fifth month of the fetus's development, the population of oogonia increases from a few thousand to about seven million. Many of these cells die, however, even before the baby is born; a human female is born with between 700,000 and 2 million primary oocytes. Of this number, only about 40,000 survive until puberty, and only about 400 are released (through the process of ovulation) in the course of a woman's lifetime.

The essential yolk

In eggs that develop outside the body of the mother, much of the large size of the oocyte is due to the yolk, which can account for more than 95 percent of the volume of the egg. Yolk is a general term, referring to the major storage material of the egg, which is rich in protein and lipids.

The process of depositing yolk in the oocyte is called vitellogenesis. In amphibians vitellogenesis begins each year during the mating season, as a result of hormonal messages from the hypothalamus in the brain, the pituitary gland, and follicle cells of the ovary (see ENDOCRINE SYSTEMS).

In most vertebrates and insects, the materials that make up the yolk are not made in the oocyte but in other parts of the body, especially the liver. These materials, which are made up of large molecules, are transported to the oocyte through the bloodstream. The molecules cannot penetrate the membrane of the oocyte, so they are taken into the cell by a process called pinocytosis (see CELL BIOLOGY). In this process tiny regions of the cell membrane move inward to form pockets, which gather in the molecules outside the cell and then pinch back on themselves to form an envelope (called a vesicle) containing the molecule.

The molecules inside the vesicles organize into large crystalline structures (ordered arrays in which the molecules are assembled at regular distances and in the same orientation), called yolk platelets. The yolk platelets accumulate from the edge of the cell's interior to near the nucleus. By the time the egg reaches maturity, the yolk platelets are larger and more tightly packed at one end of the egg, called the vegetal pole. Some animals accumulate more yolk than others: the eggs of birds and reptiles, for example, contain proportionally much more yolk than those of amphibians. Birds and reptiles develop to a more mature form inside the egg, whereas amphibians are hatched in the larval form and continue to develop outside the egg.

Mammalian embryos develop within the mother's body and get all the nutrients they need from her, so the oocytes do not need to store large amounts of yolk to nourish the egg after fertilization. Yolk proteins make up less than 5 percent of the total volume of mammalian eggs.

The oocyte stockpiles other materials during the meiotic prophase to help the embryo develop rapidly. In the nucleus oocytes steadily synthesize nucleic acids involved in protein synthesis (ribo-nucleic acid, or RNA); the "lampbrush" chromosomes that produce the RNA are easy to see under a microscope, especially in more primitive vertebrates. Lampbrush chromosomes are so named because their many loops of spread-out DNA (which are busy making RNA molecules) resemble the brushes, similar to bottlebrushes, that were once used to clean the glass chimneys of oil lamps.

After it is fertilized, the egg uses the proteins produced by the RNA as building blocks when it is going through the first of several divisions. The oocyte also forms cortical granules, found just under the plasma membrane of the cell. These granules release enzymes when the egg is fertilized, which toughen the egg's coating to ensure that no more sperm can enter. The oocyte also accumulates ribosomes, which are RNA-protein complexes used in protein synthesis, carbohydrates, and lipids (stored as oily droplets with a surrounding protein coat).

Accessory cells and layers
The oocytes of most animals develop with the help of accessory cells. In invertebrates, including insects, jellyfish, and earthworms, the accessory cells are called nurse cells. In vertebrates, as in the case of humans and mammals, the accessory cells are called follicle cells.

Nurse cells come from the same oogonia that give rise to the oocyte. The oogonium in a fruit fly called *Drosophila* divides mitotically four times, giving rise to 16 daughter cells. One of the 16 cells becomes the oocyte; the rest become nurse cells. The nurse cells are connected to the oocyte by a bridge that connects the cytoplasm of each cell. Although the nurse cells do not make yolk, they make much of the other material that the developing oocyte needs, including RNA and ribosomes. With the help of the nurse cells, the oocyte can double its volume every two hours. (Much genetic research has been carried out using *Drosophila* because some of its chromosomes are very large and easily observed under the microscope.)

In vertebrates the oocyte is surrounded by layers of ovary cells that form a primary follicle. The oocyte and the follicle cells form connections that allow the exchange of materials essential for the growth of the oocyte. The follicle cells also secrete a factor responsible for maintaining the oocytes in their arrested phase of meiosis.

Eggs of all species have an envelope, made mostly of glycoproteins, surrounding the cell. In mammals this membrane, called the zona pellucida, contains sperm receptors and other components important in fertilization. Other vertebrate and invertebrate eggs have a vitelline (yolk) layer. This layer helps protect the cells from mechanical damage, and in some species it acts as a barrier to sperm from an animal of a different species. The eggs of other animals form yet other types of layers. For example, as frog eggs pass from the ovary to the tube that carries them outside the body, they acquire

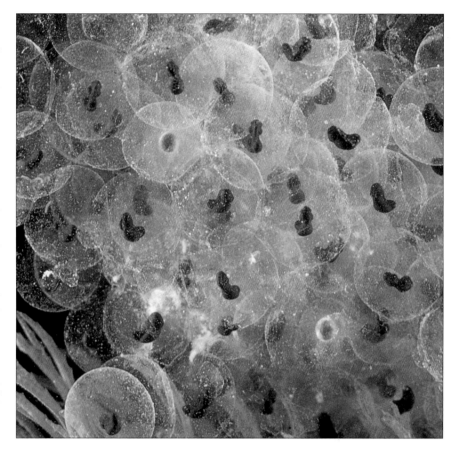

several layers of a gel-like coating. The eggs of insects are surrounded by a tough coat called the chorion. The egg white, shell membrane, and hard shell of bird eggs are all formed after fertilization.

Frog eggs, showing the gel-like coating, which helps protect them from damage.

Increasing genetic diversity
At sexual maturity, the oocytes begin their next stage of development, egg maturation. In humans a few of the follicles begin to grow dramatically at puberty in response to hormones secreted by the pituitary gland and the follicle cells. The follicle presses against the ovary, and the oocyte begins to complete the meiotic division begun so many years earlier.

First, the chromosome pairs (one inherited from the father and one from the mother) line up next to each other. They frequently cross over, exchanging DNA in the process. In this way, some of the DNA from the X chromosome ends up on the father's chromosome, and vice versa. The result is increased genetic diversity (see the box opposite).

Then the two chromosomes in a pair are pulled to opposite sides of the cell, and the cell splits into two daughter cells. However, this time, the daughter cells are not equal. One, the secondary oocyte, is destined to become a mature egg cell. The other, smaller and nonfunctional, is called a polar body. The secondary oocyte has the diploid number of chromosomes: because it duplicated the DNA content before meiosis started, it still contains twice as much DNA as it needs. Therefore, the oocyte must undergo a second meiotic division.

In most mammals, the second meiotic division occurs only after the egg is fertilized by a sperm cell. Other animals complete the division before the process of ovulation. In the second meiotic division, the sister chromatids separate to produce two daughter cells. Again the daughter cells are unequal in size, with one of the two destined to become a nonfunctional polar body.

After the first meiotic division, a hormone causes the oocyte to be released from its follicle, signaling the beginning of ovulation. In humans ovulation occurs about every 29 days. Most mammals ovulate at specific times of the year in response to internal circannual rhythms and environmental cues (see BIORHYTHMS). Rabbits and mink ovulate in response to sexual intercourse itself.

Although as many as 50 oocytes may begin the maturation process in each human menstrual cycle, normally only one reaches the point of ovulation; the rest die. Multiple births result when more than one egg matures and is fertilized successfully. Scientists believe that the follicle capable of producing the most estrogen is the one that prevails. The remaining primary oocytes stay in their arrested state of development until the next menstrual cycle, when some of them will go through the same process.

The mature oocyte, now called an ovum, is ready for fertilization (see FERTILIZATION). The human ovum remains healthy and ready for fertilization for only about 24 hours.

EGG CELLS IN PLANTS

Egg production in plants can vary widely, depending on the type of plant. Primitive plants, such as mosses, lower vascular plants (see FERNS AND FERN ALLIES), and gymnosperms (see CONIFERS; GYMNOSPERMS) produce eggs in a structure called the archegonium (see the diagram below). Angiosperms (the familiar plants, shrubs, and trees; see ANGIOSPERMS) produce eggs in a specialized embryonic sac.

All plants exist in two alternating generations: the gametophyte generation, which is haploid (having a single set of unpaired chromosomes), and the sporophyte generation, which is diploid (having a paired set of chromosomes). The sporophyte is the form that has roots, leaves, and a stem: in short, the form that comes to mind when one thinks of a plant. The gametophyte generation arises from cells in the sporophyte, called

sporangia, that divide meiotically. The egg arises from the gametophyte generation.

The reproductive organ of the flowering plant is the flower itself. At the center of the flower is the carpel. At the base of the carpel is the ovary, which contains one or more ovules. The ovules are the site of egg production.

Early in the development of the ovules, a cell begins to enlarge and differentiate. This cell is called a megasporocyte. It divides meiotically to form four megaspores, although only one survives. The surviving megaspore then divides mitotically so that it produces eight nuclei, all held together in a common embryonic sac. Three of these nuclei, called the antipodals, are gathered at the top of the sac; two, called the polar nuclei, are paired in the center, and three gather at the bottom . One of the nuclei at the bottom is the egg; the other two are called synergids (see EMBRYO).

The antipodal nuclei eventually disintegrate. However, after fertilization the polar nuclei, along with a sperm nucleus, form a specialized tissue called the endosperm. The endosperm, like the yolk of an animal cell, provides the growing embryo with essential nutrients. The synergids contain a large number of organelles and ribosomes, suggesting that their job is to make proteins and other materials. Scientists also believe that the synergids secrete a chemical that directs the pollen tube (the origin of the sperm) to grow in the direction of the ovule. Now the egg is ready for fertilization by the sperm nuclei.

S. LATTA

See also: AMPHIBIANS; ANGIOSPERMS; BIORHYTHMS; CELL BIOLOGY; CONIFERS; DNA; ENDOCRINE SYSTEMS; FERNS AND FERN ALLIES; GENETICS; GYMNOSPERMS; POLLINATION; REPRODUCTION; REPRODUCTIVE SYSTEMS.

Further reading:

Carlson, B. 1999. *Human Embryology and Developmental Biology*. 2nd ed. St Louis: Mosby.
Deeming, D. C., ed. 2002. *Avian Incubation: Behaviour, Environment and Evolution*. Oxford: Oxford University Press.
Parker, S. and A. Ganeri, Wallace, H. 2001. *Survival and Change: Life Processes*. Crystal Lake, Ill.: Heinemann Library.

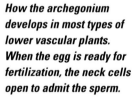

How the archegonium develops in most types of lower vascular plants. When the egg is ready for fertilization, the neck cells open to admit the sperm.

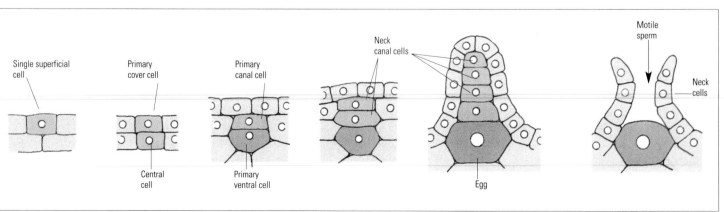

EHRLICH, PAUL

Paul Ehrlich was a renowned bacteriologist and pharmacologist who developed a cure for syphilis

Sometimes referred to as the father of chemotherapy, Paul Ehrlich was a pioneer of modern medicine. Although chemotherapy is now closely associated with cancer, during Ehrlich's lifetime chemotherapy was simply a new way of fighting fatal diseases. Ehrlich spent many years researching the effects of chemicals on various tissues and developing his theory that cells had side-chains, or specific receptor molecules, on their surfaces. He was also a brilliant hematologist. His early work staining and identifying different types of white blood cells contributed to his winning a Nobel Prize in 1908, but his greatest success was finding a cure for syphilis.

Early life

Paul Ehrlich was born on March 14, 1854, in Strehlen, Silesia, Prussia (now Germany). He was the only son and fourth child of Ismar Erhlich and Rosa Weigart. At school he was not a particularly outstanding student. However, he developed a strong interest in chemistry and biology, no doubt encouraged by his cousin and close friend Carl Weigart, a distinguished pathologist, who was nine years his senior. Ehrlich attended several universities, including Breslau, Strasbourg, and Leipzig, eventually obtaining a medical degree in 1878.

As a student he experimented in his cousin's laboratory with dyes that could be used to stain particular cells and microorganisms. His skill in interpreting the reactions between these dyes and biological materials led to his later successes. He also used stains to identify mast cells, large cells in connective tissue that release chemicals causing allergic reactions. He was already becoming aware that chemical affinities controlled biological processes.

After he graduated, Ehrlich continued with his research and became chief assistant to Freidrich von Frerichs at the Charité Hospital in Berlin. He developed a stain called methylene blue, a selective stain for nerve endings and ganglia. Working with A. Leppmann, he used methylene blue to reduce pain in patients with neuralgia. He also stained and identified a variety of white blood cells; his work made it possible to identify leukemia and anemia according to the prevalence of particular cell types.

CORE FACTS

- Ehrlich used dyes to stain and identify certain cells and microorganisms.
- Ehrlich's discovery of a rapid staining technique for the tubercle bacillus that causes tuberculosis allowed much easier diagnosis of the disease.
- Ehrlich studied chemotherapy—the design of chemical compounds to treat disease—and discovered a drug that could cure syphilis, a sexually transmitted disease.

In 1883 Ehrlich married Hedwig Pinkus, daughter of a prosperous textile manufacturer and 10 years his junior. They had two children, Stephanie, born in 1884, and Marianne, born in 1886.

Working on tuberculosis

Between 1887 and 1889, Ehrlich studied tuberculosis (TB), a chronic and highly infectious lung disease. German bacteriologist Robert Koch had isolated the microorganism, *Mycobacterium tuberculosis*, that causes the disease, using a lengthy and laborious staining technique. Koch had difficulty finding a stain that could penetrate the outer coating of the bacterium. Ehrlich developed a rapid staining technique for the microorganism by using basic dyes in an aqueous-aniline oil solution. This technique helped greatly in the diagnosis of tuberculosis and rendered Koch's discovery all the more important. Koch and Ehrlich then worked together on the etiology (cause) and possible treatment of tuberculosis.

In working with a contagious disease, Ehrlich contracted a mild form of pulmonary TB and was forced to move his family to Egypt between 1888

Ehrlich's discovery of a cure for syphilis was praised by the scientific world but criticized by some people who considered the disease to be the result of sin.

CONNECTIONS

● **CHEMOTHERAPY** is the treatment of disease using chemical agents (drugs).

● Most **BACTERIA** can be divided into gram-positive or gram-negative forms, based on their response to the Gram stain.

and 1889. He soon recovered and never suffered a recurrence. Whether Ehrlich's recovery was due to the warm, dry climate of Egypt or to receiving Koch's new treatment for TB on his return to Berlin remains a mystery.

Other bacteriological research

When he arrived in Germany, Ehrlich set up his own laboratory to continue with his studies on bacteria and other microorganisms. Soon after, Koch offered him a post at the new Institute for Infectious Diseases, and Ehrlich received a professorship from the University of Berlin.

While at the Institute, Ehrlich collaborated with Emil Adolf von Behring and Shibasaburo Kitasato. They worked on a cure for diphtheria, a contagious disease causing the formation of a membrane in the throat and inflammation of the heart and nervous system. They developed a safe and effective dosage of vaccine and conducted successful clinical trials. Their success led to the establishment of an Institute for Serology in 1896, with Ehrlich appointed as its first director. The Institute was a dilapidated, single story building, but Ehrlich took great pride in it and did some excellent work there. For example, he suggested that an international unit for antitoxin be adopted by which serum samples could be assayed. This recommendation was adopted and the term *Ehrlich's L* for test dosages survives to this day.

International recognition

By now Ehrlich's work was receiving international acclaim. Freidrich Althoff, Director of the Prussian Ministry of Educational and Medical Affairs, realized Ehrlich needed better facilities for his research work and persuaded the Lord Mayor of Frankfurt am Main to arrange for a more suitable building to be constructed near the city hospital.

The Royal Prussian Institute for Experimental Therapy opened in 1899, and Ehrlich was its director until his death in 1915. Here Ehrlich developed his side-chain theory, which explains the way in which a toxin creates its effect, leading to the production of a certain immune response in mammals. In Ehrlich's theory, cells have side chains (specific receptor molecules) on their surfaces that attach to particular chemical groups in toxin molecules. These cells produce more side chains: those that are released act as antibodies. For his contributions to bacteriology and immunology, Erhlich shared the 1908 Nobel Prize in physiology or medicine with Elie Metchnikoff, a Russian bacteriologist.

Discovering salvarsan

Ehrlich spent the rest of his career devoted to chemotherapy: investigating the design of chemical compounds to treat disease. He established that compounds containing arsenic have therapeutic qualities and started to survey all such compounds. In 1910 he announced that compound number 606 destroys spirochetes, the microorganisms that cause syphilis. Ehrlich named his new drug salvarsan, but it

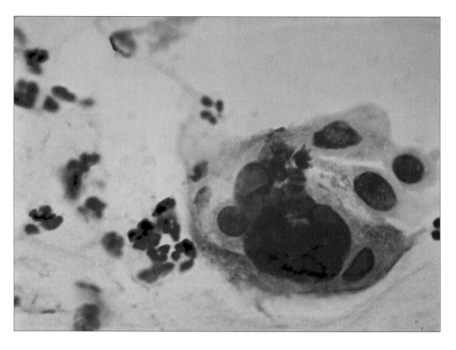

A giant cell, composed of several macrophages (phagocytotic white blood cells, which engulf and then consume foreign material and debris). The macrophages have fused together to form a large, multinucleated cell. In 1908 Paul Ehrlich was awarded the Nobel Prize in physiology or medicine, partly for his work in staining and identifying the different types of white blood cells.

is also called arsphenamine. Although a patient often needed more than one dose, the drug could cure syphilis, a painful and eventually fatal sexually transmitted disease that had plagued people for centuries. Ehrlich's discovery was greeted with acclaim within the scientific community, and he was nominated for another Nobel Prize in both 1912 and 1913.

Those infected with the disease were given hope, but keeping up with demand for the drug was difficult. Ehrlich was careful to administer the drug properly, but controversy still arose. Some people objected to the concept of a cure for a disease they associated with divine punishment for sin. Others asserted that the drug did not live up to Ehrlich's claims and was misused.

In March 1914, matters came to a head, and the case was put before the Reichstag (the German legislature). It declared the drug a "valuable enrichment of the remedies against syphilis." In May of the same year, Ehrlich was a defense witness for the Frankfurt Hospital, which won a libel suit against a newspaper claiming that prostitutes had been forced to take the drug salvarsan.

Ill health, the controversy over salvarsan, and the outbreak of World War I (1914–1918) took their toll. Ehrlich suffered a stroke at the end of 1914 and another the following year that proved fatal. He died on August 20, 1915, in Bad Homburg, Hessen, at the age of 61 and was buried at the Frankfurt Jewish Cemetry.

KIM BRYAN

See also: ALLERGY; CELL BIOLOGY; MICROBIOLOGY; PHARMACOLOGY; TUBERCULOSIS.

Further reading:
Baumler, Ernest. 1984. *Paul Ehrlich: Scientist for Life*. New York: Holmes and Meier Publishers.
Zannos, Susan. 2002. *Paul Ehrlich and Modern Drug Development (Unlocking the Secrets of Science)*. Bear, Del.: Mitchell Lane.

ELEPHANTS AND MAMMOTHS

Elephants, like the extinct mammoths, are the world's largest land mammals

An African bull elephant (Loxodonta sp.). Its huge ears help keep it cool in hot weather and are also extended to frighten off rival elephants or predators.

CORE FACTS

■ There are two genera of elephants, *Loxodonta* from Africa and *Elephas* from Asia.

■ The largest elephant known, an African bush elephant, stood 13 feet (nearly 4 m) high and weighed 16,500 pounds (7,500 kg).

■ Elephants have six sets of cheek teeth. When the last is worn out, the elephant starves to death.

■ Despite international legislation regulating ivory trading, elephant populations worldwide are still being threatened.

CONNECTIONS

● **CONSERVATION** of elephants includes protection from poaching and the establishment of reserves.

● Elephants' feeding habits can have a significant effect on the **ECOSYSTEM**, by changing wooded areas into **SAVANNA**.

The largest land animals alive today are African bush elephants. They are some million times larger than one of the smallest mammals, the European pygmy shrew, and among the largest of all mammals (some whales are larger).

All elephant species are classified in the family Elephantidae in the order Proboscidea, a reference to the elephant's proboscis, which is a flexible elongation of the upper lip and nose made up of thousands of muscles arranged in pairs. There are only two genera of elephants alive today: the African *Loxodonta*, which contains two species, *L. africana* (the bush, or savanna, elephant) and *L. cyclotis* (the forest elephant), and the Asian *Elephas*, which has only one species, *Elephas maximus*, but several subspecies. Genetic evidence has shown that the two species of African elephants are as genetically distant from one another as either is from the Asian species.

The direct ancestor of the elephant is the small, pig-sized *Moeritherium*, which lived about 50 million years ago. Thus, the elephant is a distant relative of the rabbit-sized hyrax, or coney (family Procaviidae), found in Asia and Africa, and of the aquatic manatees, or sea cows (family Trichechidae), found in tropical waters. All are thought to have evolved from *Moeritherium*, and although very different in size, they have similar bone and body structures.

At the next stage of evolution, about 25 million years ago, the Proboscidean family tree divided into two groups. The first group, the mastodons (Mastodontidae), possessed tusks and a proboscis but were a completely different group from today's elephants; they died out about 10,000 years ago. The second group, the Elephantidae comprise the now-extinct mammoths (*Mammuthus* spp.) and all living African and Asian elephants. There are about 160 species of fossil proboscids, and there is still a great deal of discussion about their relationships.

Mammoths

Mammoths and their cousins the elephants roamed most of the continents (except for Antarctica and Australia) during the last ice age, which ended about 10,000 years ago. Mammoths became extinct some 3,000 to 4,000 years ago. Most information about mammoths comes from northern Asia and North America, where deep-freeze conditions have preserved nearly complete carcasses for thousands of years. There were nine species of mammoths: the imperial mammoth (*M. imperator*) was the largest, standing about 14 to 15 feet (4.5 m) at the shoulders. It roamed the western and southwestern United States and Mexico. The woolly mammoth (*M. primigenius*) was about 10 feet (3 m) high and had huge tusks up to 16½ feet (5 m) long that spread outward from the jaw and curled back. It ranged over North America, Europe, and Asia.

The rabbit-sized rock hyrax (Procavia capensis) is descended from the same prehistoric ancestor as the elephant. The two animals are linked morphologically (structure of the feet).

No one really knows why mammoths became extinct. One theory is that they died out when the climate changed. As the ice age glaciers melted and retreated, the mammoths' habitat changed. Another idea is that a fast-spreading disease could have wiped them out, but this theory is unlikely because no "graveyards" of mammoths (indicating a massive die-off) have ever been found. Some populations may simply have become too small to be viable. One theory suggests that while climate changes led to huge reductions in the mammoth population, the animals were driven to extinction by overhunting by primitive hunter-gatherer people. There is probably no single reason why the mammoth became extinct; the cause is likely to vary from region to region.

ELEPHANTS AS PART OF THEIR HABITAT

African and Asian elephants have a considerable impact on their environment because of their large size, the extent of the herds, and the amount of space they need to live. During a drought, elephants dig holes in riverbeds that provide water for other animals. By pounding their bodies against rock (usually to scratch), they form shallow caves, which are used by smaller animals—such as monkeys, bats, amphibians, birds, and insects—for shelter. As they eat their way through an area, elephants can change wooded areas into savannas; different species of animals then move into the modified habitat.

Elephant excrement also influences the ecosystem. Because only 40 percent of the food an elephant eats is digested, whole pieces of fruit or seeds pass through in the elephant's gut little changed and are then eaten by other animals, such as monkeys. Whole seeds may eventually grow, the dung being used as fertilizer: some seeds do not germinate unless they have passed through an elephant's digestive system. Insects such as dung beetles also feast on the undigested nutrients and often lay their eggs in the elephant's dung.

Sick, old, or dying elephants are part of the food chain of the local habitat, and are often food for carnivores, such as lions and crocodiles (depending on where the elephants are located). Even the remains of a dead elephant become part of the ecosystem, their carcasses being eaten by scavenging wildlife such as jackals, hyenas, and vultures.

A CLOSER LOOK

Elephants

Elephants, like mammoths, are herbivores, eating as much as 660 pounds (300 kg) of food per day, including flowers, grasses, leaves, fruits, and—in drought conditions—bark and twigs. They spend as much as 20 hours a day feeding. In their nomadic search elephants often ruin as much food as they eat by knocking down trees and trampling vegetation. The elephant's digestive tract allows the plant food to travel quickly through the animal's stomach and then pass into a sac, called the cecum, at the junction of the small and large intestines. Here microbes break down the plant cell walls (cellulose), releasing the nutrients so that the elephant can utilize them. However, about 40 percent of the original food passes undigested through the elephant. Elephants also need a great deal of water to survive—about 20 to 40 gallons (75 to 150 l) per animal per day.

Elephant herds constantly use the same migration path (usually following a river or through low-lying land) every year because of the large amounts of food and water they need. In the dry season, they often dig water holes near rivers and swamps to find enough to drink and bathe. Most elephant herds have a home range close to 300 square miles (770 km²)—larger if there is a drought. The typical habitats of African bush elephants are forests, river valleys, and grasslands, mainly in southern, central, and eastern Africa. Some areas fluctuate between woodland and savanna, depending on the number of elephants present. The African forest elephant, as its name suggests, favors forest areas and is restricted to western and central Africa. Asian elephants roam tropical grassy plains and rain forests, especially in northern and southwest India, Sri Lanka, and southern Asia.

The elephant's body is well adapted to its habitat. Its wrinkled, sparsely haired skin traps and retains water to help keep the animal cool. The elephant does not sweat but flaps its two large ears to cool itself down during hot weather, losing heat through dilated blood vessels near the surface of the skin. The skull, although massive, contains numerous sinus cavities that lessen its weight. The short neck helps the elephant support heavy tusks and cheek teeth, which are high-crowned premolars and molars.

Most elephants have a maximum of 24 cheek teeth (six large teeth in each side of the upper and lower jaws) during their lifetime. Four teeth (two in both the upper and lower jaws) are volleyball sized and weigh about 9 pounds (4 kg) each. They grind vegetation as the lower jaw is moved back and forth. The cheek teeth are replaced, in a conveyor belt fashion, from behind. The older teeth move forward and are worn away or drop out at the front of the jaw. When the last molars are ground down, the animal can no longer eat and dies of starvation.

The tusks are large upper incisor teeth. They are made of ivory, a mixture of dentine, cartilage-type material, and calcium-salt deposits. Depending on the species and sex, tusks erupt at between 6 and 12 months of age and continue growing over the elephant's lifetime. The tusks are used to dig up roots, excavate salt from rocks and soil, peel tree bark, and move branches. They are also used for defense or for courtship and mating displays. Digging helps wear down the tusks so they keep to a reasonable length.

The elephant uses its trunk to smell (this is the animal's most highly developed sense)—it can even detect underground water during the dry season. The muscular trunk has no bones or cartilage and has numerous other uses, including gathering hard-to-reach food; drinking, by sucking water up the trunk, then squirting the water into its mouth; and powdering its thick, sensitive skin with dust or spraying it with water. At the end tip of the trunk, one (in the Asian) or two (in the African) fingerlike protrusions can gently touch and feel objects. Elephants also communicate using their trunks, beating them against the ground when threatened and trumpeting through them when surprised or to communicate over long distances. They may also comfort others by putting the tip of the trunk in the other's mouth.

At the ends of the massive columnar legs are the elephant's huge feet, large enough to allow the animal to spread its great weight over a broad area. Despite its great weight, the structure of the elephant's foot is such that, like many animals, it walks only on its toes (digitigrade locomotion). The two species of African elephants have five toes on the front legs and three toes on the hind legs; the Asian elephant has five toes on the front legs and four toes on the hind legs. The average speed of an elephant is less than 15 miles per hour (24 km/h), but it can charge an enemy or take flight at more than 20 miles per hour (32 km/h).

Elephant herds of about 30 to 50 animals have a complex social structure. Most of the elephants in the herd are closely related adults, with the herd

COMPARING AND CONTRASTING ELEPHANT SPECIES

There are numerous differences between the Asian and African elephants. The largest species is the African bush elephant, *Loxodonta africana*, which averages 10 feet (3 m) at the shoulder; *L. cyclotis*, the forest elephant, is smaller and usually averages a height of 8 feet (2.4 m) at the shoulder. The Asian elephant (*Elephas*) averages about 9 feet (2.7 m). The largest known African bush elephant measured 25 feet (7.5 m) in length, including the trunk, stood about 13 feet (nearly 4 m) high at the shoulder, and had a 4.5 foot (1.3 m) tail; it weighed 16,500 pounds (7,500 kg), and its one unbroken tusk was 8 feet (2.4 m) long. The largest known Asian elephant measured 20 feet (6 m) in length, including the trunk, stood about 11 feet (3.3 m) high at the shoulder, and had a 5 foot (1.5 m) tail; it weighed 11,000 pounds (5,000 kg).

There are other visible differences between the two elephant genera: the Asian elephant's ears are relatively small, and the top of its head has a hump, unlike the African elephants, which have large ears and smooth heads. The Asian male elephants have long tusks, but females have small tusks or none (there is a subspecies of the Asian elephant in Sumatra in which both sexes are tuskless); in contrast, both male and female African elephants possess tusks. However, the forest elephants' tusks are straighter, thinner, and directed downward so they can move unhampered through the trees. The trunks are also different: the end tip of the Asian trunk has one "finger," while the African elephants have two.

divided into three or four family groups made up of cows and young, led by the oldest female, the matriarch. Subadult males also form groups, but mature males tend to be more solitary. A great deal of interaction takes place among the elephant herds. When danger is near or another elephant is hurt, the other herd members help; it is also common to see groups of elephants wallowing together in a mudbath or shallow waters during the day.

During the three months of the mating season, the bulls undergo a change in body chemistry called musth in India. At this time a clear secretion leaks

African elephant cows stand guard over their calves. Bull calves leave the family in their early teens, but the young females remain with the other cows, help raise new infants, and eventually bear their own young.

from the musth gland on the side of the head. The bulls become aggressive and sexually active and compete for whichever female is presently in heat. Once the female is pregnant, she ignores the bull or drives him away. The gestation period for elephants averages between 18 and 22 months. African elephants stop traveling when a calf is to be born and encircle the mother, and a cow acts as a helper. When an Asian elephant calf is born, the mother and "midwife" clear a spot for the birthing, while the others stay nearby, keeping away predators. A young calf is about 3 feet (90 cm) tall and weighs about 200 pounds (90 kg) at birth, and it is on its feet in about an hour.

Cows raise, teach, and protect their young over several years. To protect the young, the adults herd the calves into "kindergartens" at the best feeding grounds, guarded by adults that act as babysitters. Bull calves leave the family herd in their early teens; females remain in the group and are taught essential skills, such as how to find water and help raise the infants, under the guidance of the matriarch.

Elephants can live up to 70 years. The lifespan is the same for all three species. Calf mortality is high in the first year—up to 36 percent in some areas. Elephants appear to respond to the death of other elephants. They will try to "comfort" a dying elephant by touching the victim with their trunks; when an elephant dies, the others often attempt to bury the dead with tree branches and dirt. When elephants come across the bleached bones of a dead elephant, they will often stroke the bones with their trunks, pick up and hold smaller bones, and even carry away pieces of bones in their mouths or on their tusks.

P. BARNES-SVARNEY

See also: ANIMAL KINGDOM; MAMMALS.

Further reading:
Moss, Cynthia. 1997. *Little Big Ears: The Story of Ely.* New York: Simon and Schuster.
Pringle, Laurence. 1997. *Elephant Woman: Cynthia Moss Explores the World of Elephants.* New York: Atheneum.

PEOPLE AND ELEPHANTS

Elephants' relationships with people have continued for more than 3,500 years. The Asian and forest elephants were used in battle for centuries; the Carthaginian general Hannibal crossed the Alps with 37 African forest elephants to fight the Romans around 200 BCE, and in Hindu mythology, the god Ganesh has the head of an elephant and guards the door of the god Shiva's sacred shrines.

The smaller Asian elephants—usually females—are easier to train than African elephants and are often domesticated. During the reign of the Mogul emperors of India, from the 16th century to the beginning of the 19th century, elephants were trained to fight, a popular spectator sport. The elephants were not usually hurt during the fight, but the mahouts, or riders, often did not survive. Elephants are still dressed in elaborate costumes or brightly painted and used in ceremonies or festivals on the Indian subcontinent.

Some Asian elephants are used to carry out heavy labor in areas that are inaccessible by vehicle. For example, trained elephants harvest trees and push and stack logs. At a busy and noisy work site, a trained elephant responds only to its trainer's voice; the young calves learn to work by following their mothers.

Elephants have no natural enemies except humans, although baby elephants are sometimes prey for lions in Africa and for tigers in Asia. Elephants used to be hunted for their meat and ivory with little impact on their numbers. However, in the early 1970s, as the value of currencies around the world collapsed and items that would retain their value, such as gold and ivory, were much sought after, many more elephants were killed, and the world population declined drastically. In 1981 there were about 1.2 million African elephants; by 1991 there were less than half this figure.

Many countries have made an effort to protect and conserve elephants. When the ban on ivory trading was agreed upon in 1989, after the UN Convention on International Trade in Endangered Species (the Washington Convention) had declared the African elephant endangered, more of an effort was made to herd the elephants into protected areas. However, a major problem with protected elephants is their tendency to overpopulate and defoliate

Asian elephants with their drivers in Bangladesh. The elephants are still used for heavy labor, particularly in forestry work.

their limited range, mainly because of the lack of predators and space. Some elephants leave the national parks and raid farm crops and thus are unpopular with local people. The situation has now improved to the extent that African elephants are currently categorized as vulnerable, rather than endangered. However, the position may alter now that the population has to be split between two species, of which about one third are forest elephants.

SCIENCE AND SOCIETY

EMBRYO

The embryo is an early phase in the development of an organism from a single fertilized cell to a mature adult

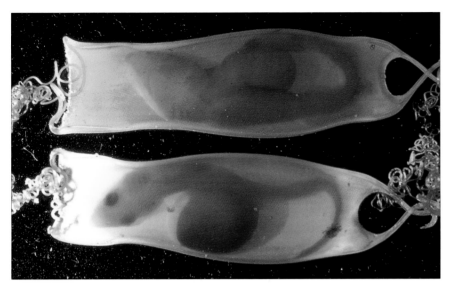

Embryos of the lesser spotted dogfish (Scyliorhinus canicula) at a late stage of development within the egg case. Fish eggs contain a large yolk reserve.

CONNECTIONS

● An embryo develops from a single **CELL** after **FERTILIZATION**.

● In animals that lay **EGGS**, both **INVERTEBRATES** and **VERTEBRATES**, the development of the embryo can be observed under the microscope.

● The later stages of human embryo development and the subsequent fetus can be observed using **X RAYS** or **ULTRASOUND**.

The development of a complex organism from a single fertilized cell takes place in many stages, each ordered and controlled by the organism's DNA. The embryo is one part of this stepwise process. It is the most important growing phase of the organism because, as the embryo develops, it forms all the early tissues and structures that will make up the mature adult. If early development goes astray, there are always drastic consequences.

Embryologists make a distinction between the embryo stage and the pre-embryo stage. In flowering plants, the embryo is not established until the cotyledons (seed leaves) begin to develop. In animals, the developing organism becomes an embryo on formation of either a ball of cells or, in many vertebrates, an embryonic disk, with its two layers of cells. In the case of mammals, the developing organism is called an embryo until the organs have been formed, after which it is called a fetus.

In both plants and animals, the pre-embryo usually develops from the fertilization of an egg by sperm (see EGGS; FERTILIZATION). However, this step is not always necessary for the formation of an embryo: many male insects, for example, develop from unfertilized eggs, and fertilization is also unnecessary in some fish and reptile species. However, an embryo usually receives chromosomes from both parents. The single fertilized cell from which the embryo develops is called a zygote.

ANIMAL EMBRYOS

Scientists in the 19th century were struck by how alike the early embryos of many different vertebrates appeared: superficially, different species could hardly be told apart. They even suggested that the fetuses of the most highly developed vertebrates went through all the stages of natural evolution (fish to amphibian to reptile, and so on), as reflected in the classic phrase "ontogeny recapitulates phylogeny," that is, early development of the individual repeats the evolution of the species). For example, scientists pointed out that the human embryo begins as a single cell, like protozoans and then becomes a small colony of cells, like sponges. After passing through stages similar to other invertebrates such as cnidarians and echinoderms, the human embryo develops a notochord like a primitive chordate (see CHORDATES), then gill pouches like a fish, and later body hair and a tail.

The single fertilized egg, or ovum (plural, ova), progresses through a number of stages, to the point where all organs and tissues are present, even if only in immature form: cleavage (repeated cell division and formation of a ball of cells called a blastula); gastrulation (rearrangement of the cells to form two or three cell layers); neurulation (formation of the first specialized tissues); and organogenesis (organization of the cells into tissues and organs).

Invertebrates

Most invertebrates develop from eggs to larvae and from larvae (which usually have a completely different body form from adults) to juveniles or, in some insects, pupae, from which they transform into fully formed adults. This process may take very different lengths of time, depending on the animal, but can be extremely rapid in some species.

The fruit fly *Drosophila,* which has been studied extensively, provides a good example of invertebrate embryo development. As in other insects, development of the *Drosophila* embryo does not begin with cell division but with a series of divisions of the nucleus without cell division. The divided nuclei form a syncytium, in which they are contained in a single cell's cytoplasm. The first nine divisions produce 512 nuclei, most of which migrate to the outer surface of the egg, where they form a single layer called the syncytial blastoderm. After four further nuclear divisions, membranes begin to grow in from the egg surface to enclose the nuclei individually so that the blastoderm now consists of some 8,192 separate cells. Gastrulation now begins. Some cells migrate to the interior and form the gut endoderm, extending the length of the embryo. Other cells (now called mesoderm) begin

CORE FACTS

■ The embryo is an early stage in the development of a complex living organism.
■ It is the most important developmental phase, in which all the tissues and organs of the mature adult are formed.
■ Both animals and plants develop from embryos.
■ The embryonic stages of many species of animals share several similarities. The same is true of plant embryos.

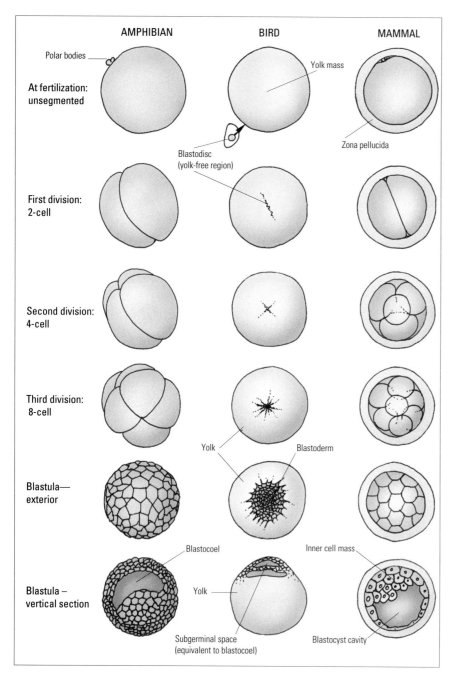

AMPHIBIAN   BIRD   MAMMAL

Polar bodies

At fertilization:
unsegmented

Yolk mass

Blastodisc
(yolk-free region)

Zona pellucida

First division:
2-cell

Second division:
4-cell

Third division:
8-cell

Yolk   Blastoderm

Blastula—
exterior

Blastocoel   Inner cell mass

Blastula –
vertical section

Yolk

Subgerminal space
(equivalent to blastocoel)

Blastocyst cavity

Comparison of the stages in cell cleavage leading to formation of the blastula, in an amphibian, a bird, and a mammal. The amphibian and mammal pre-embryos are viewed from the side, the bird (in all but the last pre-embryo), from above.

to fill the space between the gut (endoderm) and the outer layer of cells (ectoderm). In five to eight hours gastrulation is complete, and the forms of the eventual head, thorax, and abdomen are visible in the embryo. Within one day, the larva is ready to hatch from the egg as a maggot that feeds and grows.

Vertebrates

Vertebrates do not have a syncytial phase, and the fertilized cell almost immediately begins normal cell division. Many of the stages through which the embryo passes are similar in all vertebrates, although the time taken for each can be very different. The embryo of the frog, for example, is ready to hatch as a larval tadpole some 14 days after fertilization, but the human embryo takes two months to reach a similar state of development.

● **Cleavage:** The first stage of embryological development begins with cleavage, the division of the single-celled zygote. In mammals and other

cells with little yolk, cleavage is complete, passing through the entire fertilized egg. Successive divisions take place rapidly and without cell growth so that, at the end of cleavage, the ball of cells, called the blastula, is no bigger than the original ovum. In most species, cleavage takes place almost immediately, but mammalian cleavage is delayed by up to 24 hours, while the zygote is in the oviduct (the fallopian tube in humans) on its way to the uterus. In birds considerable development of the embryo may take place before the egg is laid.

In mammals, at the third cell division, the resulting eight cells of the pre-embryo are pressed closely against each other. By the time the pre-embryo reaches the uterus (day 4), the embryo has reached the 12- to 16-cell stage, or morula (the Latin word for "mulberry," which describes the appearance of the cells). The morula breaks out of its enclosing coat and divides into 32 to 64 cells by day 5. It is now called the blastocyst. An inner group of isolated cells, the inner cell mass, is the future embryo; the outer cells form structures outside the embryo (the placenta, for example). Once the blastocyst reaches the body of the uterus, it is ready to implant in the endometrium (uterine lining) and develop there, supplied with nutrients by the placenta.

Fish, reptile, and bird zygotes undergo a different form of cleavage because of the large size of their yolk reserves. Called discoidal cleavage, embryo formation occurs on a circular yolk-free region of the zygote called the blastodisc. In the chick, the first sign of cell division is a furrow in the blastodisc. The next few divisions are all on the same plane, forming a blastoderm one cell thick. The cells then divide across the embryo's equator and become raised slightly from the yolk surface, creating the subgerminal space. As the embryo enters gastrulation, the blastoderm separates into two layers, the top epiblast layer and the bottom hypoblast layer, separated by the cleft space.

● **Gastrulation:** Gastrulation has been studied in great detail in amphibians, particularly the African clawed frog (*Xenopus laevis*). The first indication that the globe-shaped blastula is entering the gastrulation phase is the appearance of a depression, called the blastopore, the site of cell movement to the interior of the blastula. As migration proceeds, a layer of cells inside the gastrula (as it is now called) arches upward to form a cavity, the archenteron, the primitive digestive tract.

The blastopore is sealed with a yolk plug, and the embryo cells form three distinct primary germ layers from which the body's tissues and organs develop: the outer ectoderm, which gives rise to the skin and nervous system (brain, spinal cord, and nerves); the mesoderm, which becomes the bone, muscle, connective tissue, heart, kidneys, reproductive organs, and blood; and the endoderm, which forms the digestive organs.

Gastrulation in reptiles, birds, and mammals starts with the appearance of the "primitive streak" on the cup-shaped embryonic disk. This thickening of the ectoderm is caused by the migration of cells toward the center to become the mesodermal pouches. As the primitive streak extends forward, the cells form the mesodermal head and notochord (a rod of cells that, in vertebrates, becomes the spine). Eventually, the primitive streak moves backward again, and notochord formation follows it.

● **Neurulation:** Neurulation and the formation of rudimentary organs begin at the head end of the embryo and continue in the direction of the tail. A broad, shield-shaped "neural plate," which becomes the central nervous system, spreads across the back of the embryo. Its margins become raised to form the neural folds and a long central indentation, the neural groove, runs the length of the neural plate. The neural folds rise and roll toward the center, where they fuse to form the neural tube.

Ectodermal cells on either edge of the neural folds are also lifted up with the folding margins and join above the neural tube. This neural crest divides down the middle, and the two sections move sideways. The neural crest cells give rise to many parts of the central nervous system, the brain, and the spinal cord. Other crest cells contribute to skin pigment cells, the center of the adrenal glands, and some of the skull and facial muscles.

● **Organogenesis:** The vertebrate embryo begins to change shape to accommodate the emerging organ systems. The body becomes longer, a tail appears, and the head and trunk become distinguishable. During this phase, the mesoderm begins to divide into paired tissues on either side of the neural tube, called somites. These paired tissues, present in all vertebrate embryos, form the vertebrae, ribs, breastbone, and skull, as well as many associated muscles and some skin tissue. In birds the first pair of somites appears some 20 hours after the egg has been laid. In the human embryo the first pair appears on day 20 after conception; eventually there will be around 42 pairs.

The embryo now enters a period of dramatic change. It curves at the head and tail, and the forerunners of the organs begin to take shape. The sides of the embryonic disk come together to form a tube shape. The embryonic endoderm closes up, with a central digestive tract incorporating part of the yolk sac and with a cavity or coelom on either side.

The heart and a simple blood vessel network make up the first embryonic organ system. In humans this system appears approximately three weeks after fertilization. Below the neural plate, the primitive heart is formed as a hollow tube from surrounding tissues. As the embryo's head lengthens and curves, the swelling heart is pushed back under the foregut. The beating heart tube folds over on itself into an S-shape. Primitive blood from the wall of the yolk sac circulates around a simple vascular system to provide the new tissues with oxygen and nutrients.

Gradually, the lungs, kidneys, liver, pancreas, and gallbladder take shape. In humans, six weeks after fertilization, the eyes begin to develop. In the

GENETIC CONTROL OF EMBRYONIC DEVELOPMENT

For a long time, embryology remained mainly a descriptive science—patterns of embryonic development became known, but how the processes were controlled remained a mystery. Since the late 1970s, geneticists have made great progress in understanding how genes act together to transform a single cell into a complex organism. A large proportion of any organism's genes are control or regulatory genes that switch other genes on or off (see GENETICS). Many control genes act in embryonic development and form a complex "chain of command." For example, in many animals there is a single "master" gene that gives the instruction to grow an eye. When activated, this gene switches on other genes, initiating a complex process by which cells multiply and differentiate to create the fully formed eye.

There are different ways that one gene can control another. In embryonic development, the protein that is coded for by a particular control gene often forms a concentration gradient across the embryo. Cells in an area of high concentration develop in one way, while cells experiencing a lower concentration develop in another. By such mechanisms the early embryo "knows" which part of it should become its head and which its tail, for example. (In many animals, these very early stages are controlled by the mother's genes.)

Many of the secrets of how genes act in development were first worked out by studying the fruit fly Drosophila. Mutants exist in which the fly grows an extra pair of legs in place of its antennae. By studying such mutations, biologists discover much about the underlying control mechanisms of development. These studies also provide new evidence for the shared ancestry of very different groups: many developmental genes are practically the same in mammals, insects, and worms.

A CLOSER LOOK

Cross sections showing development of a frog embryo, from the blastula phase through neurulation.

Blastoderm
Blastocoel
Dorsal lip of the blastopore
Blastopore

Archenteron
Mesoderm
Dorsal lip of the blastopore
Blastocoel

Neural plate
Archenteron
Mesoderm

Neural fold
Archenteron

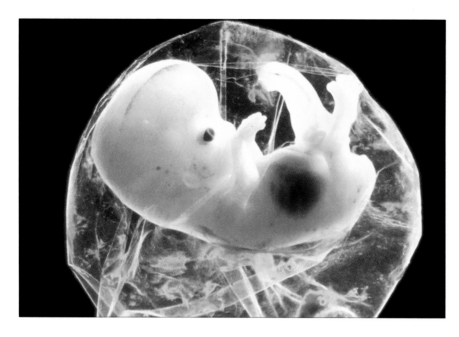

At six weeks, the human embryo has developed many of its organs, and the general form of the mature individual can already be observed.

as tadpoles. Chickens remain within the egg, nourished by the yolk, to hatch as almost fully-formed birds. Mammals continue their development in the mother's womb, nourished by the placenta, until they are born.

The end of the human embryonic stage

The human embryo at eight weeks has pigmented eyes covered with eyelids, tiny external ears, distinct, if webbed, fingers and toes, and a recognizably human face. The tail has gone. The single neural tube develops into a brain of increasing complexity. The rudimentary eyes grow as out-pocketings of the forebrain. The cells lining the central canal, a leftover from the neural tube, become the spinal cord.

The heart muscle, once differentiated, begins to beat spontaneously. At eight weeks, the heart has four chambers: blood vessels from the lungs lead into the left atrium and the aorta, which takes blood around the body, leaves from the left ventricle. However, the fetus's blood is still oxygenated by the placenta, and most of it bypasses the lungs via shunts that close during or just after birth. The brain has developed its own blood vessels.

An esophagus, an expanding stomach, and a duodenum (the first part of the small intestine) develop from the foregut. Crowded down into the abdominal cavity by the liver (where the blood is now being manufactured), the midgut repeatedly folds over itself, forming the small and large intestines. The rectum is formed from the hindgut.

Branching off the pharynx, or throat, the bronchial buds give rise to the airways, or bronchi (singular, bronchus), and lungs on either side of the heart. At eight weeks, there are two secondary bronchi on the left side and three on the right; these make the future lobes of the lungs. Finer bronchi branch out; each one will form a lung segment.

The limb buds appear at around week 4. There is a region of tissue at the tip of the limb that forms cartilage, first in the shoulders and arms and then in the pelvis and legs. By week 8 the cartilage is being replaced by bone formation (see BONE.) From week 5, thousands of renal tubules (nephrons) have begun to branch out through the tissue that will become the kidneys. Urine production begins at around eight weeks. By the time the development of the embryo is complete, all the organ systems of the adult are in place, at least in a rudimentary form. What is now the fetus will continue to grow and develop.

PLANT EMBRYOS

Many growing plants develop two types of reproductive cells: the megaspore (so called because it is large, from *mega*, "great"), which becomes the female gametophyte (the sexual generation), and the microspore (from *micro*, "small"), which becomes the male gametophyte. The female gametophyte develops within a structure called the ovule, which forms the seed in seed plants. The male gametophyte is made up of the microspore and a pollen tube with many nuclei.

neck region, the head structures, including the jaws and bones of the middle ear and the muscles of the face, begin to form. From this point on, the paths of development of the vertebrate embryo begin to diverge. The larvae of amphibians and fish are almost ready to emerge from the egg and continue development in their free-swimming larval stage

THE RESEARCH CONTROVERSY

For years human embryo research has been a political hot potato. Those in favor say it could yield important insights into the causation of such things as cancer, birth defects, and genetic disorders, as well as paving the way for improved infertility treatments and methods to grow organs for transplantation from the host's own tissues (see STEM CELLS). Opponents believe it is immoral to expect to make such gains at the cost of the lives of thousands of embryos—potential people. At the heart of the controversy are widely divergent views on when life can be said to begin. At conception? At implantation, when the blastocyst, or early embryo, attaches to the wall of the uterus (at about six to eight days in humans)? Most human embryo research is carried out on the blastocyst, a pinpoint clump of cells that has not yet taken on recognizable human form.

In the United States the Human Embryo Research Panel, which drew up guidelines on the issue pending a change in the law, recommended two weeks as the cut-off point for research because at this time the "primitive streak" appears, the first intimation of what eventually becomes the nervous system. At the two-week stage, most of the cells present are destined to form the placental tissue rather than the embryo. These guidelines rule out some of the more alarmist suggestions put forward, such as the creation of human-animal hybrids and the cloning of human embryos to produce twin copies on demand.

In studying the early embryo, scientists have begun to discover the steps in the complex genetic coding that governs the transition from a featureless clump of cells to the highly differentiated tissues comprising the human organs and body systems. The hope is that, as the sequence is laid bare, it will provide important clues as to why the system can malfunction and result in birth defects.

It is also hoped that unspecialized embryonic cells (stem cells) may be used to grow new organs for transplantation. Such methods are now beginning to be developed, and it may be possible to use them to cause stem cells in adults to grow replacement organs and thus eliminate the current serious problem of rejection of organs transplanted from others. Research in the United States using human embryonic stem cells is limited to that using established embryonic cell lines. No newly developed human embryonic cell lines can be used in federally funded research in the United States.

In gymnosperms, such as conifers, the gameto-phytes develop on different parts of the tree. In flowering plants (angiosperms), both gametophytes are usually inside the same structure, the flower; a few flowering plants have only male and female flowers on one individual, for example, holly and ginkgo trees. The mechanism of fertilization is similar in both types of plants, but the development of the embryo has been studied in greater detail in flowering plants.

Flowering plants

Before the female gametophyte is ready for fertilization, its nucleus divides three times, resulting in eight nuclei. Only five of these nuclei play a further part in development; two, called the polar nuclei, move toward each other in the center of the embryo sac; of the remaining three, the largest is the egg-cell.

Flowering plants are unique in that two male gametes are needed for fertilization. One fertilizes the female gamete, and the other causes the two polar nuclei to fuse into one cell with three nuclei (a condition called triploidy). This triploid cell divides and eventually forms a food reserve called the endosperm for the growing embryo. Within hours, the zygote triples in length. One end contains the nucleus and is densely packed with cytoplasm; it is bathed in the sac fluid, which is rich in growth-promoting substances. The zygote then enters a resting (quiescent) phase.

In most plant species, the zygote next divides across the middle, forming an apical (upper) cell reaching into the embryo sac, which is the first cell of the embryo, and a basal cell at the other end, which forms the suspensor, or supporting stalk. The apical cell then divides lengthwise, while the basal cell splits across the middle, giving the embryo three layers.

The radicle (first root) and hypocotyl (first stem) grow from the lower layer of cells. The cotyledons (seed leaves; one or two, according to the species) and plumule (first shoot) grow from the upper layer. At the next division, the cells begin to develop into the three major types of plant tissue. The pre-embryo now has 16 cells and is globe shaped, with 8 outer cells (the epidermis) and 8 inner cells, which develop into both the procambium (from which the vascular system—the plant's transport system—develops) and the meristem (from which all the remaining structures of the embryo develop).

Further cell division produces regions of meristem that become the shoot and the root. As the shoot apex forms the cotyledons, the embryo becomes broader at the top. This stage is called the heart stage because of the shape of the embryo. As the cotyledons start to grow, the embryonic shoot tip (hypocotyl) appears. As cell division continues, the embryo lengthens. The vascular tissues of the procambium now reach from the shoot end to the root end of the embryo, but the xylem and phloem (the two main tissues of plant structure) have not yet developed.

The growing embryo is now tightly enclosed in its rigid ovule and is forced to double over as it grows longer. The radicle and the stem, first true leaves, and terminal bud now point in the same direction. The seed accumulates rich energy stores of fats, starches, and proteins either in the endosperm or in the swollen cotyledon, depending on the plant. This flow of food comes from the parent plant, but when the seed coat forms, the ovule becomes a closed system. The cells surrounding the ovule harden to make the seed coat, or testa. Finally, the embryo loses most of its water and enters the dormant phase of the typical seed. Further growth is inhibited chemically until the seed germinates.

E. SAREWITZ

See also: BONE; CHORDATES; GENETICS: PREGNANCY AND BIRTH; STEM CELLS.

Further reading:

Bard J. 1994. *Embryos: Color Atlas of Development*. London: Wolf.
Bier, Ethan. 2000. *The Coiled Spring: How Life Begins*. New York: Cold Spring Harbor Laboratory Press.

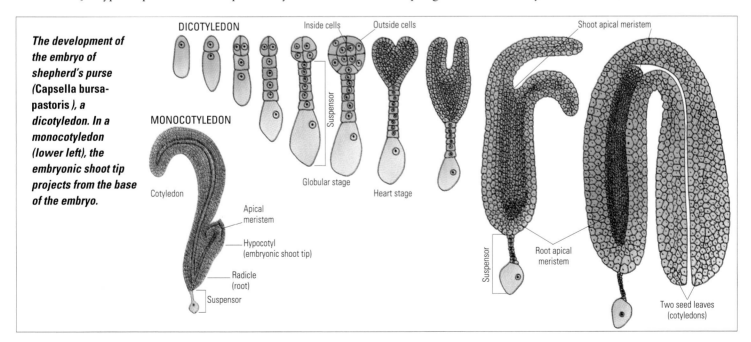

*The development of the embryo of shepherd's purse (*Capsella bursa-pastoris*), a dicotyledon. In a monocotyledon (lower left), the embryonic shoot tip projects from the base of the embryo.*

DICOTYLEDON

Inside cells   Outside cells

Shoot apical meristem

Suspensor

Globular stage

Heart stage

MONOCOTYLEDON

Cotyledon

Apical meristem

Hypocotyl (embryonic shoot tip)

Radicle (root)

Suspensor

Suspensor

Root apical meristem

Two seed leaves (cotyledons)

EMOTIONS

Emotions are feelings, such as fear, love, and anger, experienced by humans and higher vertebrates

Emotions are those feelings to which scientists give names such as fear, love, hate, anger, sadness, and happiness. Defining emotion is not easy because it is subjective: an individual's internal feelings cannot be observed or measured objectively. For example, one person's fear may not be the same as another person's fear. The word *emotion* is so subjective that many psychologists prefer to use the term *emotionality* to describe behavior that can be observed. Emotionality in animals can be characterized by such behavior as crouching, trembling, urination, and defecation. In humans, changes in the heart rate, breathing rate, and levels of various substances in the blood can all be measured as indications of strong emotions. Someone's facial expressions and tone of voice can also be interpreted as indicators of emotional states.

What are emotions?

Until the end of the 19th century, most people believed that these outward signs were the result of specific emotions generated by the brain. Then it was proposed instead that the feeling of the bodily responses to an occurrence is the emotion itself.

An individual perceives some external event (for example, standing on the railroad track, someone sees an approaching train). This event produces both immediate bodily responses (in this case, running to safety) and physiological responses through the autonomic nervous system (a sudden rush of the arousal hormones, increased heart rate, perspiration). It was suggested that the emotion experienced (fear) is due to perceiving all these responses. However, it has been shown that the same set of physiological responses can be associated with very different emotions. Until well into the 20th century, no one could agree whether people are sad because they cry or cry because they are sad.

Then, during the 1920s, researchers began to study the working of the brain directly. In 1928 W. B. Cannon and Philip Bard, who had been studying the function of areas of the brain called the thalamus and hypothalamus (see BRAIN), "separated" the emotion from the physiological response. They proposed, wrongly, that awareness of the emotion was controlled by the hypothalamus but that at the same time the thalamus sent signals to the brain cortex that resulted in various bodily responses to produce an emotional response. In other words, both the feeling and the action are produced by the brain at the same time—one does not produce the other.

In the 1960s Stanley Schachter, a psychologist from Columbia University, proposed a theory to resolve the differences between the various theories of emotion. Schachter found that feeling aroused is one of two factors in experiencing an emotion. In addition to arousal, thoughts or interpretations are

In adult life, the attachment experienced by the infant to his or her mother is replaced by what is called "falling in love."

CORE FACTS

- Emotions are feelings such as fear, love, rage, and sadness, accompanied by physiological and, frequently, behavioral and cognitive changes.
- Some methods by which emotions can be studied include measuring levels of epinephrine and other substances in the blood, recording the effects of brain injury on specific emotions, and laboratory studies of animal behavior.
- Several areas of the brain, such as the limbic system and the hypothalamus, appear to be involved in the perception of emotions.

CONNECTIONS

● Emotions are accompanied by physiological changes such as the release of **EPINEPHRINE** and changes in **BEHAVIOR.**

● **ANXIETY** disorders may be characterized by emotional states, such as depression.

necessary to label someone's feeling. If a person is aroused while being entertained that person may feel happy, but being aroused by an insult will make that person angry. Thus thoughts and perceptions provide a cognitive label for the arousal, and both these processes together create an emotion.

Most recently, emotions have been studied by evolutionary theorists interested in how emotions have developed that help humans and other species to survive. In 1980 U.S. scientist Robert Plutchik proposed a "wheel" model of eight emotions consisting of four pairs of primary emotions that are opposites: joy/sadness, acceptance/disgust, fear/anger, and surprise/anticipation. Plutchik argues that similar primary emotions become blended into more precise secondary emotions as the individual develops. For example, joy + acceptance = love. Other theorists propose that emotional reactions are produced first, and thought processes follow. Feelings lead a person to act in adaptive ways—fleeing from a threat, for example. Related thoughts are produced afterward, such as self-reflection, judgment, and planning.

Studying emotions

There are several methods of studying emotions:
- monitoring physiological effects by measuring levels of hormones, such as epinephrine, in the blood;
- recording how accidental injury to particular brain areas results in specific emotions;
- recording conscious patients' emotional changes during surgical stimulation of the brain;
- studying of animal emotional behavior;
- recording emotion patterns in psychiatric patients.

Studying emotion is not easy. Scientists hope their methods are impartial and independent, but they frequently project their own attitudes into their observations. Studies of animals are even more problematical. Guessing what an animal is feeling from its behavior can be misleading: the chimpanzee "grin" for example, indicates fear, not pleasure.

Another problem is that many of the methods used to study emotions are themselves emotive and, in some cases, cruel. Removing a baby animal from its mother to see how it reacts, for example, may be scientifically valuable, but it is an area of study now considered cruel and unethical.

Emotions in animals

The question of which groups of animals feel emotion is more than just a scientific debate. It is central to the animal rights movement and is itself an emotive subject (see ANIMAL EXPERIMENTATION).

Biology has not yet come up with an answer. It is reasonable to assume that most vertebrates can feel pleasure and pain. Their behavior seems to show such feelings, and the sensations are important for survival: animals must learn to avoid painful experiences (such as being bitten or stung) and to repeat pleasant ones (such as feeding and sex). Scientific studies on wild primates, especially apes, seem to show that these animals experience a broad

MANIPULATION OF THE EMOTIONS FOR PLEASURE

Because human emotion has a cognitive (thinking) element to it, people can often manipulate their emotions for their own pleasure.

Many terrifying activities, such as motor racing, rock climbing, skydiving, and bungee jumping, are also pleasurable and exciting because people's brains can reason through their fear. There is the knowledge that they have a realistic chance of surviving, the enjoyment of their own skill, and the prospect of the admiration of others. Many people also admit that the epinephrine (adrenaline) rush—the rapid increase in blood pressure and supply of blood to the muscles that prepares the body to face danger—can become addictive.

More serious addiction results from manipulating the emotions with drugs. Some drugs, such as alcohol, caffeine, and nicotine, are currently widely used, socially acceptable drugs. Others, such as LSD, cocaine, and heroin, are not socially acceptable in most communities, and pose a huge public health problem throughout the world (see HALLUCINOGENS). For some people the continued use of any of these drugs, whether socially acceptable or not, may eventually be accompanied by serious physical and psychological deterioration.

The fear and exhilaration of a dangerous sport and the accompanying epinephrine, or adrenaline, rush can become addictive for some people.

range of emotions, including anger, fear, pleasure, boredom, and affection.

Laboratory studies have also indicated that animals feel emotion. In a famous series of experiments published in 1958, U.S. psychologist Harry Harlow examined the bond between infant rhesus monkeys and their mothers. Previously, most scientists had believed that the biological basis of affection or love was the physical benefits that the object of this emotion could provide. They argued that infants sought contact with those who provided food and satisfaction, no matter who it was.

Harlow tested the theory by separating infant rhesus monkeys from their mothers at an early age. The distressed infants were offered a choice of surrogate mothers: dummy mothers made from wire mesh, with feeding bottles attached, or towel-covered, cuddly dummy mothers, with no bottle. The infants persisted in clinging to the cuddly mothers, rejecting the wire mothers, even though only they could offer food. This study demonstrated that infant rhesus monkeys form an emotional bond with the mother entirely separate from their need for food, but it provided important backup for the attachment theory suggested by German ethologist Konrad Lorenz (1903–1989) in the same year.

Attachment theory has greatly influenced the psychology of close relationships. Stable relationships are a source of enjoyment and security, but separation, loss, and the threat of losing someone all arouse anxiety, anger, sadness, or depression.

Many behavioral scientists now believe that the need to form emotional ties with one or a few other individuals is part of people's genetic makeup. In childhood this need is focused on the mother (or another caregiver), and the effect is to bring the child close to the mother and keep it there (hence, attachment behavior). Separation causes anguish and protest, which diminishes as the child gets older. In later life, the focus shifts to an adult partner—a process that people call falling in love.

Although biologists would not use the word *love* when speaking about animals, attachment behavior occurs in the young of almost all species of mammals and in many birds. In addition, in a number of species, attachment behavior continues throughout adult life. The importance of attachment behavior to survival may be that it helps to provide protection, particularly from predators.

The function of emotions

For years scientists believed that emotions represented human nature in the raw and are a remnant of human's supposed animal ancestry. Many modern psychologists believe that emotions are not necessarily remnants of an animal past. Rather, they are important parts of an active, thinking person.

Emotional events are different from other events because people often also become physiologically aroused (see the box on page 605). The theory is that memories that are stored after people have been aroused in this way are labeled with a mental marker and are therefore more easily retrieved. Since emotional events tend to be those that have special significance, the body has a built-in search facility for important events. These events can then be learned from and may serve to influence future behavior.

How are emotions evoked?

Scientists still do not understand how the brain generates emotions or exactly where this process happens. There appear to be several areas of the brain involved, including the limbic system and the hypothalamus (see BRAIN). The limbic system is a small region at the center of the brain, directly connected to the hypothalamus. It seems to have a role in generating emotions.

Stimulation of certain parts of the limbic system produces a range of intense emotions in the patient, such as fear, loneliness, disgust, sorrow, ecstasy, and depression, depending on the area stimulated. Sometimes the difference in the emotions produced by different areas is quite subtle: stimulation of one area may produce fear; stimulating another may produce a feeling of dread.

Dr R. G. Heath, operating on conscious psychiatric patients in New Orleans, found that stimulating a part of the limbic lobes called the septal area induced pleasure and a feeling of optimism in many patients. Several patients described sexual feelings. One patient, on the verge of

Experiments with rhesus monkeys (Macaca mulatta), such as this female and her baby, showed that an infant will always choose a cuddly substitute for its mother, rather than a wire mesh frame that would provide milk.

tears and blaming himself for his father's near-fatal illness, immediately changed focus as the doctor stimulated his septal area and with a broad grin started discussing his plans to date a girl-friend that evening.

The hypothalamus, which controls many of the body's automatic functions, may also be involved in producing emotions. As well as controlling the sympathetic and parasympathetic nervous systems, the hypothalamus organizes "packages" of behavior, such as sex and aggression, with the emotions that go with them. In experiments on animals, when certain neurons of the hypothalamus are stimulated electrically, the animals show rage and attempt to attack any living thing in sight.

Expression of emotions

Facial expression, bodily gestures, and verbal communication all provide a means to express emotions. Facial expressions are surprisingly consistent across the whole human race, the evidence suggesting that they are genetically determined. The smile of an Australian aboriginal means roughly the same as the smile of an Inuit. Learning also has a part to play. However, facial expressions can also show regional and class differences, rather like speech accents.

English naturalist Charles Darwin (1809–1882), in his book *Expression of the Emotions in Man and Animals*, suggested that human facial expressions that now have purely social meanings originally had a functional purpose: frowning shaded the eyes, drooping of the mouth rejected bitter or poisonous fruit, widening of the eyes improved vision for emergencies, and so on.

Blushing, like crying, occurs only in people. In his book Darwin suggests that blushing is a warning that an individual is not to be trusted because he or she has committed some crime or violated the social conventions of the group. Perhaps other primates do not blush because, although they have a range of social conventions, they do not monitor (or care about) their success and failure in the same way that humans do.

H. BYRT

The smiles of children, as signs of happiness, are the same throughout the world.

See also: ANIMAL EXPERIMENTATION; BRAIN; CHILD DEVELOPMENT; DEGENERATIVE BRAIN DISEASE; EVOLUTIONARY PSYCHOLOGY; HALLUCINOGENS; NEUROSCIENCE; PERSONALITY DISORDER; PHOBIAS; PSYCHOLOGY.

THE PHYSIOLOGY OF EMOTIONS

All acute emotions are accompanied by evident physiological changes, mediated by the sympathetic nervous system, which is controlled by the hypothalamus in the brain. The sympathetic nervous system prepares the body for work or an emergency. It shunts blood from the digestive organs to the muscles, increases the heart rate, raises blood sugar levels, and releases epinephrine from the adrenal medulla—the epinephrine further increases the heart rate, inhibits salivation (causing a dry mouth), and relaxes the airways to allow easier breathing. Researchers have recently confirmed what they have long believed, that negative emotions, such as fear and anger, can be factors in provoking or contributing to disease (see EPINEPHRINE AND NOREPINEPHRINE).

A CLOSER LOOK

Further reading:

Damasio, Antonio. 2000. *The Feeling of What Happens: Body and Emotion in the Making of Consciousness.* New York: Harvest Books.

Evans, D. 2001. *Emotion: The Science of Sentiment.* Oxford: Oxford University Press.

Goleman, Daniel. 1997. *Emotional Intelligence.* New York: Bantam Books.

LeDoux, J. E. 1994. Emotion, memory, and the brain. *Scientific American* (June), 270, 50–57.

Pert, C. B., and D. Chopra. 1999. *The Molecules of Emotion: Why You Feel the Way You Feel.* New York: Simon and Shuster.

Russell, James A. 1997. *The Psychology of Facial Expression.* New York: Cambridge University Press.

ENDANGERED SPECIES

Endangered species are species that scientists have classified as likely to become extinct in the near future

Every year the enormous diversity of life on this planet is reduced as more species of living organisms become extinct. To a certain extent, this extinction is quite natural: it is an essential part of English naturalist Charles Darwin's theories that species develop and disappear. There have been periods of mass extinction in the past, in which vast numbers of organisms have died out (see EXTINCTION). These extinctions happened over a period of millions of years. However, the activities of humans, especially over the past 250 years, are leading to the extinction of species across the globe, a process that worries and frightens many observers.

The term *endangered species* has been used since the the early 1900s, when scientists and policymakers began to realize that many once common species were either extinct or disappearing rapidly. However, it was not until the 1960s that scientists began to systematically classify species threatened with extinction. At this time, the IUCN (World Conservation Union—then called the International Union for Conservation of Nature and Natural Resources) published its first red data books. The red data books and their companion red lists are catalogs of threatened species from around the world. Many other organizations and governments have published regional and national red lists of threatened species.

Threatened species

Many people are confused about the terms *threatened* and *endangered*. These terms have very specific meanings when used by conservation organizations and governments. Endangered species are the most at risk in becoming extinct. Threatened species are at risk of becoming listed as endangered. The IUCN red lists place these species in one of four categories of threat:
• Endangered species are species in danger of extinction.
• Vulnerable species are species that are likely to become endangered in the near future.

Northern white rhinoceroses at a water hole. These animals are almost extinct in the wild, and attempts to breed captive populations have so far been unsuccessful.

CONNECTIONS

● The attempt to save endangered species, generally described as **CONSERVATION**, is powered by various motives. The two most important motives are that it is immoral for humanity to wipe out other creatures in pursuit of economic growth and that the **EXTINCTION** of so many species may, in the end, be dangerous for the continuation of human life on Earth.

CORE FACTS

- Endangered species are the most at risk of becoming extinct. Species defined as threatened are at risk of becoming listed as endangered. Less at risk are species described as vulnerable and rare.
- Most species endangered in the modern world are endangered as a result of human activities.
- There are many reasons why species become endangered. The most common pattern is of habitat destruction because of human socioeconomic activities (making the species vulnerable), followed by specific threats such as hunting, pollution, or a sudden outbreak of disease.

• Rare species are species that have small populations but are not yet endangered or vulnerable.

• Indeterminate classification is reserved for species that are thought to be rare, vulnerable, or endangered but that cannot be classified because of lack of information.

Under this classification, endangered species are a minority of all threatened species. Of more than 5,400 species placed in different categories of the IUCN 2000 Red List of Threatened Animals, around 25 percent (approximately 1,350) of these are considered endangered.

Most endangered species have a declining population that lives in an area much smaller than its original range. The population becomes broken up into small fragments, which become isolated from one another. These small isolated populations are more vulnerable than large ones. They tend to become inbred, losing their genetic diversity; any catastrophe, such as a disease, epidemic, or flash flood, is likely to kill a large proportion of the animals. When a population falls to 10 or 20 individuals, animals may have trouble finding mates or plants may have difficulty in becoming pollinated. When all the small population fragments collapse, the species becomes extinct.

The factors that lead to extinction interact in a complex way, creating what biologists describe as an "extinction vortex." Like water spinning down a drain, numbers in a population spiral downward: population numbers decline because of overhunting or habitat loss; individuals get isolated in small populations of 40 to 50 and begin to inbreed, which may lead to fewer births; and a reduced number of individuals may make it more difficult to find a mate, the result being further inbreeding. The final blow may be caused by a random environmental event such as an epidemic, drought, or pollution.

Why do species become endangered?
Many factors are involved when people cause a decline in numbers and fragmentation of habitats. Some species, for example, have always been rare. Endemic species are found only in a specific area. These species have never been numerous, so they are very vulnerable to changes, such as the arrival of agriculture or the development of land for building.

Other species, some of which may be very numerous and widespread, may become classified as endangered for a number of reasons. Destruction of habitats is probably the most significant factor, but for widespread species, this factor alone is rarely responsible for their extinction. Sometimes population numbers are dramatically reduced by sport hunting, poaching, or direct harassment.

The introduction of a new predator or competitor, an alien or exotic species, into the same habitat can also threaten a species. Another agent of extinction is disease, which rarely kills every member of a population but may reduce it to a fraction of the original numbers, making it more vulnerable to other factors.

Most endangered species become endangered for a number of reasons, and often it is the interaction of factors that can push a vulnerable species into the endangered category. The best way to understand this problem is to study case histories of endangered species.

CASE STUDIES
Habitat loss and hunting:
The tiger
The tiger (*Panthera tigris*) was at one time among the most successful predators in the world. In 1900 eight subspecies of tigers ranged across Asia and Southeast Asia. Tigers hunt in relatively dense

THE ROLE OF CAPTIVE BREEDING

One of the most important debates within the conservation community concerns the role of captive breeding: should people preserve endangered species by protecting them in the wild or by bringing them into captivity and trying to breed them? This problem is especially critical when populations fall very low. With only 10 or 20 individuals, bringing animals or birds into captivity would compromise the wild population. With so few individuals, however, an oil spill, a disease epidemic, or a mild increase in illegal hunting could wipe out the species. Debates on how to save the whooping crane (*Grus americana*) in the 1950s were resolved in favor of protecting the wild population, with ultimate success.

However, in the case of the California condor (*Gymnogyps californianus*), a victim of DDT that was nearly extinct in the wild, the threat of extinction was averted by developing a breeding population of 26 captive birds, some of which were caught when the population became very small. The species is being reintroduced to the wild. The northern white rhinoceros (*Ceratotherium simum*), in contrast, has never bred in captivity. When in 1983 the last population, living in Zaire, Africa, fell to 18 individuals, many scientists argued that a captive breeding program was the rhinoceros's only hope. They argued that all remaining wild animals should be caught and used to raise the captive population. Yet the captive population has slowly declined, and the wild population has doubled. The argument must be resolved in terms of what is best for the individual species, but it is clear that captive populations should be established when hundreds, rather than dozens, of animals remain.

The California condor, a species that was saved from extinction by captive breeding.

AT RISK

The tiger (Panthera tigris) is an example of an endangered species whose plight has been given a high public profile. Despite the vigorous campaigning on its behalf, a combination of habitat destruction and overhunting makes it unlikely that this largest of the big cats will survive in the wild far into the 21st century.

forests, and before they became endangered, at least a million animals roamed the Asian forests. in 2002, as few as 5,000 individuals remained. By the 1940s, the Bali tiger was already extinct, probably the result of habitat loss and overhunting; in the 1970s, the Caspian tiger, which ranged through Iran, Afghanistan, Turkestan, and Turkey, was declared extinct for the same reasons. In India, hunting for sport was blamed for local extinction of the Indian tiger, while other groups of tigers in India, Java, Southeast Asia, and China disappeared as their forest homes were felled.

Zoologists began to notice that tigers were also rapidly disappearing from forests where much good habitat remained. They eventually realized that the animals were being hunted, usually illegally, for their bones, skin, and flesh, which are particularly valued in oriental medicine. The tiger is unlikely to survive to 2030 unless this consumption is curbed because there are billions of potential consumers and only a few thousand tigers left.

Habitat loss and hunting: The whooping crane

The whooping crane (*Grus americana*), or whooper, is North America's tallest bird, at over 4 feet (1.25 m) tall. This bird once lived and bred in a small population on the wet interior grasslands of the East Coast. Whoopers overwintered across states bordering the Gulf of Mexico, north and east into North Carolina. Only one wintering ground, Arkansas National Wildlife Refuge, Texas, and one breeding area, the Wood Buffalo National Park, Canada, remain.

The species has never been abundant, and by 1870 only around 1,400 individuals remained. At first much of their decline was blamed on the expansion of agriculture and cattle farming, which took over the whoopers' wet grassland habitats. However, habitat loss alone was not responsible for the decline in the number of whoopers.

The biology of the whooping crane made it particularly vulnerable. Whoopers mate for life, and a pair will produce only one or occasionally two offspring per year. The young die easily, and those that survive take four to six years to reach maturity. Populations grow at a maximum of 2 to 3 percent per year. The adult birds have few natural enemies, but any rise in the death rate severely affects population stability. If only four birds in a population of 100 are killed each year, it is enough for the population to enter a slow steady decline. In the late 1940s an ecologist named Robert Allen determined that the decline in whoopers was due to four or five birds being shot for sport by hunters each year.

The early attempts of conservationists to breed whoopers in captivity were marred by political infighting and lack of expertise, and the decision was eventually made to protect the wild population. Whoopers are now one of the best protected and most intensively managed population of wild animals, and their numbers rose from just 14 individuals in 1940 to over 300 in 2000.

Massacre with political motives: The buffalo of the great plains

Until the middle of the 19th century, the forests and open plains of the American west were packed with herds of buffalo (*Bison bison*). Up to 60 million individuals roamed the plains. Yet by 1890, the species was nearly extinct. There were estimated to be only about 600 buffalo in existence, 250 of them in Yellowstone National Park.

The rapid decline in buffalo numbers resulted from ruthless killing of the animals by people. The slaughter was partly for meat, particularly to feed workers building the transcontinental railroads. It was also partly for luxury goods: hunters shipped hides back east for carpets, robes, and leather.

Many people believe the slaughter of the buffalo was more for political than commercial reasons. The Native Americans who lived on the plains were nomads and relied on the buffalo for their meat, clothing, and material to build shelters. By killing the buffalo, the authorities could starve the Native American tribes and force them onto reservations.

The buffalo was saved by the foresight of the New York Zoological Society (now the Wildlife Conservation Society), which runs the Bronx Zoo. In 1907 the society sent 15 buffalo to Wichita Mountain Reserve in Oklahoma and, in 1909 a second herd was established in Ravalli, Montana. The buffalo is now safely reestablished with about 35,000 individuals in national parks and refuges throughout the United States and Canada.

Habitat destruction and collection: The Venus's-flytrap

The Venus's-flytrap (*Dionaea muscipula*), which can trap and digest insects (see CARNIVOROUS PLANTS), is found in the bogs of the southeastern United States in North and South Carolina. These plants are a favorite with plant collectors and are now endangered as a result of overcollection and the destruction of their habitat. Many of the bogs of the southern states are being drained and reforested with pine trees to support a growing demand for timber.

The Venus's-flytrap is easy to cultivate but expensive to produce on a commercial scale—more profit can be made from collecting plants in the wild than growing them in captivity. It is quite possible that one day the Venus's-flytrap may exist only in botanical gardens and private collections.

Overcollection: "Flower of the Gods"

The orchid called "flower of the gods" (*Disa uniflora*), grows in the small mountain streams around Cape Town, South Africa. When it flowers, it transforms into a spectacular plant with four to five red blossoms. The orchid once had considerable commercial value because of the beauty of its blooms. By the early 1900s it was exported to Europe, where it became a favorite with gardeners. The natural populations were being destroyed by commercial demand, despite eventual legislation to protect them.

Today, botanists from Sweden have determined the requirements for this orchid's seed germination, and South African botanists have developed successful cultivation techniques. Despite these efforts, the wild populations of the "Flower of the Gods" have dwindled and their long-term survival is at risk.

Taking action

There have been campaigns by organizations and individuals, which have been successful in some cases, to rescue threatened and endangered living organisms. It is quite clear, however, that government action is essential where difficult decisions about habitat exploitation must be made. In 1973 the U.S. Congress enacted the Endangered Species Act, which authorized the government to compile a list of threatened and endangered animal and plant groups. Despite certain limitations, the act has been one of the most valuable pieces of legislation for protecting endangered species.

Internationally, getting governments to agree on how to deal with endangered species has been more difficult. There has, however, been some progress in trying to limit the trade in products from endangered species. In 1973 the Convention on the International Trade of Endangered Species of Wild Fauna and Flora (CITES), was implemented. CITES has three appendices of plants and animals, depending on how threatened they are. For example, those on Appendix I are the most endangered and cannot be traded for commercial reasons. Trade in Appendix II and III species requires permits. By 2002, 158 countries had signed the convention.

J. GINSBERG

See also: CARNIVOROUS PLANTS; ECOLOGY AND ECOSYSTEMS.

Further reading:
Czech, B. and P. R. Krausman. 2001. *The Endangered Species Act: History, Conservation Biology, and Public Policy*. Baltimore: Johns Hopkins University Press.
DeBlieu, Jan. 1991. *Meant to be Wild: the Struggle to Save Endangered Species through Captive Breeding*. Golden, Colo.: Fulcrum Publishing.
Endangered Wildlife of the World. 1993. New York: Marshall Cavendish Corporation.
Glen, William, ed. 1993. *The Mass-Extinction Debates: How Science Works in a Crisis*. Stanford, Calif.: Stanford University Press.
Primack, R. B. 2000. *A Primer of Conservation Biology*. Sunderland, Mass.: Sinauer Associates.

The Venus's-flytrap (Dionaea muscipula) has long fascinated collectors. The result is that wild populations have become seriously depleted. Attempts to revive wild populations have met with difficulties because the bogs of the southeastern United States, the plants' natural habitat, are being drained and planted with pine trees.

ENDOCRINE SYSTEMS

Endocrine systems are made up of the organs, tissues, and cells that control body functions by secreting hormones

What makes an animal wake up after a winter of hibernation or stimulates the alteration in a woman's body during pregnancy or signals a young man's voice to crack? These profound physiological changes are regulated by hormones, chemical messengers released by the glands, tissues, and cells that make up the endocrine system.

Until the mid-19th century, when endocrinology (the study of the endocrine glands) began to emerge as a branch of physiology, scientists knew little about endocrine systems. Although anatomists had discovered glands such as the adrenals and the pancreas, they had no notion of the existence of hormones. For many centuries, the pituitary gland, which lies at the base of the brain, was thought to be the source of nasal mucus. Its significance within the endocrine system was recognized only in the early years of the 20th century. The word *hormone* (from the Greek word *hormon*, "to excite") only entered the English language in 1905.

The endocrine system is the recognized as one of the two great control systems present in multicellular organisms, working in partnership with the nervous system to coordinate life processes.

Relationship with the nervous system

The main difference between the endocrine and nervous systems is in their duration of action. Nerve transmission is rapid but is over quickly; nerves must receive repeated stimulation if their "messages" are to be prolonged. In the case of hormones, the effects can last from under a minute to several days.

The nervous system generally brings about short-term changes, such as adjustments to breathing and heart rate or changes in pupil size in response to available light. The endocrine system, meanwhile, is involved with longer-term processes, including the maintenance of a stable internal environment (or homeostasis; see HOMEOSTASIS), the regulation of energy production (see ATP PRODUCTION; KREBS CYCLE; METABOLISM), growth and development, and reproduction (see REPRODUCTION).

However, the two systems are closely interrelated. The nervous system secretes hormones of its own as well as controlling the output of various

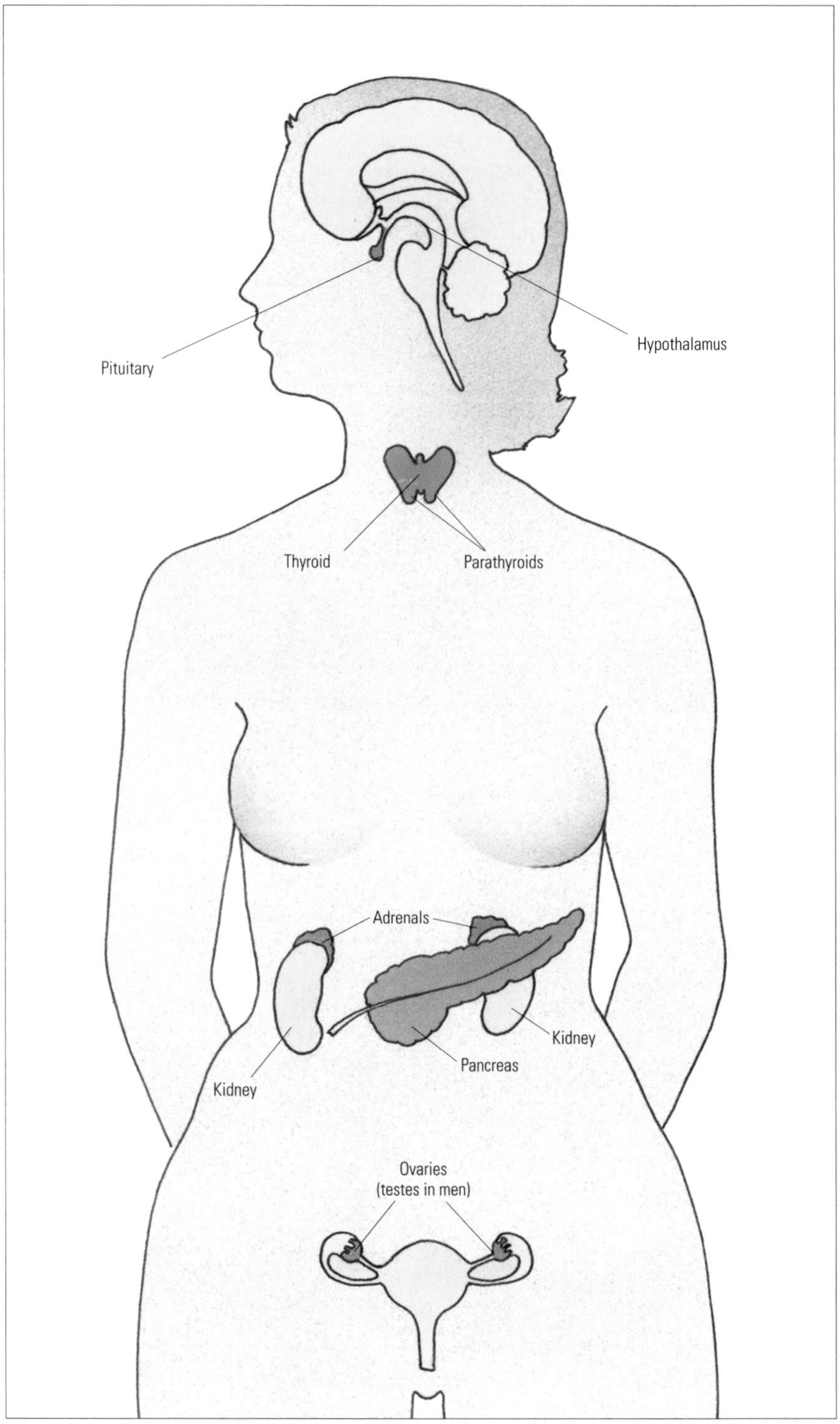

This diagram shows the principal glands of the endocrine system in the female body (males have testes).

endocrine glands. For their part, the endocrine glands alter nerve function and exert a powerful influence on many types of behavior. Among the unexpected discoveries in this area has been that some chemicals serve as messengers in both systems. For example, several substances first identified as gastrointestinal hormones, such as gastrin and secretin, also act as neurotransmitters in certain regions of the brain.

CORE FACTS

- The endocrine system works with the nervous system to control life processes in multicellular animals.
- The endocrine glands, which secrete hormones to control body functions, include the pituitary, hypothalamus, pineal, thyroid, parathyroids, and adrenal glands and the pancreas, gonads, and probably also the thymus.
- Diseases of the endocrine system are generally due to genetic defects or the presence of tumors.

CONNECTIONS

● The **NERVOUS SYSTEM** deals with rapid, short-term changes. **HORMONES** in endocrine systems control longer-term body processes.

Distribution of endocrine glands

Endocrine glands or tissues have been identified in all vertebrates, although they vary considerably in size, shape, and distribution between the classes of these animals. The endocrine glands common to all the major groups—from cyclostomes (the most primitive living vertebrates: the fishlike lampreys and hagfish) to mammals—are the pituitary, thyroid, pancreas, adrenals, and gonads (sex glands). Molecules that are identical to or closely related to, vertebrate hormones have also been identified in many invertebrates and even in plants.

Endocrine glands, which are present in the head, neck, and trunk of all vertebrate species, are sometimes called ductless glands because they release their hormones directly into the bloodstream. In contrast, exocrine glands, such as the salivary and sweat glands, discharge their secretions into ducts. Hormones enter the general circulation, where they are transported to target organs elsewhere in the body. In some cases target glands secrete hormones that inhibit the output of the secreting gland, employing a negative feedback mechanism (see INFORMATION SCIENCE), which helps to maintain chemical stability.

Some endocrine glands, including the pituitary, thyroid, parathyroids, and adrenals, are concerned only with hormone production. Other glands, such as the pancreas and gonads, also produce exocrine secretions. There are also hormone-producing cells in some organs that are not normally associated with the endocrine system. These organs include the gastrointestinal tract, heart, liver, and kidneys, and in the pregnant mammal, the placenta.

The pituitary and hypothalamus

The pituitary is a pea-sized structure that nestles in a bony depression of the skull toward the back of the neck called the *sella turcica*. It is attached to the hypothalamus (the hind part of the vertebrate forebrain; see BRAIN) by a stalk of nervous tissue.

The pituitary is really two glands in one. It consists of two lobes: the anterior (front) pituitary, or adenohypophysis, and the posterior (behind) pituitary, or neurohypophysis. The anterior pituitary secretes six different hormones, five of which stimulate secretion, elsewhere in the body, of other hormones that are involved in a wide range of physiological activities, including growth, salt and water metabolism, and reproduction. Only one anterior pituitary hormone, prolactin, has a direct effect on a target tissue: its principal function is to stimulate milk production in nursing mammals.

Most vertebrates, but not humans, also have an intermediate lobe in the pituitary. This lobe secretes melanocyte-stimulating hormone (MSH), which makes skin cells change color in response to the environment. In humans MSH is produced by the anterior lobe of the pituitary.

The posterior pituitary releases only two hormones: oxytocin, which, among other things, stimulates the pregnant uterus to contract, and antidiuretic hormone (ADH, also called vasopressin), which instructs the kidneys to retain water. Both of these hormones are synthesized in the hypothalamus, a part of the brain that is a regulatory center for many vital functions. The hypothalamus is also an important endocrine gland. Its hormones, manufactured in neuron (nerve) terminals, are sometimes called neurohormones.

The hypothalamus also secretes hormones that control production of all the anterior pituitary hormones. These hypothalamic-releasing hormones are delivered to the anterior pituitary through a circulatory branch line, a network of blood vessels that seems to exist only for the purpose of this transfer. Such is the influence of these hormones that, if the hypothalamus is destroyed, production in the anterior pituitary falls dramatically, and the effects brought about by its hormones, with the exception of prolactin, are no longer apparent.

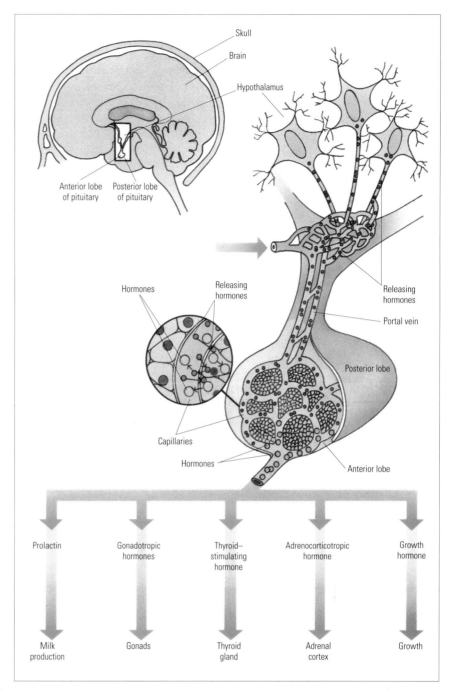

The hypothalamus–pituitary connection. The hypothalamus secretes releasing hormones, which reach the anterior lobe of the pituitary through the portal veins. The releasing hormones stimulate the pituitary to synthesize specific hormones, which are then secreted into the bloodstream.

The thyroid gland

The anterior pituitary releases its thyroid-stimulating hormone (TSH) to prompt the production of thyroid hormones. The thyroid is a two-lobed gland encircling the trachea (windpipe) at the front of the neck. It can function effectively only in the presence of the mineral iodine, which is acquired in tiny amounts from the diet. Thus, the thyroid disease goiter occurs most often in people living in regions far from the sea, where this mineral is sometimes lacking. The thyroid hormones are essential to metabolism, growth, and development.

Behind the thyroid, or sometimes embedded within it, are the parathyroid glands, usually present in one or two pairs (two in the case of humans). Parathyroid hormone, or parathormone (PTH), is essential to the regulation of calcium levels in the blood and also in phosphate metabolism. High calcium levels can cause muscle weakness; low calcium levels cause severe muscle spasms (a condition called tetany).

The significance of the parathyroid glands began to emerge only with the spread of thyroid surgery in the late-19th century. It soon became obvious that total removal of the thyroid gland, with loss of the parathyroids, could prove fatal.

The pancreas

The pancreas is a large gland in the abdomen, partially resting in the loop formed by the duodenum (the first part of the small intestine). Most of the pancreas is given over to its exocrine function (secreting powerful enzymes to aid in digestion), but scattered in the tissue are clusters of endocrine cells called the islets of Langerhans. The two main hormones the islets produce are insulin, which decreases levels of glucose in the blood, and glucagon, which increases blood-glucose levels.

Lack of insulin gives rise to diabetes mellitus (see DIABETES; INSULIN; PANCREAS). It was the prevalence of this once-fatal disease that drew attention to the pancreas. A link between diabetes and pancreatic disorder was first made in 1788, although insulin was not isolated until the early 1920s. Other substances have since been isolated from the pancreas, including the hormone somatostatin, which inhibits secretion of growth hormone from the pituitary gland.

Scientists first identified a hormone, secretin, in 1902, isolating it from the digestive tract. Since then considerably more hormones have been discovered, and it has become obvious that the digestive tract is the largest and most diffuse of all the endocrine organs. All digestive hormones have a role in regulating digestive activity, whether in the stomach or intestine. However, instead of issuing from distinct clumps of endocrine tissue, these substances are released from single cells scattered along the digestive tract.

The adrenal glands

The adrenals, which are paired in mammals, are named for their location close to the kidneys (renal means "relating to the kidney"). In humans, the adrenals are triangular structures positioned on top of each kidney. Each gland consists of two distinct parts: the outer cortex and the inner medulla. The yellowish cortex is stimulated by anterior pituitary hormones to secrete corticosteroid hormones. Corticosteroids are involved in protein and carbohydrate metabolism and in regulating the concentration of fluid in the body. The cortex also secretes small quantities of sex hormones (androgens and estrogens). The medulla secretes two hormones for use in highly charged or threatening situations, the result being the "fight or flight" reponse. These hormones are epinephrine and norepinephrine (see EPINEPHRINE AND NOREPINEPHRINE).

A classic paper by British physician Thomas Addison, published in 1855, first highlighted the disease resulting from failure of the adrenal cortex, which was named Addison's disease. However, it was not until 1913 that scientists concluded that it is the adrenal cortex, not the medulla, that is essential to life. Doctors were soon successfully treating patients dying of Addison's disease with extracts from the adrenal cortex.

The gonads

The sex hormones (and their associated hypothalamic and pituitary hormones) are involved in reproduction, from conception through menopause. The gonads (testes in the male, ovaries in the female) are usually paired in mammals. In most species, including humans, the testes (singular, testis) are suspended outside the abdominal cavity in the scrotal sac; the ovaries are in the lower abdomen.

The bulk of the testis is devoted to production of spermatozoa, but it is also responsible for the synthesis of androgens (male sex hormones), of which the most important is testosterone. The androgens are concerned both with sperm production and with the initiation and maintenance of male

ENDOCRINE GLANDS IN INVERTEBRATES

Most hormones in invertebrates are secreted by neurons rather than endocrine glands. However, both crustaceans and insects have endocrine glands as well as neurosecretory cells (see CRUSTACEANS; INSECTS).

In crustaceans hormones regulate molting, reproduction, heart rate, and metabolism. In insects endocrinal and neurosecretory hormones interact to regulate reproduction, metabolism, growth, and development. An environmental factor (such as temperature change; see THERMOREGULATION) affects neurosecretory cells in the brain; they produce brain hormone (BH), which is stored in the paired corpora cardiaca in the head of the insect. When released from the corpora cardiaca, BH stimulates the prothoracic glands, which are endocrine glands in the front end of the thorax; these glands then secrete a molting hormone called ecdysone to stimulate growth and molting.

Immature insects also have paired endocrine glands, called corpora allata, which secrete juvenile hormone. This hormone suppresses metamorphosis at each larval molt, allowing the insect to grow larger but remain immature (see GROWTH). Metamorphosis occurs when the concentration of juvenile hormone drops (see METAMORPHOSIS; MOLTING).

characteristics, including a deep voice and facial hair. The testes increase in size at puberty, when testosterone production intensifies.

The ovaries are concerned with the production of ova (egg cells). The ovarian follicles, in which the ova develop, synthesize progesterone and estrogens, steroid hormones produced cyclically. These hormones control female sexual development and also work to prepare the uterus for pregnancy and to maintain it once established.

The placenta, the organ by which the developing mammalian fetus is attached to the wall of the uterus, also has an endocrine function, in addition to its role of supplying nutrients to the fetus. In some species the placenta produces gonadal steroids to help support pregnancy. In humans it secretes human chorionic gonadotrophin (HCG), progesterone, and estrogens, which regulate the pregnancy by stimulating mucus production by the cervix and growth of the uterine lining and relaxing the muscles of the uterus so that the fetus is not expelled too soon. HCG is secreted by the membranes around the embryo, and the presence of HCG in the urine is used as the basis for most pregnancy tests.

The pineal body and thymus gland

Other tissues that have an endocrine function include the pineal body, which is present in the brain in nearly all vertebrates. In 1959 scientists discovered that the pineal gland secretes the hormone melatonin. Melatonin is of interest to physicians, drug manufacturers, and animal breeders for its involvement in daily and seasonal rhythms (SEE BIORHYTHMS). The pineal body receives information from the eyes about the photoperiod (the light-dark cycle) and secretes melatonin only during the hours of darkness. Changing levels of the hormone in the bloodstream enable the body to distinguish night from day and also to make changes appropriate to the season. In photoperiodic species, such as sheep and deer, whose lives are governed by the seasons, the hormone is influential in everything from mating to the growth of a winter coat.

In some species, especially lizards, the pineal body has an associated structure called the parapineal, which penetrates the braincase to lie just beneath the skin. In fish, amphibians, and reptiles (but not snakes), the pineal and parapineal contain photoreceptor (light-sensitive) cells. Many scientists believe the parapineal gland evolved from a sensory structure in fish to an endocrine gland in birds and mammals. However, it also has the same endocrine function, production of melatonin, in the less developed vertebrates.

Another structure that may have endocrine status is the thymus gland, which is involved in the development of immunity. This gland, found in all vertebrate groups, is situated in the neck or upper thorax. It is more prominent in young and larval forms than in adults, and in some species, including humans, the thymus gland may shrink after puberty. Some biologists have suggested that the biologically

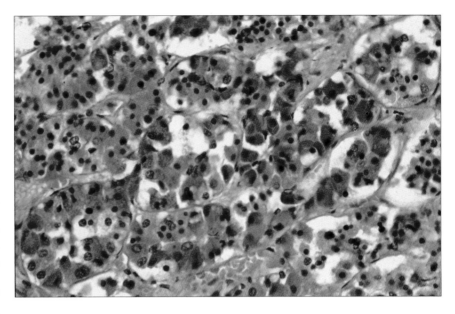

A cross section of the anterior lobe of a human pituitary gland (light micrograph x 50).

active substances isolated from the thymus, sometimes called thymic hormones, may initiate development of immune "awareness" in some white blood cells and bone marrow.

Human endocrine disease

Endocrine diseases can be genetic or acquired. Most of them arise from either too much or too little of a specific hormone being available when it is needed. Diabetes mellitus, for example, the best known of the endocrine disorders, is caused by a lack of the pancreatic hormone insulin (see DIABETES; INSULIN). Gigantism is owing to an over-secretion of growth hormone (GH) by the pituitary gland during childhood. Dwarfism, the reverse of gigantism, is due to a lack of GH (see GROWTH DISORDERS).

The reasons for too much or too little hormone vary. There may be over- or under-production by the gland, due to a tumor. Hormone-secreting tumors (mostly benign; noncancerous) can occur in all endocrine organs, especially the pituitary, thyroid, or parathyroids. Hormone synthesis may also be impaired by a missing or defective enzyme.

Many endocrine diseases, including primary ovarian or testicular failure, are autoimmune, that is, the body attacks itself. Autoimmune diseases occur in every major endocrine organ, the most prominent example being Type 1 (insulin-dependent) diabetes. More common in women, these conditions have a genetic connection.

P. PRATT

See also: ATP PRODUCTION; BIORHYTHMS; BRAIN; CRUSTACEANS; DIABETES; EPINEPHRINE AND NOREPINEPHRINE; GROWTH DISORDERS; HOMEOSTASIS; INFORMATION SCIENCE; INSECTS; INSULIN; KREBS CYCLE; METABOLISM; METAMORPHOSIS; MOLTING; PANCREAS; REPRODUCTION; THERMOREGULATION.

Further reading:
Griffin, J. E. and S. R. Ojeda. 1996. *Textbook of Endocrine Physiology.* 3rd ed. New York: Oxford University Press.

ENDORPHINS

Endorphins are morphinelike painkillers naturally produced by the body

Endorphins are chemicals, produced naturally by the central nervous system that suppress the perception of pain. Researchers studying why the synthetic painkiller morphine affects the body eventually discovered the body's natural painkillers. Endorphins were first isolated in 1975; the word endorphin is an abbreviation of "endogenously manufactured morphinelike substance"—that is, a morphinelike chemical manufactured by the body.

Most endorphins are produced in the pituitary gland and certain areas of the hypothalamus in the brain. They are opioid peptides, substances structurally similar to proteins but of much shorter chain length. The endorphins have pain-killing properties similar to some drugs, such as morphine, which is derived from opium. There are different types, named alpha-, beta-, and gamma-endorphins. Another type of opioid peptide is called enkephalin, which is produced mainly in the adrenal glands and certain areas of the brain. In the nervous system of most vertebrates, these natural painkillers interact with certain nerve cells on sites called opiate receptors, just as opiate drugs such as morphine do. They control the nerve impulses across the nerve synapses, reducing or relieving pain.

The release of endorphins has been connected with many body functions and responses and is thought to lead to significant changes in the pain regulation system. They have been associated with changes in blood cholesterol levels, memory, learning, sexual activity, depression, and schizophrenia. A well-known effect of endorphins (in particular beta-endorphins) occurs after vigorous exercise—the so-called runner's high. This phenomanon may be the body's way of coping with the strain of exercise by raising the pain threshold.

Beta-endorphins are unique: unlike the other opioid peptides, which are present in a number of regions of the brain, beta-endorphins have been found only in a group of cells in the brain's hypothalamus, the highest levels being in the pituitary gland. This gland releases the peptide at the same time as it releases adrenocorticotrophic hormone (ACTH), a hormone that is produced when someone is under stress. During World War II (1939–1945), surgeons found that wounded soldiers required a lower dose of painkillers than civilians when undergoing surgery, even though their wounds were extensive. Researchers have shown that the stress of combat increased the release of endorphins, as well as ACTH and thus altered the soldier's perception of pain. Researchers believe that some people have abnormally low levels of natural pain-killers. These low levels may explain some types of addiction, as a person tries to compensate for the lack of natural painkillers by consuming a substance that produces or intensifies the same

A well-known effect of the release of endorphins is the so-called runner's high, which may be a part of the body's way of coping with the pain of intense exercise.

effect. Normally, the endorphins occupy most of the receptor sites, and narcotics occupy any unfilled receptors, giving additional relief to the pain. However, the presence of narcotics reduces the production of natural painkillers, and as more sites become unoccupied, the craving for narcotics to fill the "holes" intensifies, leading to addiction.

P. BARNES-SVARNEY

See also: ADDICTION; ALTERNATIVE MEDICINE; BRAIN.

Further reading:
Marieb, Elaine Nicpon. 2000. *Human Anatomy and Physiology.* 5th ed. San Francisco: Benjamin/Cummings.

CONNECTIONS

- Endorphins are chemicals produced by the **NERVOUS SYSTEM**, which reduce the sensation of pain.

- The effects of these painkillers are similar to the effects of opiate **DRUGS**.

HELPING THE RELEASE OF ENDORPHINS

Alternative therapy makes use of alternatives to drugs for healing and pain relief. Acupuncture, the ancient Chinese healing art, is the insertion of needles at specific lines on the body (called meridians). According to acupuncturists, the needles allow the body's natural energy (or qi, pronounced "chi") to flow, and the method is used to eliminate imbalances in the body, leading to pain relief. Researchers believe that acupuncture may be effective because the stimulating needles cause the release of endorphins. Other alternative health methods may act in the same way, including reflexology, a technique that includes applying gentle pressure to the feet, hands, and ears, and acupressure, a method of using pressure on the body (the meridians) to treat specific symptoms or disorders (see ALTERNATIVE MEDICINE).

ENERGY

To be able to do work, people need energy. Even a person mentally solving a problem is doing work because thinking uses energy. Information is transferred through the nervous system, using the energy of shifting electrically charged particles, such as sodium and potassium ions, to carry signals. Biological work cannot always be observed in the same way as the moving of an object, but something is moved from one location to another within an organism whenever energy is used. In each cell and across each cell membrane, molecules and ions can move, and such movement often requires energy. Molecules can be rearranged when ions, atoms, or other molecules are added to or subtracted from them. Energy makes things happen in the world and within every living organism. Energy comes in many forms, all of which are interchangeable.

Laws of thermodynamics

The immediate source of energy for any living organism depends on its type. The farmer's cabbage is an energy source for the local rabbit; the little fish supplies food energy for the big fish. Whatever its source, scientists have concluded that the total energy of the Universe is constant. Energy can be changed from one form to another, but it can be neither created nor destroyed. This generalization is the first law of thermodynamics and is also called the law of conservation of energy.

The first law of thermodynamics states that energy can be changed only from one form to another. Windmills turn the energy from the wind into mechanical energy.

CORE FACTS

■ All forms of energy—mechanical, electrical, chemical, light, heat, and nuclear—can be changed from one form to another form.

■ The entire food web depends on energy from the Sun, stored in plants by photosynthesis.

■ The main energy carrier in all living systems is a molecule called adenosine triphosphate (ATP).

■ Complete metabolism of one molecule of glucose results in the formation of 36 molecules of ATP by the process of cellular respiration.

Light, heat, electrical, mechanical, nuclear, and chemical energy are all forms of energy that can change from one form into another. Light energy from the Sun (solar energy) can become heat energy when it is absorbed by Earth. Solar energy is also transformed into chemical energy, through photosynthesis: the process by which plants make food.

When fossil fuels are burned, the heat and light energy obtained was originally stored in plants many millions of years earlier as chemical energy. Chemical energy can also be converted to light in bioluminescent organisms, such as the firefly (see BIOLUMINESCENCE).

When energy changes from one form to another, some of it is always wasted and is usually lost as random heat. There is no perfect system in which some energy is never lost, whether it is a mechanical, chemical, or biological system.

Entropy is the term used to describe the energy that is not used to do work and measures the state of disorder in a system. One example of an increase in entropy is when molecules and ions in a solid enter a solution and immediately diffuse randomly to produce an equal concentration throughout the solution. The second law of thermodynamics states that entropy increases with every spontaneous change.

CONNECTIONS

● The first stage of energy transfer in living organisms is the process of **PHOTOSYNTHESIS.**

● **KREBS CYCLE** (tricarboxylic acid cycle, or citric acid cycle) is the central biochemical process that harnesses energy from food to be used by cells.

Visible light is just one part of the electromagnetic spectrum. The light in each band of color seen in a rainbow has a different energy value.

Potential and kinetic energy

There is another way of looking at energy. One form of energy is called potential, or stored, energy. This is energy that can be used but is not at that moment doing any work. An example would be a skier at the top of a ski jump waiting for the signal to race to the bottom. Work was done to get the skier to the high position. That work is now stored as potential energy. Carbohydrates (sugars), produced by photosynthesis in plants, are an example of stored energy in biological systems. Work was done to synthesize the carbohydrates, and that work is stored as potential energy.

Energy that is not potential is called kinetic energy. The term *kinetic* means "of motion." The skier going down the slope is an obvious example of kinetic energy. An example of kinetic energy that is not visible to people is the breaking down of glucose in the living cell by the process of glycolysis.

In the skier's race down the hill, not all the potential energy is converted to motion. Some energy is lost to entropy as heat in the friction of the skis on the snow. This lost heat energy cannot be used to carry out work—it is the energy of the random movement of molecules and is one of the most disorganized forms of energy.

Thermal energy, heat, and temperature

In every substance all particles are moving all of the time. The collective random movement of the particles is called thermal energy. The total thermal energy of a system cannot be measured, but scientists can measure changes in the total energy.

Temperature is a measure of the average kinetic energy of the randomly moving particles in a system. If two systems having different temperatures come into contact, kinetic energy of the faster-moving particles of the warmer system will be transferred to those of the cooler system. In time an intermediate common temperature will be reached (this phenomenon is called thermal equilibrium). The quantity of energy transferred in an exchange of thermal energy is called heat. Heat is measurable because temperature is measurable.

Heat is most commonly measured in calories. A calorie (cal) is the amount of heat that is necessary to raise the temperature of one gram of water one degree Celsius. Because a calorie is a very small unit, the kilocalorie (kcal or, in nutrition, calorie) is more often used, which is the amount of heat required to raise a kilogram of water by one degree Celsius. Calories are used for more than a measure of energy as heat or within foods; indirectly, they can also be considered a unit of metabolic energy (see CALORIES; METABOLISM).

Solar energy and photosynthesis

Solar energy is the primary source of energy, directly or indirectly, for most living organisms. Visible light is only one part of the complete electromagnetic spectrum, which also includes gamma rays, X rays, ultraviolet radiation, infrared radiation, microwaves, and radio waves. The spectrum extends from radiation of extremely short wavelength (such as gamma rays) to radiation of very long wavelength (such as radio waves). Short wavelengths have greater energy than long wavelengths.

Within the visible range is the spectrum of the familiar rainbow, ranging from violet through blue, green, yellow, orange, and red. Violet has the shortest wavelength and highest energy. Red has the longest wavelength and lowest energy. Wavelengths of light are measured in nanometers (nm); one nanometer is one billionth (10^{-9}) of a meter. Visible light ranges from violet at 380 nm to red at 750 nm.

Solar energy travels to Earth through space. However, about a third of the energy from the Sun is reflected back into space by clouds, snow, ice, and the oceans. Most of the solar energy that reaches Earth's surface is in the visible range, and this energy warms the atmosphere and drives the winds and ocean currents.

Less than 1 percent of sunlight that reaches Earth is absorbed by certain organisms such as plants and algae, which use the solar energy to convert carbon dioxide and water into complex organic molecules in the process of photosynthesis. Such organisms belong to a group called autotrophs. Autotrophs are organisms that make their own food, either by photosynthesis or chemosynthesis (a process by which energy is provided by chemical reactions).

A number of pigments are involved in photosynthesis. The pigments absorb photons (units of light energy) of certain wavelengths and reflect the rest of the wavelengths received. The principal pigments in plants are chlorophylls. Chlorophylls absorb light in the violet, blue, and red range but reflect green light. Thus, the predominant color of plants appears green.

When chlorophyll molecules in plants absorb photons of light, electrons in the molecules are excited—that is, those electrons are raised to a higher energy level (relative to the nuclei in the atoms of the molecules of chlorophyll) than they normally occupy. This change of state is the source of the energy used in photosynthesis.

Chemical energy

In addition to photosynthesis, hundreds of other important chemical reactions take place in living organisms. All of these reactions depend on the energy of electrons, and energy exchanges occur when chemical reactions take place.

A neutral atom (one that is not ionized to be positively or negatively charged) has a number of positively charged protons in the nucleus and an equal number of negatively charged electrons held in stable orbits around it. When an electron absorbs energy, as from a photon, it is raised to a higher energy orbit. If enough energy is absorbed, the electron may move away from the atom altogether and become part of another atom.

When a substance burns it combines with oxygen and gives up electrons. Any chemical reaction that involves the loss of electrons is called oxidation. The reverse of oxidation is called reduction, and an atom or molecule that receives an electron is said to be reduced. If an atom loses an electron (is oxidized), it will then have a net positive charge. The atom is then a positive ion, while the atom receiving the electron becomes a negative ion. If the atom is part of a molecule, the whole molecule will be a positive (or negative) ion, and some molecules lose or gain several electrons and thus become highly charged. Oxidation-reduction reactions involving the exchange of electrons are essential in energy transfer throughout biological systems.

Most chemical bonds can be classified as ionic or covalent. Ionic bonds form between oppositely charged ions. Covalent bonds form when atoms share a pair of electrons. Organic molecules are carbon based, and carbon can form up to four covalent bonds. Organic molecules can be large and complex and, in biological systems, often have very specialized functions.

If a chemical reaction between molecules is to occur, they must interact with sufficient energy to break or form one or more bonds. This energy is called activation energy. If the total energy of the products is less than the reactants, the reaction releases energy and is called exergonic. If the total energy of the products is more than the reactants, the process is endergonic and absorbs energy from the biological system (see the diagram below). Photosynthesis is an endergonic process because energy is absorbed by the Sun to produce complex organic molecules from simple starting materials.

In either endergonic or exergonic reactions, the activation energy may be very high. In biological systems, the activation energy is often too high for many reactions to occur in any reasonable time, were it not for catalysts. Catalysts provide alternate and lower energy-demanding pathways for chemical reactions. They speed the rate of a reaction, but they do not change the outcome. Catalysts are used but not consumed by the reaction.

Most biochemical reactions are catalyzed by proteins called enzymes (see ENZYMES). To work as a catalyst, some enzymes need a coenzyme, which often acts as the carrier of either electrons or protons in a catalyzed reaction. The reactant in an enzyme-catalyzed reaction is called the substrate.

Energy pathways in photosynthesis

Photosynthesis takes place in chloroplasts in plant cells (see PHOTOSYNTHESIS) and initially involves light-dependent reactions, followed by those that are independent of light. In the first stage of light-dependent reactions, in a complex structure called photosystem II, photons are absorbed by a reactive form of chlorophyll (called P_{680}), which is sensitive to light that has a wavelength of 680 nm. Its electrons are energized by the light, and it is

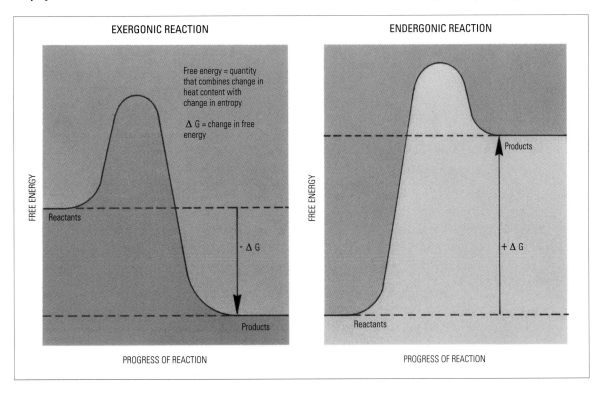

EXERGONIC REACTION

Free energy = quantity that combines change in heat content with change in entropy

Δ G = change in free energy

FREE ENERGY

Reactants

$-\Delta$ G

Products

PROGRESS OF REACTION

ENDERGONIC REACTION

FREE ENERGY

Products

$+\Delta$ G

Reactants

PROGRESS OF REACTION

Energy changes in exergonic (left) and endergonic (right) reactions. In exergonic reactions the products have less energy than the reactants, and energy is released. In endergonic reactions the products have more energy than the reactants: there is a net input of energy.

A computer graphics model of an ATP molecule bound to phosphoglycerate kinase, a glycolytic enzyme. The carbon backbone appears as yellow, with ATP highlighted in green. The bonding of oxygen, carbon, and nitrogen atoms in ATP are shown as red, white, and blue, respectively. ATP supplies energy for many biological cellular processes by undergoing enzymatic hydrolysis (interaction with water), especially to ADP.

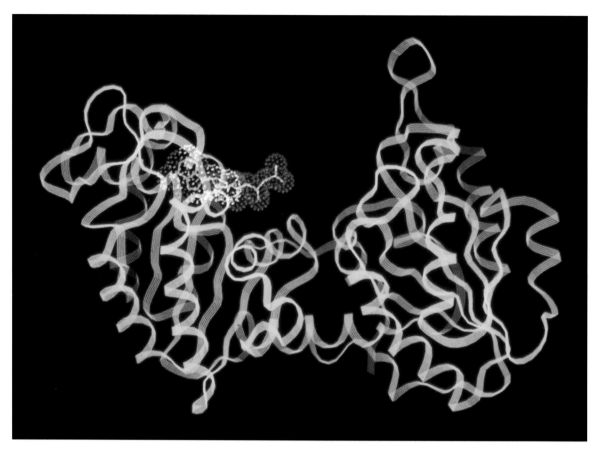

oxidized, thus losing electrons; it then recovers electrons from water molecules (H_2O), releasing hydrogen ions (H^+), and producing oxygen (O_2).

Electrons from P_{680} move through a series of oxidation-reduction reactions, giving up energy with each transfer. Some of the released energy is used to convert ADP (adenosine diphosphate) to ATP (adenosine triphosphate) by the addition of a phosphate ion. ATP is an important energy-carrying molecule in light-independent reactions and many other biochemical reactions.

At the end of these reactions, the electrons are donated to a second system called photosystem I. The reactive chlorophyll is P_{700}, which is sensitive to light with a wavelength of 700 nm. P_{700} is oxidized by light, and its energized electrons go through a series of oxidation-reduction reactions that end with the reduction of $NADP^+$ (oxidized form of nicotinamide adenine dinucleotide phosphate) to form NADPH (an important coenzyme in other processes). P_{700} is regenerated with electrons from photosystem II. These light-dependent reactions provide the chemical energy (stored in ATP and NADPH) that is needed to reduce carbon from carbon dioxide to carbohydrates in the light-independent reactions (see PHOTOSYNTHESIS).

ATP—the energy carrier

The main energy carrier for all metabolic pathways —including photosynthesis—is ATP, adenosine triphosphate. It stores large amounts of energy within its chemical structure, and it is continuously synthesized and degraded as needed in response to the energy needs of the cell. Each ATP molecule has

three main parts: adenine, also found in nucleic acids (see DNA); a five-carbon sugar called ribose; and three phosphate groups (phosphorus surrounded by oxygen atoms). When ADP, adenosine diphosphate, gains a phosphate ion, energy is absorbed and ATP is formed. This process is called phosphorylation, energy for which often comes from electron transfer in oxidation-reduction reactions. The bonds holding the phosphate groups are weak and break easily. Many biosynthetic reactions are endergonic (that is, energy demanding). ATP provides energy for these reactions when it breaks down to ADP, releasing energy in the process.

In another process, chemiosmosis, synthesis of ATP is driven by a force similar to osmosis. Energetic reactions from NADH (the reduced form of nicotinamide adenine dinucleotide, NAD^+) and $FADH_2$ (the reduced form of flavin adenine dinucleotide—FAD) drive hydrogen ions (H^+) from an area of lower concentration to one of higher concentration. The energy generated as the ions move back to lower concentration regions is used for the synthesis of ATP from ADP and phosphate ions.

Energy pathways in catabolism

Getting energy from glucose by aerobic respiration is a multistage process. In the first stage, glycolysis, two molecules of ATP are used to convert a molecule of six-carbon glucose into two three-carbon pyruvate molecules. Along the way, the two molecules of ATP are regenerated, two more are produced from available ADP and phosphate ions, and hydrogen atoms are picked up by two molecules of coenzyme NAD^+ to form two NADH molecules, which will be needed in a later stage. Glycolysis and the next step, which produces yet two more NADH, take place in the cytoplasm of cell, and do not require oxygen.

The third stage of aerobic respiration takes place in mitochondria, which are organelles within each cell. Oxygen is required by mitochondria, where a series of reactions called the citric acid cycle (see KREBS CYCLE) produce more ATP and NADH, FADH$_2$, and carbon dioxide. Mitochondria have two membranes. The last stage of the cycle takes place at the inner membrane and is the chemiosmotic process described above, using NADH and FADH$_2$. The net gain in ATP in the breakdown of glucose molecules depends on cell conditions and the particular pathway followed, but on average, 36 ATP are gained for each glucose molecule.

Aerobic respiration is about 38 percent efficient in energy terms; that is, 38 percent of the energy of each glucose molecule is stored in the ATP, and the remaining energy is released as heat.

Other catabolic pathways generate less energy. Fermentation, the anaerobic (in the absence of oxygen) breakdown of glucose (see FERMENTATION) yields just two ATP molecules for each molecule of glucose. Yeasts, bacteria, and certain fungi carry out fermentation. Because anaerobic respiration is less energy efficient, it requires large amounts of fuel. Anaerobic cells need about 20 times as much glucose as aerobic cells do to carry out the same amount of work.

Energy storage in plants and animals

Through photosynthesis, green plants manufacture carbohydrates from carbon dioxide and water, storing the energy absorbed from light in chemical bonds. Carbohydrates are organic molecules made of carbon, hydrogen, and oxygen (see CARBOHYDRATES). Simple carbohydrates are soluble in water and move through plants by a process called translocation: movement through the phloem, the tissues used to conduct nutrients to all parts of growing plants. If carbohydrates are not needed for plant metabolism, they are stored in locations throughout the plant. An important carbohydrate transported and stored in plants is the soluble disaccharide (double sugar molecule), such as sucrose. Other important storage carbohydrates in plants are relatively insoluble polysaccharides called starches. They are stored in microscopic granules in seeds, roots, and fruits and are the principal food storage substance in plants. Familiar starch sources in food include corn, wheat, rice, and potatoes.

Some glucose is converted to fats and oils (lipids). Lipids are water insoluble and can be differentiated by their melting points. Plants store fats and oils in fruits and seeds; olives, peanuts, corn, and coconuts are familiar sources.

Animals depend on plants directly or indirectly for their food, and carbohydrates provide the most immediate source of energy. Sucrose, which readily breaks down into fructose and glucose, supplies about 13 percent of the energy needed by an average active person. Other carbohydrates and fats and oils supply most of the rest of the necessary energy. When vertebrates such as humans have an excess of glucose in the bloodstream, as occurs after eating a carbohydrate-rich meal, the surplus is stored as glycogen in the liver and in muscles. Glycogen is a polysaccharide and a primary food storage substance in animals.

Surplus food energy is also stored in animals as fat and oils. Fat contains more than six times the energy of an equivalent weight of glycogen. An average adult stores enough glycogen for a day but enough fat for a month. If this energy had to be stored as glycogen, the average body weight would be increased by about 60 pounds (27 kg).

Migrating birds may double their weight with stored fat before migration to supply the energy reserve for the flight, because the weight of an equal amount of energy stored as carbohydrates would make the birds too heavy to fly. Animals such as walruses, seals, and whales use thick layers of stored fats or oils for insulation, as well as for energy reserves, in their cold environments.

Proteins make up about half the dry weight of cells and are very complex molecules containing nitrogen. There are many different proteins with a wide variety of different functions. Some proteins serve structural roles in cells. Enzymes, hemoglobin, antibodies, and the contractile structures of muscles are also proteins. Other proteins are stored in beans, peas, nuts, seeds, and eggs. Animals depend on plants and other animals as protein sources. When they need their stored energy, proteins are the last source to be used.

M. NAGEL

See also: BIOLUMINESCENCE; CALORIES; CARBOHYDRATES; CELL BIOLOGY; DNA; ENZYMES; FERMENTATION; METABOLISM.

Further reading:
Brown, Guy C. 2000. *The Energy of Life: The Science of What Makes Our Minds and Bodies Work.* New York: Free Press.

The action of the cat leaping after its prey uses energy. If the cat catches and eats the bird, this meal provides energy for its future activity.

ENTOMOLOGY

Entomology is the scientific study of insects

*A migratory locust (*Locusta migratoria*) mass above a marsh in Botswana, southern Africa. Locust swarms have caused devastation to crops since biblical times. A swarm may be as dense as 100 to 200 million insects per square mile (260 to 500 million per km²).*

CONNECTIONS

● Some systems of **BIOLOGICAL CONTROL** may use insects to prey on insect pests: the habits of both insect species are studied by entomologists.

● **INSECTS** are of great ecological importance because two-thirds of all flowering plants depend on them for **POLLINATION**.

● The information gathered by entomologists has been crucial in **MEDICINE** to help doctors find ways of combating certain serious diseases.

● There is considerable evidence that many chemicals used as **PESTICIDES** to kill insect pests can cause diseases such as **CANCER** in the farmers that use them and the consumers that eat sprayed products.

Although insects are among some of Earth's smaller creatures, they are by far the largest class of animals. There are around 900,000 known species, and it is estimated that a similar number of species is yet to be discovered. Insects belong to their own class of the phylum Arthropoda, which also includes crustaceans, spiders, ticks, and centipedes, and are the most successful group of animals ever to have evolved on Earth. The scientific study of insects is called entomology. Entomology is an important branch of science because insects are of great significance to people. Throughout the world insects are responsible for an enormous amount of food loss, including damage to crops and stored foods, and also transmit diseases to people, plants, and animals. In nature insects play a vital role as scavengers and pollinators and are also providers of economically valuable products, such as honey and silk.

People and insects

People have long recognized the importance of insects. Early people undoubtedly had fleas and lice and were pestered by mosquitoes and flies. Large insects may have been an important part of their diet. When people changed from a hunting-gathering to an agriculturally based lifestyle, their relationship with insects took on a new significance. Crop cultivation meant that high concentrations of plants were grown in particular areas, resulting in a buildup of large insect populations. The devastating effects of locust swarms on crops are recorded from ancient times, and when people began to plant and store food, insects homed in on these large sources of nutrition.

However, while insects have harassed people since ancient times, they have themselves been exploited for just as long. Production of silk by silkworms has been utilized by people since about 2500 BCE, while management of bees for wax and honey is thought to have first been practiced by the ancient Egyptians.

The history of entomology

In the 4th century BCE, Greek philosopher and naturalist Aristotle (384–322 BCE; see ARISTOTLE) described the biology of insects and recognized that their anatomy is based on three major body parts. The science of entomology got its name from Aristotle's work: *entomon* is the Greek word meaning "insect." However, after Aristotle's time, entomology did not really develop much further until 1602, when Italian naturalist Ulisse Aldrovandi (1522–1605) published a major work called *Of Insect Animals* (*De Animalibus Insectis*). In the mid-17th century, the invention of the microscope led to major advances in all the life sciences, including entomology. Two naturalists, an

---

CORE FACTS

■ Entomology is the scientific study of insects.
■ Entomologists have identified around 900,000 species of insects and believe there are just as many more still to be discovered.
■ Insects are extremely important because they pollinate flowers; some transmit disease and damage crops.

Italian, Marcello Malpighi (1628–1694) (see EXCRE-
TORY SYSTEMS), and a Dutchman, Jan Swammerdam
(1637–1680) (see CELL BIOLOGY), conducted the first
accurate studies of insect anatomy.

In Europe toward the end of the 17th century and
into the 18th century, interest in natural history, particularly entomology, increased. By the middle of the
18th century, biological nomenclature had become
extremely cumbersome. Names of species consisted of
long phrases or descriptions, all in Latin, and often
used inconsistently. The binomial nomenclature of
Swedish naturalist Carolus Linnaeus (1707–1778) (see
TAXONOMY) was applied to animals in the 10th edition
of his *Systema Naturae* in 1758, and this system greatly
simplified the naming of insect species.

The first outstanding insect taxonomist was Johann
Fabricius (1745–1808) from Denmark. He based his
taxonomy on mouthpart structure and tried to cover
the entire insect fauna of the world in his book *Systema
Entomologica*. It soon became obvious that insect taxonomy was too large a task for one person. Since then,
most workers have studied just one group of insects
or insects from only one country.

Modern entomology

Modern entomology is often divided into two main
parts: one concerned purely with scientific research
and the other with the applied aspects of entomology.
Scientific entomology is concerned purely with the
basic taxonomy, ecology, behavior, and physiology of
insects. Applied entomology (often called economic
entomology) is concerned with pest management and
economically important insect producers. Applied
entomologists also study how populations of predatory insects might be manipulated as a means of biological control (see BIOLOGICAL CONTROL).

Applied entomology is of such importance,
especially to agriculture, that governments, agricultur-
alists, and chemical companies spend millions of dollars on the study of pest species.

Medical entomology

A branch of applied entomology, medical entomology, emerged in the 19th century as a result of a series
of discoveries that identified insects as the carriers
responsible for transmitting some of the world's worst
diseases. In 1898, British physician Ronald Ross
(1857–1932) showed that mosquitoes transmitted
malaria, and in 1900, U.S. army surgeon Walter Reed
(1851–1902) proved that they carry yellow fever.
Many more diseases have now been associated with
insect vectors, for example, African sleeping sickness,
transmitted by the tsetse fly, and bubonic plague, which
is carried by fleas (see INFECTIOUS DISEASES).

Applied entomology in action

A great deal of research by applied entomologists is
directed at finding ways of controlling the insects
responsible for transmitting disease. For example,
malaria kills more than 1 million African children
under the age of five, produces symptoms in more
than 150 million people, and threatens a further

2 billion people in tropical countries. Malaria is caused
by four species of *Plasmodium*, a single-celled protozoan
transmitted by about 30 species of *Anopheles* mosquito.
Early scientists studying this insect soon discovered that
mosquitoes rely on stagnant water in which to breed. A
combination of massive drainage programs and the use
of insecticides began to reduce the number of cases of
malaria. For example, by 1986, clearing cesspits, open
drains, and swamps near Pondicherry, South India, had
reduced the incidence of mosquito bites by 90 percent
and led to a dramatic drop in the incidence of malaria.

However, both *Anopheles* mosquitoes and the
malaria parasite easily develop resistance to insecticides
and drugs. Studies on vaccines have had mixed results.
Applied entomologists involved in the problem may
next turn their efforts toward genetic engineering to
find ways to wipe out the mosquitoes.

K. McCALLUM

See also: ARISTOTLE; ARTHROPODS; CELL BIOLOGY;
EXCRETORY SYSTEMS; FLEAS; FLIES; INFECTIOUS DISEASES;
LICE; TAXONOMY; WASPS AND BEES.

Further reading:
Waldbauer, G. 1998. *The Handy Bug Answer Book*.
Detroit: Visible Ink.

THE DEVELOPMENT OF AMERICAN ENTOMOLOGY

It was not until around 1800 that
U.S. scientists began to study U.S.
insects. Before then some studies had
been included by English naturalist
Mark Catesby (1679–1749) in his book
*A Natural History of Carolina, Florida,
and the Bahama Islands*, which
contained representations of the
"Birds, Beasts, Fishes, Insects, and
Plants": European entomologists had
also collected and described a few
species. A major breakthrough for
American entomology came in 1812,
when a group of naturalists set up the
Academy of Natural Sciences of
Philadelphia. One of them was the
outstanding entomologist Thomas Say
(1787–1834). From 1817 to 1828, Say
published in three volumes the
*American Entomology, or Descriptions
of the Insects of North America*.
This work quickly became a classic

*Thomas Say, who has been called the
Father of American Entomology.*

entomological text. Because of the extremely high quality of his work, Thomas
Say has been called the Father of American Entomology.

Another landmark of American entomology came in 1841, when Thaddeus
Harris (1795–1865) published *Report on Insects Injurious to Vegetation,* which
became the first textbook of applied entomology. The work of Say and Harris
had a great influence on future entomologists, and before long many
scientists began publishing papers on every aspect of insect biology. Since
the middle of the 19th century, state and federal funding has supported
considerable research in insect biology.

A CLOSER LOOK

ENVIRONMENTAL DISASTERS

Environmental disasters are events that seriously damage ecosystems

A forest fire on the Caribbean island of Trinidad. In many regions of the world, forest fires are part of the natural cycle, in spite of having seemingly disastrous short-term effects. In some areas of the world, however, fires have been used by people to clear rain forest for farming, and in these cases they really have been a disaster for a rich environment and the species within it.

CONNECTIONS

● Some scientists theorize that one of the largest environmental disasters to affect Earth was a meteorite impact that led to the extinction of **DINOSAURS**.

● An environment in grave danger from human activities is the **TROPICAL RAIN FOREST BIOME**. Conservationists fear that if too much rain forest disappears, many species will become extinct.

Environmental disasters can be due to many different causes, both natural and human made, but they all damage the life-forms in an ecosystem. Disasters caused by human activities can be either sudden or more long term in their effect. The worst of these disasters are connected to an increase in industrial and economic growth or to powerful technology that is misused or gets out of control.

Human activities and natural events

Nuclear power is the single most powerful energy source scientists have discovered. Ionizing radiation from nuclear materials has been a source of potential environmental disasters since the 1940s. The most notable incident was the nuclear reactor explosion at Chernobyl, in the Ukraine, on April 26, 1986. This explosion released a dust cloud 50 times as radioactive as those from the nuclear bombs dropped on the Japanese cities of Hiroshima and Nagasaki at the close of World War II in 1945. More than thirty people were killed immediately at Chernobyl, many more later developed cancer, and 135,000 people were evacuated from the contaminated zone.

Modern industry creates and uses many materials, besides nuclear materials, that can cause severe environmental damage: in March 1989, for example, the supertanker *Exxon Valdez* polluted hundreds of miles of coastline with the oil it was carrying when it ran aground in Prince William Sound, Alaska (see the box on page 623).

It seems that sudden human-made environmental disasters, such as toxic waste spills, sewage release, and radiation leaks, are becoming an increasing consequence of modern life. Also extremely important are human activities that have disastrous effects on the environment that become apparent only after many years.

For example, DDT, a pesticide once widely used, is now banned in the United States because of its severe impact on the ecosystem. The populations of some species of birds have been critically reduced because of DDT contamination. Ingestion of DDT interferes with the way birds can use calcium and causes the shells of their eggs to be too thin, so they break easily. The impact has been greatest on fish-eating seabirds, such as pelicans, and birds of prey,

CORE FACTS

■ Environmental disasters are events that result in serious damage to an ecosystem.

■ Typical natural events that seriously affect the environment are volcanic eruptions, floods, droughts, winds, and sometimes collisions with other bodies in the Universe, such as asteroids or comets.

■ Human activities that have sudden adverse effects include oil spills and chemical or nuclear contamination.

■ Other human activities, such as the use of pesticides, may have serious effects that take longer to recognize.

because these birds are at the top of the food chain, where the pesticide becomes concentrated (see BIRDS OF PREY; CARSON, RACHEL LOUISE; DDT; FOOD WEBS).

Deforestation is another progressive environmental disaster. In some forested areas in countries such as Sri Lanka and New Caledonia, only 10 percent of the original trees remain. Even in areas where much of the forest is intact, the deforestation rate is accelerating rapidly. Clear-cutting vast forests results in the extinction of countless species and loss of habitat. It also has a severe impact on the cycling of oxygen, carbon, and water in the biosphere. Removal of the forests may even change the reflectance of Earth's surface, increasing temperatures around the world (see GLOBAL WARMING).

Another environmental disaster is the depletion of the ozone layer in the atmosphere, which acts as a shield against ultraviolet radiation from the Sun. An increase in ultraviolet radiation reaching Earth's surface could result in widespread crop failures and an increase in skin cancers and epidemic diseases.

In the late 1970s, scientists found extensive evidence that chemicals called chlorofluorocarbons (CFCs) were gradually destroying the ozone layer. CFCs were then used in a variety of industrial applications, from aerosols to refrigerator coolants. Since 1996, CFCs have been banned globally and phased out of use. Although this ban will not reverse the ozone depletion, it has slowed down. It may take until the middle of the 22nd century for ozone levels in the Antarctic to return to 1970 levels.

There are also many natural events that can adversely affect the environment, such as fire, volcanic eruptions, earthquakes, hurricanes, floods, drought, and other weather changes. The effects of these events, however, are soon absorbed by the ecosystem or have limited impact. They seem massive to people because of the damage they cause to human society and property. However, these broad-scale disturbances are important natural processes that keep ecosystems healthy and diverse.

Fire

Each year in the United States, 1 to 2 million acres (40,500 to 81,000 hectares) of the approximately 225 million acres (9,105,000 hectares) of forests are burned in forest fires. Most fires are started by lightning storms; some fires are started by human activity. Such fires can be temporarily devastating to wildlife, destroying their sources of food and protection and killing many animals directly.

For most ecosystems, however, fire is a means of renewal. Sweeping through grassland, scrub, or forests, it clears out old dead plant material and returns the nutrients to the soil. The seeds of some plants need to pass through the heat of the fire in order to germinate (see DORMANCY). California's chaparral habitat is so reliant on periodic fires that it is called a "fire community." Only when people build their homes there does the chaparral fire become a disaster—not for the biome but for the people who live there (see CHAPARRAL BIOME).

CLEANING UP AFTER THE *EXXON VALDEZ*

One of the most disastrous oil spills of all time, the *Exxon Valdez* incident was also one of the most difficult to clean up. Strenuous efforts were made to prevent the oil from reaching the coast. There are several methods that can be employed. Sometimes detergents are sprayed to help break up the oil slick before it reaches the shore. Then special oil-collecting boats skim the oil from the surface of the water. Floating containment rings are also used near inlets to restrict the movement of the slick. However, containing the oil from *Exxon Valdez* was hampered by high winds and waves, which caused the oil to wash over the rings.

On rocky parts of the coastline, hot steam was used to soften the oil so that it could be removed by working crews; on sandy beaches the entire surface of the beach was scraped off and removed by hundreds of workers. Yet in spite of these efforts, the 10 million gallons (nearly 38 million liters) of oil killed thousands of seabirds, hundreds of marine mammals, and countless invertebrates.

Animals and birds covered with the oil had to be cleaned laboriously with detergents. Those that had tried to clean themselves and so ingested the oil could not be saved. They died of poisoning.

Cleaning a seabird thoroughly coated with oil in the wake of the Exxon Valdez *disaster. Some birds were saved even when covered with oil, but they inevitably died if they swallowed too much oil in trying to clean themselves.*

LETTING FIRES RAGE

Yellowstone National Park in Wyoming has always had occasional wildfires. In 1988, however, wildfires raged through a great deal of the park, scorching 1 million acres (40,500 hectares) of land—or about one half of the park and 45 percent more than in any year since its founding in 1872. Scientists held back from putting out most of the fires because they decided that such "disastrous" events were part of the natural life cycle of the region.

However, letting Yellowstone burn was not an easy decision. Before the 1970s, fires were suppressed if possible; more recent policy has been to allow fires to burn. It has been suggested that the park's earlier policy of putting out fires may have increased the seriousness of the fire because fuel (wood) accumulated in the forest. Some 10 years later, Yellowstone had repaired itself naturally in many of the fire-scorched regions. The scientists' decision appeared vindicated, but the complex role of fire in the environment is still debated.

Volcanoes and earthquakes

These expressions of massive forces within Earth may seem disastrous when they occur, but the local damage they do is usually soon made up. The Mount St. Helens eruption in Washington State in 1980 flattened every tree for over 230 square miles (600 km^2) and killed an estimated 5,000 black-tailed deer, 200 black bears, 1,500 elks, and countless birds. However, vegetation soon took root, thriving on the fertile soils produced by the volcanic ash, while outside the area the ecosystem was hardly altered.

Earthquakes destroy people's property, but unless they are accompanied by tidal waves, they rarely have more than a minor effect on the ecosystem.

Winds, tidal waves, and floods

Strong winds and flooding can cause changes in ecosystems. For example, a hurricane that struck the New England coast in 1938 dramatically flooded the coastline. Rivers can change their course and wetlands can flood completely because of the sudden influx of water. Such changes affect wildlife and vegetation in the area. However, as with fire, the effects of regular flooding or strong winds can be absorbed into an ecosystem, and even the strongest tornadoes have little long-term impact.

Drought and weather changes

A period of sudden drought is difficult for ecosystems to cope with. In Africa the Sahara Desert is

A satellite image of deforestation in Rondonia Province, Brazil. The blue lines are areas where farmers have cut down the rain forest. Rain forest destruction may change weather patterns across the entire planet.

DISASTER FROM SPACE

Is it possible that an asteroid, comet, or large meteorite will ever strike Earth again? The answer is yes; but no one really knows when. Astronomers do know there are certain asteroids that come close to Earth. In the past few years, several such bodies have come within hundreds of thousands of miles (close in astronomical terms), but none struck the planet. Comets also come close to Earth: scientists believe that, in 1908, a comet or meteorite vaporized above a forest in Siberia, knocking down trees and killing wildlife within a few-mile radius.

About 65 million years ago, the dinosaurs, along with about 50 percent of all other species, became extinct. Many scientists believe that a comet or asteroid (or a shower of comets and asteroids) struck Earth, causing tons of material to enter Earth's atmosphere. This environmental disaster could have changed the climate because dust particles in the upper atmosphere reflected some of the Sun's radiation out into space, cooling the global climate, and causing changes in vegetation and thus in food sources.

---

moving south year by year, taking over previously fertile land. This desertification process is accelerated with local human use of land for cultivation or for general living purposes (see DESERTIFICATION).

Droughts can be a disaster for the ecosystems affected. However, drought as a natural event must be put into the context of general weather changes. Earth's weather is always changing and may affect temperature and rainfall, which in turn affect life-forms. Whether they should be classed as disasters depends on whether the changes radically limit the number of life-forms in an ecosystem.

The impact of space objects

Whereas forces from within Earth may be absorbed into ecosystems, the impact of objects from space is unpredictable. It is no surprise that such objects —asteroids and comets miles wide and smaller meteorites—have struck Earth in the past. The best evidence is the more than 100 nearly-circular land features called impact craters, such as the Meteor Crater, near Winslow, Arizona. There are probably even more impact craters on the ocean floor.

Large impacting space objects could cause a major environmental disaster. An impact in the oceans would probably change the local weather for weeks, as the steam from the hot object rose. Marine wildlife within the area would also die. An impact on land would be even more devastating. If a sufficiently large object hit Earth, many life-forms could be wiped out. Such an impact is what some scientists think affected the dinosaurs (see the box above).

P. BARNES-SVARNEY

See also: BIRDS OF PREY; CARSON, RACHEL LOUISE; CHAPARRAL BIOMES; DDT; DESERTIFICATION; DORMANCY ECOLOGY AND ECOSYSTEMS; EXTINCTION; FOOD WEBS; GLOBAL WARMING; RADIATION AND RADIATION SICKNESS.

Further reading:

Davis, Lee A. 1998. *Environmental Disasters: A Chronicle of Individual, Industrial, and Governmental Carelessness*. New York: Facts on File Incorporated.

ENVIRONMENTAL DISEASES

Environmental diseases are caused by factors in the environment

Environmental diseases come from a variety of sources. They can be divided into three general groups: diseases caused by conditions or substances that exist in the environment outside the home, both naturally and through the direct action of people, either deliberately or accidentally; diseases caused by home environments; and finally, diseases caused by working environments.

Whatever the causes of environmental diseases, society spends huge sums of money to cope with them. In 1992 alone, for example, $120 billion in public money was set aside in the United States to help protect the environment.

The atmosphere

The air people breathe is close to the top of the list of concerns about the natural environment. On October 27, 1948, a combination of weather patterns trapped industrial and other pollutants over Donora, a Pennsylvanian mill town. By the time the air cleared, 20 people were dead and 6,000 others had fallen sick. In December 1952, a "killer fog" (a thick layer of smog full of industrial pollutants) settled over London, England, killing more than 4,000 people. Air in the United States improved after the passage of the Clean Air Act in 1970, but it has a long way to go.

The air can contain many unhealthy components:

● **Particulates:** These are tiny bits of solid and liquid matter suspended in the air. When people breathe particulates into their lungs, respiratory problems may occur. Most particulates come from industrial smokestacks and vehicle exhaust pipes. U.S. legislation on the control of emissions has resulted in considerable improvement of air quality with respect to particulates in the United States.

● **Sulfur dioxide:** Most atmospheric sulfur dioxide (SO_2) comes from burning fossil fuels that have high sulfur contents, especially by utility companies. High concentrations of the chemical can cause death as a result of respiratory failure, as well as bring about chronic respiratory diseases. Sulfur dioxide also causes acid rain (see ACID RAIN).

● **Nitrogen dioxide:** Another product of combustion, or burning of fossil fuels, is nitrogen dioxide

Uncontrolled smoke emission releases many contaminants into the atmosphere, including particulates, sulfur dioxide, and nitrogen dioxide.

(NO_2). It can irritate people's lungs and lower their resistance to respiratory infections. It also contributes to smog, the blend of smoke and chemicals that hangs over many densely populated and industrial areas, as well as to acid rain.

● **Ozone:** The role of ozone (O_3) is complicated. The gas, formed by the action of ultraviolet (UV) radiation on ordinary oxygen (O_2), exists naturally high in the atmosphere and performs a valuable function. In the upper atmosphere, the ozone layer filters out the Sun's harmful UV radiation before it strikes Earth. Reduced ozone in the upper atmosphere ("holes" in the ozone layer) means an increase in UV radiation, which heightens risks of skin cancer, eye damage, and harm to the immune system.

Ozone can also be formed in the lower atmosphere, however, by the action of sunlight reacting with nitrogen dioxide. Ozone then contributes to photochemical smog and may cause respiratory problems and damage to plant life.

● **Carbon monoxide:** Motor vehicles and most other burners of fuel produce carbon monoxide (CO), an odorless, colorless gas that prevents the absorption of oxygen by the hemoglobin in red blood cells. Carbon monoxide is highly poisonous. Breathing carbon monoxide produces drowsiness, confused thinking, and eventually death.

● **Lead:** Most lead in the atmosphere came from car exhausts, a product of the antiknock compound tetraethyl lead. However, leaded gasoline is no longer used in cars in the United States. Lead steadily builds up in the body. It can seriously damage the kidneys, and in young children it can produce mental retardation and cerebral palsy.

CORE FACTS

■ The natural environment, as well as people's homes and workplaces, may be contaminated with substances that can produce disease.

■ The United States has set aside $4.5 billion for global climate change-related activities for the year 2003.

■ One in five Americans is believed to suffer from allergies, many of which are caused by environmental hazards.

■ Government scientists estimate the cost of treating asthma-related diseases at $14.5 billion a year.

CONNECTIONS

● Environmental contamination can result in a wide variety of human diseases, as well as harming **ECOSYSTEMS.**

● Diseases attributable to environmental factors include **ALLERGIES, ASTHMA,** and **CANCER.**

● **POLLUTION** occurs when harmful substances, especially chemicals and waste, contaminate the environment.

• **Hydrocarbons:** Not all the fuel in motor vehicle engines is burned efficiently, and exhaust fumes can contain residues of hydrocarbons (compounds that contain only carbon and hydrogen), capable of causing cancer. Since 1975 most cars in the United States have been fitted with catalytic converters, which reduce the emission of hydrocarbons, as well as nitric oxide and carbon monoxide.

Agriculture

Agricultural methods used by farmers and farm workers in the United States can lead to problems of environmental disease that span all three main categories. Farmers use massive amounts of chemicals, many of which are poisonous because they are used to kill pests and weeds. U.S. farmers spend approximately $4 billion a year on pesticides and put more than 400 million pounds (180 million kg) of these chemicals on their crops. Many pesticides have toxic effects on laboratory animals and harmful effects on humans.

Farmers are themselves exposed far more than most people to pesticides, as well as to dust, solvents, fuels, and animal viruses. Several studies have shown that farmers have a higher risk for certain cancers and other diseases.

Less is known about the effects of agricultural chemicals on people who do not live on farms but who consume water and air contaminated by these chemicals. Many citizen groups and some state environmental agencies have sought to restrict the use of chemicals on residential lawns or at least to educate people in their use. The U.S. Environmental Protection Agency (EPA) has cautioned people to avoid contact with freshly treated lawns.

In 1993 the National Research Council found "serious deficiencies" in the nation's techniques for regulating the use of pesticides on foods. The researchers called for new ways of testing the chemicals' toxicity in children.

Radiation and electromagnetic fields

Radiation, or energy radiated in the form of waves or particles, is a part of everyday life. There would be no life on Earth, for example, if there was no solar energy. Radiation includes electromagnetic waves (from X rays through ultraviolet light, visible light, infrared or heat, microwaves, television, to radiowaves) and emitted particles, including alpha and beta particles, protons, and neutrons.

Natural radioactive sources also emit gamma rays, beta rays (free electrons), and alpha particles (helium nuclei). Excessive exposure to X rays and gamma rays can be dangerous, although a single medical X ray poses little risk. Alpha particles are even more dangerous. Artificial radioactive emissions can come from atomic plants and nuclear reactors. People exposed to these emissions can suffer radiation sickness, leading to skin cancers, loss of hair, loss of bone marrow, and even death (see RADIATION AND RADIATION SICKNESS).

There have been thousands of accidents in power plants that manufacture nuclear materials or use them to generate energy. Most have been minor, but two events stand out dramatically in recent history. In 1979, at Three Mile Island, a nuclear generating plant on the Susquehanna River in Pennsylvania, a nuclear reactor underwent a partial meltdown, threatening residents over a large area. Workers brought the reactor under control without releasing large quantities of radioactivity, but the cost was estimated at $1 billion. The outcome of another reactor accident in 1986 was far more serious. An explosion in a nuclear reactor at Chernobyl, in Ukraine, released radioactive dust and debris over much of Europe. More than thirty people died immediately, and scientists estimated that many more people would eventually die of cancer because of the explosion. Domestic and wild animals were poisoned, and large quantities of food were contaminated.

Radon is a radioactive gas that occurs naturally in certain rocks. It emits alpha particles and can cause cancer and lung damage in people. It has been detected in the air and water of homes in various parts of the United States. Radon from underlying mineral strata and from building materials enters buildings through cracks, builds up in the air, and attaches itself to airborne particles, which then can be inhaled. Scientists are still not certain of the effects of radon.

Agricultural workers engaged in crop spraying should wear protective clothing and a mask. Local communities, however, have no protection against the use of pesticides on neighboring farms and plantations, particularly when these chemicals are sprayed from airplanes.

Scientists also disagree on the possible dangers to people of electromagnetic fields. These fields are the zones of energy generated around television and radio sets, computers, hair dryers, electric heaters, power tools, and the overhead power lines that bring electricity to people's homes.

Some researchers have suspected that these fields increase the risk of cancer in people, particularly children, who are exposed to them. One study in Sweden found that the closer people lived to power lines, the greater their risk. Surveys by governmental agencies in the United States and Britain found no firm evidence of danger. However, the National Cancer Institute and the Children's Cancer Group began a long-term study, hoping to provide more detailed information.

Water

Water is one of the biggest environmental concerns. One reason is that people have long poisoned their drinking water with their own wastes. For centuries communities pumped raw or inadequately treated sewage directly into the nearest river or stream. Although that practice is all but ended in the United States, human and animal wastes can still contaminate water supplies. When they do or when such sewage trickles down into aquifers supplying well water, there is the risk of people becoming infected by bacterial diseases such as cholera and typhoid fever; viral infections such as gastroenteritis, hepatitis, and polio; and infections with protozoans such as amoebas (SEE INFECTIOUS DISEASES).

Communities routinely use chlorine or ozone to kill bacteria in their water supplies. During the 1970s researchers discovered that chlorine can react with natural substances in water to create chloromethanes, which are suspected of causing cancer. However, chloromethanes are rarely present in concentrations greater than one part per million (ppm) after water supplies have been treated with chlorine, and therefore there is unlikely to be any risk. Other chemicals, contributed to water sources by industrial and agricultural effluents, can also be carcinogenic (cancer-producing).

Most drinking water contains many natural minerals, one of which is fluoride. Researchers in the 1940s discovered that people in fluoride-rich areas had reduced tooth decay. As a result, toothpaste manufacturers now add a fluoride compound to their products. Many communities also add a small amount of fluoride (about 1 ppm) to their public water supplies so that all children are protected.

There are some occasions, however, when fluoride may be harmful. For example, someone on an artificial kidney machine might be harmed if fluoride is concentrated in their body tissues.

Many minerals in naturally occurring water from springs and wells can also be harmful. Arsenic and lead are particularly poisonous. People who have always drunk water from such sources build up a certain tolerance to arsenic, but lead poisoning can lead to lasting effects on the brain and other tissues.

The house dust mite, a small arachnid, infests homes and can cause allergies.

The home environment

The environments in which people live offer many causes for concern. People now think about the quality of the air inside their homes and offices. Indoor air sometimes contains higher concentrations of contaminants than the air outside. These contaminants can include radon (from soil, water, and construction materials); carbon monoxide, sulfur dioxide, and nitrogen dioxide (from stoves and fireplaces); airborne particles (from tobacco and other smoke); formaldehyde (a gas given off by household insulation and composite boards); microorganisms in the air; and allergens.

People attempt to save energy by insulating their homes and offices, but they may be making the indoor air even more unhealthy. Adding insulation and plugging leaks around windows reduces the dependence on fuels for heating, but insulation also cuts down the amount of fresh air that can circulate indoors. Bad ventilation can result in the build-up of lethal carbon monoxide gas from stoves and other fuel-fired appliances.

Even treated air may be contaminated. Outbreaks of Legionnaire's disease, a bacterial infection that can produce severe bronchopneumonia, have been traced to air conditioning systems. The organism that causes this disease (*Legionella pneumophila*) was first identified in the mid-1970s. Later, scientists discovered that a slightly different strain of this bacterium had caused Pontiac fever, an illness that affected some people working in Pontiac, Michigan.

Another household hazard is lead, which can enter drinking water if water pipes are made of lead. Many paints also contain lead. The symptoms of lead poisoning include vomiting, constipation, abdominal pain, and pale skin. There may also be a blue line around the gums. Lead poisoning in very young children can prevent the normal development of the brain and lower the IQ level (see INTELLIGENCE).

Allergens are part of people's living environment, and one in every five Americans is believed to suffer from some sort of allergy. Allergies can cause itchy eyes or throat, pressure along the nose

BLACK LUNG

Black lung can result when a miner breathes in coal dust over a period of several years. Eventually the dust scars and thickens the tissue in the worker's lungs and turns them black (see the picture below). Symptoms are a chronic cough, fatigue, and shortness of breath; the disease can cause early death.
A similar disease, silicosis, is caused by workers breathing the fine dust from sand and powdered rock. Brown lung, or byssinosis, can afflict textile industry workers who lack proper ventilation and breathe cotton dust over long periods.

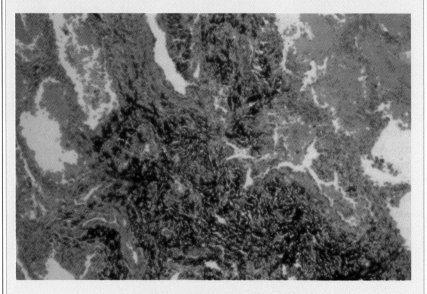

A CLOSER LOOK

or forehead or under the eyes, or perhaps an uncomfortable draining down the throat that leaves it sore. A congested, runny nose caused by allergy is called allergic rhinitis (more commonly called hay fever), the most common form of allergic disease. Treating allergies, such as asthma, is expensive. Government scientists have estimated that the cost of treating asthma-related diseases in the United States is over $6 billion a year, and that figure is still rising.

Allergic reactions can be triggered by almost anything: dust mites; cockroaches; fungi; pollens; wild mice and rats; and pets, most notably cats and dogs. Much allergic material, along with plant matter tracked into the house, building materials, and scales of dead skin from people's own bodies, goes into the general definition of house dust.

When allergens from these foreign sources enter the nose, eyes, or mouth, the body senses an intrusion and sends out histamines and other chemicals to fight them. The ensuing battle is what makes the tissues swell during an allergic reaction.

Work-related diseases

There are many possible causes of work-related environmental disease. Asbestos is one cause. As early as the 1930s, researchers reported a connection between asbestos and lung cancer. Asbestos is a natural mineral with microscopic fibers that is used in insulating buildings and in manufacturing a variety of

products, from roofing material through floor tiles to automobile brakes. Asbestos is harmless unless it is inhaled or ingested. When the tiny fibers enter the body, they lodge in the lung tissue, resulting in various diseases. These include: asbestosis, which scars the lung tissue and makes the organ susceptible to fatal infections; lung cancer; and mesothelioma, a cancer of the lung lining or the abdomen. Research on asbestos has shown high rates of disease among people who were exposed to heavy doses of the mineral over long periods of time. The United States asbestos industry has paid out several billion dollars in health claims.

Mining and the extraction of minerals cause many environmental illnesses, such as black lung, scientifically called anthracosis or anthrasilicosis.

Work with other minerals and chemicals—such as arsenic, lead, benzene, carbon tetrachloride, dioxins, mercury, polychlorinated biphenyls (PCBs), and tetrachloroethylene—exposes people to a number of diseases. Among these diseases are cancer, developmental and birth abnormalities, blindness, and damage to the skin, kidneys, liver, bone marrow, and central nervous system.

One of the world's worst industrial accidents occurred in Bhopal, India, in 1984, when a Union Carbide pesticide-producing plant leaked a highly toxic cloud of methyl isocynate. Three thousand people died immediately, 300,000 were injured, and up to 8,000 have died since. Many survivors suffered from partial or complete blindness, gastrointestinal disorders, impaired immune systems, post-traumatic stress disorders, and menstrual problems (in women). Doctors also noted a rise in spontaneous abortions, stillbirths, and offspring born with genetic defects.

Repetitive motion injury is another workplace problem. It affects workers who perform the same motions repeatedly and without much interruption, as in typing at computer keyboards, bricklaying, carpentry, and some factory jobs. These people may move their wrists in precisely the same way thousands of times a day, performing the same tasks over and over. Such repetition can lead to severe problems of the muscles and nerves, such as carpel tunnel syndrome (compression of a nerve in the wrist, resulting in weakness and pain in the hand).

Researchers have also questioned whether the radiation from computer terminals injures the health of people who sit before them. The displays produce electromagnetic fields. Experts advise computer users to maximize the distance between themselves and their screens or to install protective filters.

F. POWLEDGE

See also: ACID RAIN; INFECTIOUS DISEASES; INTELLIGENCE; RADIATION AND RADIATION SICKNESS.

Further reading:

Craighead, James E. 1995. *Pathology of Environmental and Occupational Disease*. St Louis: Mosby Year Book.
Nadakavukaren, Anne. 2000. *Our Global Environment: A Health Perspective*. Prospect Heights, Ill.: Waveland Press.

ENZYMES

Enzymes are molecules that act as catalysts in biological systems by speeding up metabolic reactions inside cells

Without enzymes a simple meal of bread, cheese, and beer would be impossible. Bakers, cheese makers, and brewers have exploited the action of enzymes for centuries: bread and beer are made with the help of the enzymatic breakdown of sugar by yeast cells, and cheese is made using the milk-clotting enzyme rennin.

Enzymes are molecules that act as catalysts in biological systems, changing the rate of chemical reactions. They are normally globular-shaped proteins (see PROTEINS), although other forms exist. Numerous reactions occur within a cell: the enzyme assists by reducing the activation energy (see below) required to get a reaction going. All metabolic processes are governed by enzymatic activity.

Catalysts

A catalyst is a chemical that can change the rate at which a reaction progresses, usually by speeding it up. It is not normally used up or permanently changed in any way by the reaction. Any reaction affected by a catalyst could still proceed, even if the catalyst was absent. The products of the reaction and their quantities would be exactly the same. However, without the catalyst the reaction might take hours, days, or even years.

All sorts of substances can be catalysts—for example, even common metals can act as catalysts in industrial chemical processes. Enzymes are different in that they are complex organic molecules, usually made only by living organisms. They are specific: most enzymes react with only one type of substrate (the molecule or molecules involved in the reaction the enzyme catalyzes).

Enzymes are also among the most efficient catalysts, increasing rates of reaction by factors of a million to a trillion. In addition, because the enzyme and its substrate need to be together for only a very short time, each enzyme molecule can catalyze the chemical transformation of many molecules of substrate to products. For example, a single molecule of the enzyme carbonic anhydrase (found in most types of cells) can catalyze the production of 600,000 molecules of bicarbonate ion from carbon dioxide and water every second. Finally, unlike industrial catalysts, enzymes act in the chemically mild conditions present in living cells.

German biochemist Emil Fischer put forward the "lock and key" hypothesis of enzyme action in 1894.

The discovery of enzymes

In 1834 German naturalist Theodor Schwann isolated a substance from gastric juices that rapidly digested meat protein. He called it *pepsin*, from the Greek word for "digest." At about the same time, two French chemists, Anselme Payen and François Persoz, discovered a substance in malt extract that would convert starch to sugar: they called this material *diastase* (which means "separating substance").

By the middle of the 19th century, the fact that most biochemical reactions could not be reproduced chemically in the laboratory led French chemist Louis Pasteur (1822–1895) to conclude that fermentation could occur only in living cells. The opposing view was that there were chemical substances called ferments that brought about reactions. The word *enzyme*, coined by Fredrich Kuhne in 1878 and

---

CORE FACTS

■ Most enzymes are proteins with high molecular weights.

■ Enzymes are catalysts, reducing the activation energy of metabolic reactions without themselves being used up.

■ Enzymes (with a few exceptions) are highly specific, catalyzing only one biochemical reaction.

■ Specific drugs can bind to and inhibit specific enzymes.

CONNECTIONS

● Many enzymes are produced by the **EXOCRINE GLANDS** and play an important role in **DIGESTIVE SYSTEMS**.

● Researchers in **BIOTECHNOLOGY** are experimenting with "designer enzymes," produced by **GENETIC ENGINEERING** and other processes.

derived from the Greek words *en* (in) and *zyme* (yeast), implied it was something chemically active within yeast, rather than the yeast itself. In 1897 this argument was resolved by German chemist Eduard Buchner's (1860–1917) demonstration that a cell-free extract of yeast could ferment glucose. Research into enzymes began in the early years of the 20th century, but most progress was made in the second half of that century, with the development of a range of sophisticated instruments and techniques.

Nomenclature of enzymes

When scientists first recognized and began to identify enzymes, the naming of newly discovered enzymes was left to the scientists doing the work. Very often this amounted to adding the suffix *-ase* (on the analogy of diastase) to the name of the substrate; sometimes the names were chemically uninformative, such as pepsin or catalase. As enzyme research began to advance, this haphazard system started to cause confusion, with single enzymes being given several different names independently by different groups of researchers.

Every enzyme now has three labels: a recommended name, a systematic name, and an Enzyme Commission (EC) number. The recommended name is short and suitable for everyday use; the systematic name is based on a series of classes and subclasses

and describes the reaction catalyzed; the EC number is an unambiguous identity tag and is used in scientific communications.

For example, an enzyme that is involved in the digestion of proteins (polypeptides) has the recommended name carboxypeptidase A, the systematic name peptidyl-L-amino acid hydrolase, and the number EC 3.4.17.1. The first number (3) is the enzyme's major class (hydrolases); the second number (4) denotes peptide bonds; the third number (17) denotes its sub-subclass (metallo-carboxypeptidases, since this enzyme has a zinc ion in its structure); the last number (1) is the enzyme's unique serial number in its sub-subclass.

Enzyme structure

Most enzymes are globular proteins, often far larger than their substrates. Each enzyme has a unique three-dimensional shape, thanks to its primary, secondary, tertiary, and sometimes quaternary, structures, as described below.

Like all proteins, enzymes are made up of different combinations of 20 major amino acids. The primary structure is the order in which these different amino acids are linked together to form a polypeptide chain (see PROTEINS). Each chain forms twists or bends, which make up its secondary structure. Further bending and coiling results in a three-dimensional globular protein, the tertiary structure. Some enzymes are made up of only one polypeptide chain; the intertwining of two or more chains results in a quaternary structure. The characteristic overall 3-D shape of a protein is called its conformation.

The conformation of an enzyme molecule and its catalytic function are linked inextricably. The amino acid sequence and thus the conformation are defined by the sequence of DNA in a gene that encodes the enzyme. Sometimes a DNA sequence error causes an enzyme to be catalytically inactive. Numerous genetically inherited disorders can be attributed to a single sequence error in a gene that encodes an enzyme. For example, in a condition called homocystinuria, there is a defect in the metabolism of an amino acid called methionine owing to a virtual absence of the enzyme cystathionine synthetase. This defect has widespread physiological consequences for a sufferer, including skeletal abnormalities and mental retardation.

Cofactors

Some enzymes are self-contained, relying solely on their own structures for their catalytic actions; others require one or more cofactors to be present to participate in the catalytic process. These cofactors may be metal ions, such as iron and copper, or organic molecules derived from vitamins, called coenzymes. Many of the water-soluble vitamins in a normal diet are coenzyme precursors. Niacin, for example, part of the vitamin B complex, is the precursor for the coenzyme needed for many catabolic reactions, and vitamin B_6 plays a coenzyme role in amino acid metabolism. Cofactors are often separate from the enzyme molecule, and their presence or absence allows some control over the enzyme's activity. Cofactors that are permanently linked to the enzyme are called prosthetic groups.

How enzymes work

For a chemical reaction to take place, a reactant molecule has to acquire sufficient energy to reach a transition state, where the probability is highest that a chemical bond will be formed or broken. Stable compounds will not change spontaneously into their products because their molecules do not have enough energy to reach the transition state. The difference in energy between a molecule in its initial state and an identical molecule in its transition state is called its activation energy.

To increase the rate of a reaction, it is necessary to increase the proportion of reactant molecules that can reach the transition state, either by raising their kinetic energy (by heating them) or by reducing the activation energy required. Enzymes reduce activation energy by holding the reactants close to one another (increasing their effective concentration), holding them in the correct orientation for bond formation, and putting their existing bonds under strain.

The complex three-dimensional shape of an enzyme molecule incorporates one or more active sites, asymmetrical indentations complementary in shape to specific substrate molecules. Only the intended substrate will fit a particular active site. When the substrate binds to the active site, an enzyme-substrate complex forms, and the activation energy of the substrate molecule is reduced.

The close match between active site and substrate molecule is the basis of the lock-and-key hypothesis proposed by German biochemist Emil Fischer (1852–1919) in 1894, following his discovery that glycolytic enzymes can distinguish between stereoisomeric sugars (sugars that are chemically identical but have mirror image structures). A specific substrate, he suggested, fits the active site, just as only the correct key can undo a lock.

An alternative induced-fit hypothesis, put forward in the 1950s, suggests that binding between enzyme and substrate might occur by the enzyme wrapping around the substrate, like a gloved hand

DESIGNER ENZYMES

Considerable research is directed to ways of producing synthetic enzymes to carry out specific metabolic functions. These enzymes can be made by preparing antibodies that recognize the transition states of specific chemical reactions, by taking naturally occurring substances that have been chemically modified, by making small changes to the DNA carrying the code for a specific enzyme (see GENETIC ENGINEERING), or by synthesizing the molecules that form the enzymes. Among these last are some that are not even protein based: doughnut-shaped molecules called cyclodextrins, made of six, seven, or eight glucose molecules linked into a ring. If a suitable molecule is drawn into the cavity of the "doughnut," the forces existing between the heart of the cavity and its rim can be enough to break apart the molecule. Experiments with cyclodextrins and their catalytic effect on organic molecules help to explain how natural enzymes work.

around a ball. Evidence from X-ray crystallography (determination of a crystal's structure using X-ray diffraction) suggests that the true situation is a combination of both of these concepts.

One hypothesis put forward to explain how activation energy is reduced suggests that an enzyme is not an exact fit for its substrate. This fact has been observed in the enzymes lysozyme, chymotrypsin, and papain. Another hypothesis is that the enzyme and substrate bind exactly but that chemically unstable intermediates (with low activation energies) are formed. No single hypothesis has yet been able to account for all observations.

Factors affecting reaction rates

Enzyme action is dependent on its structure, which can be modified by changes in temperature or pH. Proteins have a narrow optimum range of temperature and pH in which their catalytic action is most effective. In people, this temperature range often centers on 98.6 °F (37 °C), normal body temperature. The optimum pH range for most enzymes is pH 6 to 8; for pepsin, which has to work in the acid conditions of the stomach, the optimum is pH 2.

Enzyme-catalyzed reaction rates in cold-blooded animals (those unable to control their internal body temperature) are very slow in cold conditions because there is no external source of heat. Often these animals remain alive but immobilized because their metabolic rate slows right down, especially at night and in the winter. The

An illustration of the lock and key hypothesis of enzyme action. Two substrate constituents fit into the specific active sites of the enzyme. Once they are close together, the reaction can take place, and the two reaction products are released.

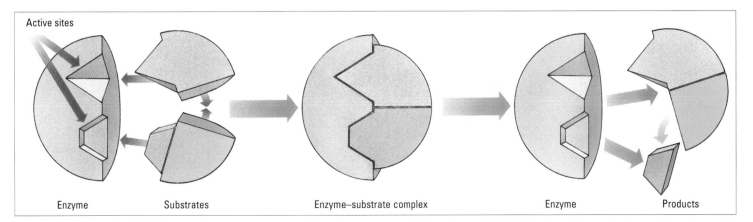

Active sites

Enzyme   Substrates   Enzyme–substrate complex   Enzyme   Products

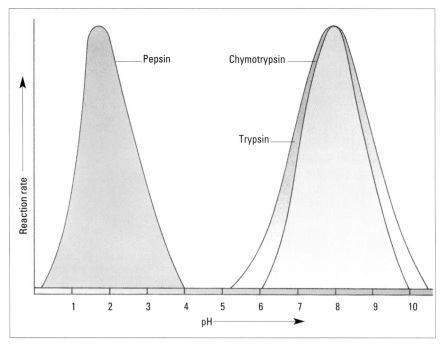

concentration of substrate also influences the reaction rates. If the substrate is present in excess, the rate of reaction increases with increasing enzyme concentration; if the substrate concentration is low and is the limiting factor in the reaction, increasing the enzyme concentration does not increase the reaction rate because there is not enough substrate to react with.

Like all chemical reactions, enzyme-catalyzed reactions are potentially reversible, so the product of the forward reaction is the substrate for the reverse reaction. If the product of the forward reaction is not used up by some other process as it is produced, in some cases its concentration will rise enough to allow the reverse reaction and thus reduce the rate at which more of it is created.

Regulation of enzyme activity

The total activity of an enzyme in a cell can be altered indirectly by changing its levels by modifying the relative rates of enzyme synthesis and degradation. The synthesis of an enzyme is controlled by

Trypsin and chymotrypsin, two digestive enzymes that work in the alkaline conditions of the intestine, are effective in only a narrow range of pH, with the optimum at pH 8. Pepsin, a stomach enzyme, is most effective around pH 2.

The metabolism of cold-blooded animals, such as reptiles and amphibians, slows down if they are unable to make use of an external source of heat. This lizard is basking on a rock to absorb some of the Sun's warmth.

a specific gene, which may be switched on by a hormone or cellular product of some kind. When the gene is switched on, the enzyme is synthesized.

Some enzymes exist in both active and inactive forms, and it is possible to regulate the relative proportions of the two. A second enzyme governs interconversion between one and the other.

Allosteric enzymes (*allosteric* means "another space") have a secondary site, distinct from the catalytic site, to which a specific metabolite can bind to alter the enzyme's activity. The shape of the enzyme molecule thus changes to affect its substrate-binding efficiency. Substances binding to allosteric sites are called regulators and can be inhibitors or activators. In a multienzyme reaction sequence, such as the citric acid cycle (see KREBS CYCLE), a reaction sequence product may inhibit an enzyme earlier in the sequence, a process called feedback inhibition.

Allosteric control is part of a broad category of control called noncompetitive inhibition. The regulating agent acts away from the catalytic site and does not compete for access with molecules of substrate. In competitive inhibition, the active site on the enzyme is occupied by a molecule that is structurally similar to but different from the normal substrate and competes with substrate molecules for access. For example, the normal substrate for alcohol dehydrogenase is ethanol (grain alcohol), but if methanol (wood alcohol) is taken in, it competes with ethanol for the active site. In this type of inhibition, an increase in the concentration of the normal substrate enables it to compete successfully for the active site, and so methanol poisoning is treated by giving ethanol.

Uncompetitive inhibition is a further regulatory mechanism, in which the inhibitor does not combine with the free enzyme or hamper its ability to form an enzyme-substrate complex. Instead, it combines with the latter, once formed, to create an enzyme-substrate-inhibitor complex, which cannot go on to yield the normal product.

These forms of inhibition are reversible. Irreversible inhibition occurs when an enzyme is exposed to agents capable of covalently bonding to it and permanently modifying its structure. For example, organophosphorus compounds (nerve gases) used in chemical warfare combine with and inactivate acetylcholinesterase. This enzyme plays an important part in the correct functioning of the nervous system because it is necessary to break down the neurotransmitter acetylcholine.

J. PAGE

See also: AMINO ACIDS; BIOCHEMISTRY; KREBS CYCLE; METABOLISM; PROTEINS.

Further reading:
Kornberg, Arthur. 1991. *For the Love of Enzymes: The Odyssey of a Biochemist.* Cambridge, Mass.: Harvard University Press.
Wong, Dominic W. S. 1995. *Food Enzymes: Structures and Mechanism.* New York: Chapman and Hall.

EPIDEMIOLOGY

Epidemiology is the study of patterns of disease in society

A COURT FOR KING CHOLERA.

The crowded conditions of the courts and alleys of London's Soho district, combined with the contamination of the water supply, accounted for the cholera epidemic of 1854. Physician John Snow's study of the outbreak was one of the first studies in epidemiology.

Epidemiology is the systematic study of patterns of disease in society. Epidemiologists seek to understand why particular groups of people are affected by particular diseases at particular times and places. With that information, epidemiologists and other medical researchers can figure out how people and whole societies can reduce their chances of developing a disease—for example, by quitting smoking to avoid lung cancer, by practicing safe sex to reduce the risk of being infected with the AIDS virus, or in certain parts of the world, by filtering water to avoid typhoid, cholera, and hepatitis. An epidemiological study may show that people have a greater chance of getting a disease (for example, heart disease) under certain conditions (for example, being overweight).

John Snow, the pioneer

One of the earliest epidemiological studies showed just how valuable this type of research can be in helping people avoid sickness and death. In 1854 London, England, was suffering from an epidemic of cholera, an often fatal disease in which the victim suffers from severe vomiting and diarrhea. John Snow, a physician, believed that people were

becoming infected with cholera from their drinking water, and he used an epidemiological study to prove his hypothesis. At the time, London had two water companies. One company used water that had been in contact with human sewage, while the other company used cleaner water that had not.

Snow analyzed London death records and found that many of London's cholera cases were coming from parts of the city that used the contaminated water. Therefore, Snow was able to show that the contaminated water was affecting London residents, even though he did not know exactly what agent in the water was harmful. (The bacterium that causes cholera, *Vibrio cholerae*, was not identified until many years after Snow's study was published.)

CORE FACTS

- Epidemiologists study why particular groups of people get sick at particular times and places.
- The work of epidemiology involves studying the health and lifestyles of large groups of people and using statistics to analyze the data.
- Epidemiological research can be descriptive or analytic.

CONNECTIONS

- Epidemics of infectious disease are now rare in the developed world, but there is always the danger of an outbreak following an **ENVIRONMENTAL DISASTER** or the **POLLUTION** of water supplies.

- The black death, was a form of bubonic plague that killed around a quarter of the population in Europe during the 14th century. This epidemic was an **INFECTIOUS DISEASE** transmitted to humans from rats via fleas.

The country of Bangladesh suffered severe floods in 2002. Unless immediate steps are taken, floods and other environmental disasters are followed by epidemics of typhoid and cholera.

Epidemiology today

Like other early epidemiologists, Snow focused on infectious diseases (those passed from one person to another) and on how people put themselves at risk of catching those diseases. In the 20th century, better sanitation and the development and use of vaccines and antibiotics cut down on the threat of dying of infectious diseases in many parts of the world. However, AIDS and occasional influenza epidemics are major exceptions. Epidemiologists study both infectious and noninfectious diseases, such as heart disease and cancer.

When a new infectious disease breaks out, epidemiologists are called in to identify its source and determine how it can be fought. A large amount of epidemiological research is carried out by the U. S. government's Centers for Disease Control and Prevention (commonly called the CDC), the headquarters of which are in Atlanta, Georgia. Working from data provided by health departments in cities and states, the CDC publishes health statistics. The United Nations' World Health Organization (WHO) also conducts its own epidemiological research around the globe.

The advent of AIDS has focused attention on the work of epidemiologists, who have carefully tracked the progress of infection in the United States and other countries. They have pieced together a picture of the groups of people most likely to be affected by AIDS and the best ways for all people to prevent the spread of the disease (see AIDS).

Gathering statistics

An important concept in epidemiology is the notion of a population. To epidemiologists, a population is a well-defined group of people who share common characteristics, such as age, occupation, or country. Some populations are very large; others are small. For example, a single population could be all the people who live in the United States. Other types of populations could be all the students in a certain school or in a particular grade or in a single classroom. Epidemiologists study the occurrence of diseases among people in the same population or among people in different populations to try to uncover exactly what is causing a disease.

Two important mathematical tools for epidemiologists are statistics called the prevalence and incidence rate. Prevalence shows how many people in a population have a particular disease at a particular time. For example, if 25 people in a population of 200 have a particular disease, the prevalence is 25 divided by 200, that is 0.125. The larger this number, the more the disease is said to have penetrated into the population at a particular time.

The second figure, the incidence rate, is calculated over a span of time, not at just one particular moment. This number helps epidemiologists estimate a person's risk of contracting the disease in question over a given period, such as a lifetime.

To calculate the incidence rate, epidemiologists count how many new cases of a disease were found during a given period (for example, a month, a year, a decade). They then multiply the total number of people who were studied by the amount of time over which they were studied and calculate the incidence rate by dividing the number of new cases by this number. For example, if 25 people in a population of 200 develop a disease over a period of 10 years, the incidence rate is 0.0125 cases per person per year, that is, 25 divided by (200 x 10).

Studying disease patterns

Epidemiological studies fall into two broad categories: descriptive and analytic.

Descriptive studies simply try to paint a picture of the patterns of disease without drawing any conclusions about what is causing the disease. For example, one type of descriptive study, called a correlational study, compares the incidence of various diseases, such as heart disease, among people from various populations.

Another type of descriptive study, called a cross-sectional survey, checks people in a single population to see both whether they have a specific disease and whether they have been exposed to certain factors that could be causing the disease. A good example is the government-sponsored Health Interview Survey. More than 100,000 people fill out questionnaires about their lifestyles and health, which provides many useful clues about trends in American health. For example, the study has shown that cigarette smoking is decreasing among doctors and nurses and that a higher percentage of nurses smoke than doctors.

A third type of descriptive study is the case report, in which a physician publishes a detailed description of a particular person suffering from a particular disease. Sometimes, case reports of people with unusual illnesses are the first hint that a new disease has been discovered, as was the case with AIDS in late 1980.

Discovering the cause

In analytic studies, epidemiologists try to find the causes of disease. One type of analytic study is the experimental study, in which people change their behavior or get a new medical treatment, and the scientists determine whether it has had any effect, good or bad, by comparing them with people who did not get the new treatment. New drugs are often tested in this way. Some people with a disease get the experimental drug, and others do not; researchers analyze the results to see if the drug made any difference. For example, some scientists have suggested that diets rich in vitamin E and beta carotene might reduce the risk of lung cancer. However, in one study released in 1994, 29,133 male smokers were divided into groups that received either vitamin E or beta carotene or both or neither. The men who received neither substance had a lower incidence of lung cancer.

Another type of analytic study is called an observational study, in which the scientist does not do anything special to the participants. Information is collected on them—sometimes before they develop a disease, sometimes after—to try to pinpoint the cause. One well-known observational study is the Framingham Heart Study, in which 5,127 men and women from Massachusetts have been tracked since the 1950s, with researchers collecting information, such as whether they smoked and their general state of health. The researchers have been following the participants to see which ones develop heart disease.

People often misunderstand one crucial thing about epidemiological studies. These studies usually show only an association (or, in mathematical terms, a correlation) between two factors, such as smoking and cancer. Epidemiological studies do not show conclusively that one thing causes another; an epidemiologist cannot prove that smoking causes cancer. Something else might be hidden—for example, some other habit or some genetic trait—that might be causing both the smoking and the cancer, and if so, the smoking would not really be the cause of the cancer. There is also the possibility that the association is a statistical fluke that does not mean anything. Some "cancer clusters" (neighborhoods with an unusually high incidence of cancer) are due to such random variation.

Medical scientists work on showing exactly how smoking causes cancer, by studying how the smoking produces changes in the body's cells that lead to the formation of cancer tumor cells. Epidemiology can point the way, indicating factors that should be studied for cause-and-effect relationships, but researchers have to go beyond the findings of epidemiology for final, convincing proof.

V. KIERNAN

See also: AIDS; ANIMAL DISEASES.

Further reading:

Gordis, Leon. 2000. *Epidemiology*. Philadelphia: W. B. Saunders.
Shilts, Randy. 2000. *And the Band Played On: Politics, People, and the AIDS Epidemic*. New York: St Martin's Press.

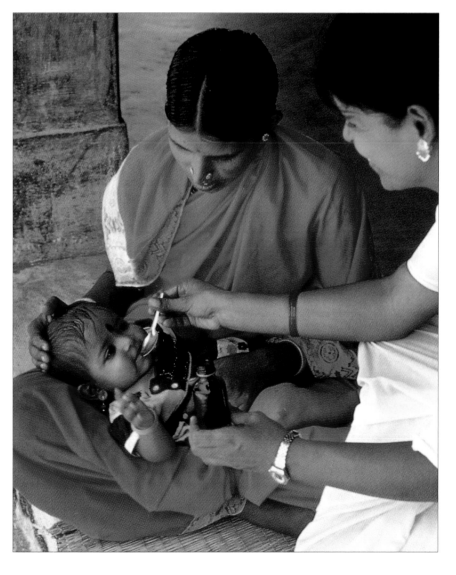

Administering oral vaccine against polio. Epidemiological studies around the world have suggested that the prevalence of certain diseases can be reduced by immunization programs. Smallpox was eradicated by such an immunization program.

EPILEPSY

Epilepsy is any disorder of the brain that causes recurrent seizures

A patient connected to an instrument called an electroencephalograph (EEG) machine. It produces a printout of the patient's brain waves; bursts of abnormal electrical activity indicate epilepsy.

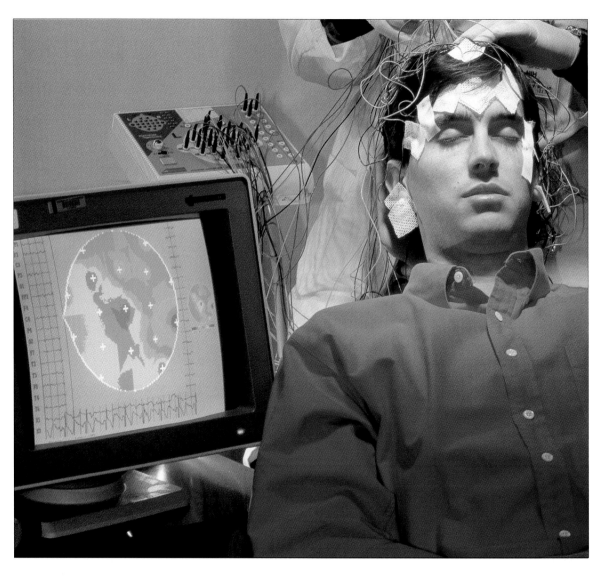

Epilepsy is not a single disease but an umbrella term for a range of different types of seizures (sudden attacks) caused by an electrical disturbance in the brain. The seizures vary from violent convulsions of the whole body to momentary lapses in consciousness or strange changes in behavior. Epilepsy is surprisingly common—about 1 in 180 people in the United States have the condition.

An ancient mystery

Epilepsy is probably one of the oldest medical conditions known, but it was misunderstood for thousands of years. In ancient times and throughout the Middle Ages, many people thought that epileptics were possessed by demons. The appropriate cure, they believed, was to cast out the demon, a task carried out by priests or religious healers with supposed magical powers. The Bible contains several stories describing how Jesus drove out the demons from people who were "possessed," probably suffering from epilepsy. Greek philosopher and scientist Hippocrates (ca. 450–377 BCE) had a good

understanding of epilepsy for his time. He wrote that "the sacred disease is no more sacred than other diseases, but has a natural cause." He argued that epilepsy was inherited and was caused by a

CONNECTIONS

● Epilepsy can result from a **BRAIN** tumor.

● **NEUROSCIENCE** deals with the **ANATOMY**, physiology, **BIOCHEMISTRY**, or molecular biology of nerves and nervous tissue, especially in relation to behavior and **LEARNING**.

CORE FACTS

- ■ Electrical disturbances in the brain are responsible for causing the seizures associated with epilepsy.
- ■ Epilepsy is a common disorder, and probably one of the oldest known medical conditions.
- ■ There are many different types of epileptic seizures that are divided into two main categories: generalized seizures that affect the whole brain and partial seizures that affect only one part of the brain.
- ■ Epilepsy is a symptom of a brain injury and can be caused by meningitis, brain tumor, stroke, or hypoglycaemia.
- ■ Treatment involves using anticonvulsant drugs to suppress brain cell activity; occasionally brain surgery is carried out or a specialized diet (ketogenic diet) is used.

disturbance of the brain. This brilliant stroke of intuition, remained unsubstantiated until the late 19th century, more than 2,000 years later.

In earlier writings, Hippocrates had even noted that injuries to one side of the head could cause convulsions on the opposite side of the body, although he did not see the connection with epilepsy. The treatment he suggested for people with epilepsy was to ensure a balanced diet and a healthy way of life to correct what he saw as physiological imbalances.

Hippocrates's teachings influenced doctors for hundreds of years, but his cure did not work, and superstitious explanations remained popular. Roman writer Pliny the Elder (ca. 23–79 CE) claimed that epileptics could be cured by drinking blood—especially the blood of gladiators. A Roman doctor, Alexander of Tralles (525–605 CE), later recommended an even more exotic cure. He told patients to take a nail from a wrecked ship, bend it into a bracelet, and decorate it with "the bone of a stag's heart" taken from the animal while still alive. This bracelet gave "astonishing results," he declared if worn on the left arm.

The Middle Ages

Theories of demonic possession were popular throughout the Middle Ages, and people continued to dream up bizarre treatments for what they thought of as a spiritual disease. French surgeon Guy de Chauliac (1298–1368) attempted to cure epileptics by getting them to write the names of the Three Wise Men in their own blood on parchment.

In central Europe mistletoe was the treatment of favor, and people hung it around their children"s necks to protect them from seizures. British chemist Robert Boyle (1627–1691), better known for his discovery of the relationship between temperature and pressure in gases, also favored mistletoe.

Discoveries and breakthroughs

The situation improved in the 19th century, when doctors began to classify and study the different forms of epilepsy. Special hospitals were built for epileptics to keep them separate from other insane people because doctors thought the condition might be infectious. The doctors attached to these institutions became experts at classifying the different types of seizures, and the terms they invented are still in use. In the mid-19th century doctors discovered that drugs called bromides could reduce the frequency of seizures, and successful medical treatment for epilepsy at last became available.

Meanwhile, neuroscientists were beginning to figure out what caused epilepsy. In 1873 pioneer British neuroscientist John Hughlings Jackson (1835–1911) called epilepsy "a sudden, excessive, and rapid discharge" of brain cells.

This definition gained strength when scientists found they could induce seizures in animals by giving their brains electric shocks. In 1875 Jackson

PROBING THE BRAIN

Neuroscientists owe much of their knowledge about the brain to a man named Wilder Penfield (1891–1976). Penfield was a leading Canadian brain surgeon who used a radical technique to treat epilepsy. He opened up the brains of his patients while keeping them wide awake and then stimulated the brain's surface with a small electrode to find the area responsible for starting seizures. Penfield was successful because there are no pain endings in the brain. He wanted to be sure that when he carried out the surgery, he did not paralyze his patients, render them speechless, or make them lose their memory.

However, he went much further. The technique gave him the opportunity to probe many areas of the brain to find out what each region did. Stimulating some areas of the brain made the patient's feet or toes jerk, while other areas made their hands quiver or made their face twitch. Penfield found parts of the brain that made people see flashing lights or hear buzzing sounds, and he even found an area that triggered dreamlike memories of the past. Penfield's discoveries allowed neuroscientists to make a better map of the cerebral cortex, the outer part of the brain. The map showed what the different areas of the brain seemed to do.

A CLOSER LOOK

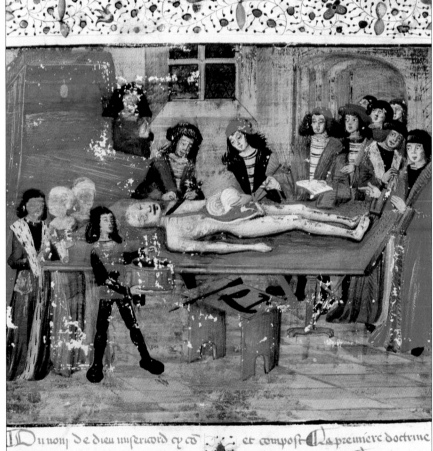

French manuscript illustration of a public dissection, from Guy de Chauliac's Chirurgia Magna. *De Chauliac thought epilepsy was a spiritual disease that could be cured by encouraging sufferers to write out the names of the Three Wise Men in their own blood.*

SPLIT BRAINS

For people with very severe and apparently incurable epilepsy, there was one drastic remedy that could sometimes stop the seizures: doctors cut their brains in half. By severing the bundle of neurons (called the corpus callosum) that connects the left hemisphere of the brain to the right, the doctors stopped the spread of electrical activity that caused generalized seizures. However, the procedure was one of the world's most controversial operations because it had some very strange side effects, called collectively split-brain syndrome.

In split-brain syndrome, the two halves of the brain sometimes acted like independent brains. The right hemisphere, for example, controls the left hand, while the left hemisphere controls the right hand. In most people, the left hemisphere also controls speech. People with split brains can recognize everything they see, but they can name things only if they see them in the right half of their field of vision (because the right half of vision is processed by the left half of the brain). However, these defects can be shown only by specialized techniques because most people use both ears and eyes in their daily activities so that information gets to both sides of the brain.

A CLOSER LOOK

discovered that one type of epilepsy, now called Jacksonian seizures, is caused by damage to a certain part of the brain's outer layer, the cerebral cortex. This important finding marked the beginning of a period in which neuroscientists began to study the brain by investigating how damage to specific areas affected its function.

The next breakthrough occurred just a few years later. During the 19th century, surgical techniques had improved by leaps and bounds thanks to the discovery of new anaesthetics and huge improvements in aseptic (sterile) techniques. The advances paved the way for the beginnings of modern brain surgery. In 1886 another pioneering British neuro-

This is a 14th-century manuscript illustration of foltas herb and its alleged properties for curing epilepsy, from the book Miscellanea Medica.

surgeon named Victor Horsley (1857–1916) cured a young man of epilepsy by surgically removing a patch of scarred tissue from his brain.

The electroencephalogram

The theory that epilepsy is caused by abnormal electrical discharges was confirmed by an instrument called the electroencephalograph, or EEG, machine. This device, first demonstrated in the late 1920s, produces a printout of brain waves (an electroencephalogram) detected by electrodes placed on the scalp. In a person with epilepsy, the brain waves show bursts of abnormal electrical activity. EEG machines are still used to diagnose epilepsy and other brain disorders. Sometimes doctors can tell from an EEG exactly where a seizure is starting. Before surgery electrodes can be implanted in the brain or directly on the surface of the brain to verify the location of the malfunctioning tissue.

TYPES OF SEIZURES

The many different types of epileptic seizures are divided into two main categories: generalized seizures, which affect the whole brain, and partial seizures, which affect only one part of the brain. Sometimes, seizures can begin as partial seizures and then generalize throughout the brain.

These two categories have several subdivisions. Generalized seizures are divided into tonic-clonic seizures (previously called grand mal seizures), which produce convulsions of the whole body, and absence seizures (previously called petit mal seizures), which cause brief lapses of consciousness.

Generalized seizures

Tonic-clonic seizures are the violent shaking fits that most people would recognize as epilepsy. For a minute or two the person becomes unconscious, the body stiffens and jerks violently, and breathing becomes irregular. An epileptic fit can be a disturbing thing to witness, but in most cases it causes no harm, provided the person does not bruise him- or herself against a solid object.

After a tonic-clonic seizure, the muscles relax, which sometimes causes incontinence, and the person regains consciousness. Sufferers have no memory of the fit and feel confused and disorientated. Often they want to sleep, which is usually the best immediate treatment. In rare cases, tonic-clonic seizures occur in rapid succession without consciousness being regained between fits. This condition, called status epilepticus, is life threatening and needs immediate medical attention.

Absence seizures are much more common in children than adults. During an attack, the child loses awareness of his or her surroundings for up to 30 seconds or so and develops a blank, staring expression that looks like day-dreaming. The child usually has no memory of the attack and so remains unaware that anything is wrong. Such seizures often go unnoticed and can occur hundreds of times a day, sometimes severely impairing schoolwork.

Partial seizures

Partial seizures are divided into simple and complex types. During a simple partial seizure, the hand, arm, or one side of the face may start twitching or tingling, or the head and eyes may turn to one side. The seizure lasts for several minutes, and the person remains conscious throughout. Some people experience hallucinations or odd smells, sounds, or tastes during a simple partial seizure. Jacksonian epilepsy is a type of simple partial seizure in which twitching spreads slowly across one side of the body.

Complex partial seizures occur in a condition called temporal lobe epilepsy. Just before an attack, the person may have an aura. Some epileptics experience a strange feeling of fear or unease or a strange smell, or they may feel they have experienced it all before a few seconds in advance of the onset of one of these seizures. Then sufferers enter a dreamlike state and start to behave in odd ways. They often look dazed or unresponsive and might smack their lips, grimace, or fidget. Afterward, they have no memory of the seizure.

Causes of epilepsy

There are many different causes of epilepsy, such as damage to the brain, whether by disease or injury. Diseases that can trigger epilepsy include the infection viral meningitis, brain tumor, and stroke. Some conditions that cause single epileptic seizures, include high fever in children, cocaine abuse, alcohol withdrawal in alcoholics, and hypoglycemia (low blood sugar). However, seizures have to be recurrent for the condition to be diagnosed officially as epilepsy.

By experimenting on animals, neuroscientists have found out a great deal about what happens in the brain during an epileptic seizure, but many mysteries remain. The brain is made up of billions of cells called neurons. Like tiny wires, neurons work by sending electrical signals to each other. When an electrical signal reaches the end of one neuron, the neuron releases a chemical called a neurotransmitter to pass the signal to the next cell. During a seizure, huge numbers of neurons send electrical signals and release neurotransmitters at the same time, causing an uncontrolled burst of activity. In a partial seizure the activity is usually restricted to one place, but in a generalized seizure this activity spreads throughout the brain.

In partial seizures the problem seems to begin in brain cells called pyramidal neurons, which excite other neurons. The pyramidal cells are normally kept in check by inhibitory neurons, which use a neurotransmitter called gamma-amino butyric acid (GABA) to pass on their signals.

Scientists have been able to trigger seizures in slices of brain tissue kept alive in a laboratory by blocking the action of GABA. If a number of pyramidal neurons are connected, a chain reaction occurs: all the brain cells start firing out of control. However, scientists do not yet understand how this activity spreads throughout the brain in a generalized seizure or how it can keep going for several minutes.

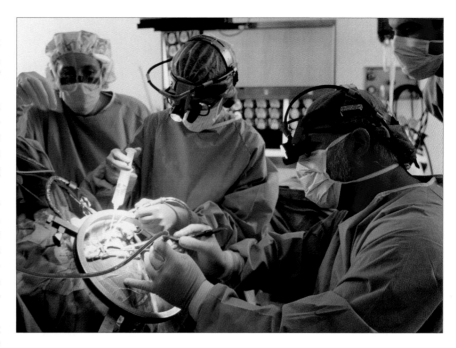

Treating epilepsy

Thanks to drugs called anticonvulsants, which prevent seizures, epileptics can lead normal lives. Anticonvulsants work by suppressing the activity of brain cells, although some of these drugs have side effects that make the person drowsy. If an underlying condition such as a vitamin deficiency or a brain tumor is causing the epilepsy, then treating that condition will also help prevent seizures. If drugs do not work and doctors know which area of the patient's brain is responsible for starting the seizures, they sometimes perform brain surgery.

People with epilepsy have to take certain precautions. For instance, they have to avoid certain things that can trigger a seizure, such as flashing lights, excessive alcohol consumption, lack of sleep, or irregular eating habits. Many epileptics are not allowed to drive, and they usually avoid dangerous sports such as skiing.

BEN MORGAN

See also: BRAIN; CONSCIOUSNESS; CT SCANNING; DEGENERATIVE BRAIN DISEASE; PERSONALITY DISORDER; SCHIZOPHRENIA.

Further reading:

Devinsky, O. 2001. *Epilepsy: Patient and Family Guide*. Philadelphia, Pa.: F. A. Davis.
Epilepsy Foundation of America Website: www.efa.org
Freeman, J. M., et al. 1997. *Seizures and Epilepsy in Childhood: A Guide for Parents*. 2nd ed. Bethesda, Md.: Johns Hopkins University Press.
Freeman, J. M. 2000. *The Ketogenic Diet: A Treatment for Epilepsy*. 3rd ed. New York: Demos Medical Publishing.
Reeves, A. G., et al., eds. 1995. *Epilepsy and the Corpus Callosum II*. New York: Plenum.
Weaver, D. F. 2001. *Epilepsy and Seizures: Everything You Need to Know*. Toronto, Ontario: Firefly Books.

Surgeons carry out delicate brain surgery. If drugs do not control a patient's epilepsy, then brain surgery may be performed to correct the problem.

EPINEPHRINE AND NOREPINEPHRINE

Epinephrine and norepinephrine are hormones produced in response to exercise, stress, or strong emotions

Imagine how people feel when confronted with a dangerous situation: their heart pounds in their chest, they break out into a cold sweat, and their hair feels as if it is standing on end. These are just some of the effects of the hormones epinephrine and norepinephrine (also called adrenalin and noradrenalin) on the vertebrate body.

Epinephrine and norepinephrine are hormones released by chromaffin cells in the adrenal glands, which are located just above the kidneys (see ENDOCRINE SYSTEMS). The cells release the hormones when they are stimulated by nerve impulses traveling from the hypothalamus in the brain (see BRAIN). In amphibians and birds, the chromaffin cells are spread throughout the adrenal glands; in reptiles, they are found on the outside of the adrenal glands; in mammals, including humans, they are in the center, or medulla, of the adrenal glands.

Norepinephrine is also secreted by nerve endings in the sympathetic nervous system (part of the nervous system that is not controlled by conscious thought; see NERVOUS SYSTEMS). The sympathetic nervous system exerts control over the chromaffin cells. When the sympathetic nerves are stimulated, they release norepinephrine, which may then travel directly to the target organs, including the eyes, heart, lungs, stomach, intestines, sweat glands, blood vessels, and bladder, or they stimulate the production of epinephrine and more norepinephrine from the chromaffin cells.

The norepinephrine that travels from the nerve endings directly to the target organ exerts its effects much faster and more accurately than the norepinephrine and epinephrine that are secreted from the adrenal medulla. In the first case, the norepinephrine affects only the target organ, while

The epinephrine and norepinephrine released during the rush of fear just before a steep drop on a rollercoaster are the same hormones that prepare animals to fight or flee when faced with a predator.

in the second case, the hormones from the adrenal medulla are released into the bloodstream and travel to all organs around the body.

Alpha and beta receptors

Hormones exert their effects by binding to specific sites called receptors on the outside of the cells of the target organ (see HORMONES). In the case of epinephrine and norepinephrine, these sites are called the adrenergic receptors. There are two types of adrenergic receptors: alpha and beta. Norepinephrine activates mainly alpha receptors, while epinephrine activates both alpha and beta receptors. Therefore, the response of a particular organ to epinephrine and norepinephrine depends on whether its cells have alpha receptors or beta receptors.

CORE FACTS

- Epinephrine and norepinephrine are hormones released in response to stressful situations.
- Epinephrine is released from chromaffin cells in the adrenal glands; norepinephrine is also released from the chromaffin cells, as well as from nerve endings in the sympathetic nervous system.
- Epinephrine binds to both alpha and beta adrenergic receptors on target cells; norepinephrine binds mainly to alpha adrenergic receptors.
- Activation of alpha receptors causes the arteries to narrow, the pupils to widen, the muscles in the intestines to relax, muscles that control body hair to contract, and the platelets in the blood to clump together.
- Activation of beta receptors causes the heart to beat faster and stronger and the arteries to widen, as well as making the airways to the lungs widen and the muscles of the intestines and bladder relax.

CONNECTIONS

- During cardiac arrest, in which the **HEART** stops beating, epinephrine may be given to stimulate the heart into activity.

- The effects of the epinephrine and norepinephrine released following stimulation of the sympathetic **NERVOUS SYSTEM** are opposite to those caused by stimulation of the parasympathetic nervous system.

Activation of alpha receptors, which is caused by the hormone binding to them, initiates a multi-stage process that results in the regulation of specific cellular enzyme levels. These changes cause many physiological responses: the arteries narrow, the pupils widen, the muscles in the intestine relax, the muscles that control body hair contract, and blood-clotting agents called platelets clump together in the blood. Activation of beta receptors makes the heart beat faster and stronger, the arteries and the airways widen, and the muscles of the intestines and bladder relax. This activation also helps make energy available, by breaking down glycogen in the muscles and the liver. Glycogen is a type of stored glucose, the sugar that provides energy for the body. Activation of beta receptors causes the breakdown of a type of fat, triglycerides, into fatty acids, which are released into the blood and used by the muscles. This energy release increases body temperature, another tangible effect of beta-receptor stimulation.

It seems contradictory that epinephrine affects both types of receptors, when alpha receptors cause blood vessels to narrow and beta receptors cause them to widen. Why would epinephrine do two opposite things at once? The answer is that certain arteries have mainly alpha receptors, while others have mainly beta receptors. For example, the arteries in the skin, intestines, and salivary glands contain alpha receptors, while those of the heart and other muscles contain mostly beta receptors, so blood is diverted to areas where it is most needed.

Fright, fight, flight

Epinephrine and norepinephrine (often called the stress hormones) are released from the chromaffin cells when the sympathetic nervous system is stimulated by stressful situations. Strenuous exercise, strong emotions such as fear and anger, major blood loss, and pain can all cause the release of epinephrine and norepinephrine. These hormones prepare the body for intense physical activity.

Think how someone feels just before an exam, at a big game, or while watching a scary movie. In all of these situations, the body is preparing to protect itself. It needs as much blood as possible going to the muscles to ferry the oxygen and nutrients vital for providing enough energy for combat or escape. The heart might pound, beating faster and stronger, to pump more blood around the body, and the arteries supplying the muscles widen while those supplying the digestive organs, salivary glands, and skin narrow. As a result, the mouth feels dry, and the person becomes "white with fear," as the blood is diverted from the skin to the muscles.

The pupils enlarge to let in more light so that the person can see better. The sweat glands in the skin increase their secretion to cool the body during exertion, and a cold sweat breaks out. The sweat glands in the armpits secrete a strong-smelling liquid: the person may notice the "smell of fear." The muscles that control the body hairs contract. This last reaction no longer has any real purpose in humans, but in other mammals it serves to raise the hairs and make the animal look larger and more threatening than it really is.

EPINEPHRINE IN MEDICINE

Epinephrine has been produced synthetically as a drug since 1900 and used to treat a range of disorders. For example, there are two medical conditions in which administering epinephrine makes breathing easier. Croup is a viral infection that makes the throat swell, and in asthma the airways to the lungs become narrowed. Inhaling a mist containing epinephrine relieves the swelling of croup, while an epinephrine injection opens the airways in acute asthma attacks. Epinephrine can also help with allergies. A severe allergic reaction may be fatal for two reasons: it can cause a severe asthma attack, and it can cause fluid to leak from blood vessels, producing a life-threatening drop in blood pressure. Epinephrine restores blood pressure by making the heart beat faster and stronger and by narrowing the blood vessels. Before sewing up incisions, surgeons sometimes inject epinephrine, which narrows the blood vessels around the cut and reduces bleeding. In addition, epinephrine combined with a local anesthetic slows the rate at which the anesthetic spreads into the surrounding tissues, so prolonging the pain-deadening effect.

There are other effects the person may not be aware of. Their blood pressure rises to pump blood quickly to the muscles and brain. The amount of fatty acids and glucose in the blood increases from the breakdown of glycogen in muscle and liver and triglycerides in fatty tissue. The airways open so the person can breathe in more air. The clumping of platelets makes the blood clot more easily, so less bleeding will occur if injured. Each of these responses has prepared the person for intense physical activity. It may be to fight. It may be to flee. This series of responses was named the "fight or flight" response by U.S. physiologist Walter B. Cannon (1871–1945).

Epinephrine does not last long in the body. Within a few minutes of release, it is broken down by enzymes in the tissues. Once the danger is past, fear and sympathetic stimulation usually subside, and the body returns to its normal state. Sometimes fear and anger persists after the real danger is past. Anger and the associated release of epinephrine may lead to high blood pressure, a rapid heartbeat, and an increased risk of heart attack.

M. ALLEN

See also: BRAIN; ENDOCRINE SYSTEMS; HORMONES.

Further reading:
Guyton, Arthur C. 2000. *Textbook of Medical Physiology*. 10th ed. New York: W. B. Saunders.

EPINEPHRINE

EPIPHYTES

Epiphytes are nonparasitic plants that grow on other plants

Epiphytes are a group of plants that grow on other plants. The term comes from the Greek words *epi*, which means "upon" and *phyton*, which means "plant." Also sometimes called air plants, epiphytes do not have roots embedded in the soil and so must obtain their water and nutrients from the air, rainwater, or the organic debris and moisture that builds up in the angles between the branches and trunks of trees or crevices in the bark.

Epiphytes grow in almost every habitat in the world that provides enough moisture: the canopies of tropical and damp temperate forests are particularly rich in epiphytes. Spanish moss (a vascular plant, *Tillandsia usneoides*, rather than a species of moss) drapes cliffs, telegraph wires, and the branches of trees—looking like strands of gray hair—in the southern United States, Central America, Argentina, and Chile. In the Amazon rain forest, many orchids (in the genera *Cattleya*, *Epidendrum*, and *Laelia*) and bromeliads (in the genera *Guzmania* and *Neoregelia*) are epiphytes. There are also species of epiphytic cacti, such as *Epiphyllum hookeri*. Epiphytic ferns and mosses also grow on tree trunks, surviving on the rain that trickles down the bark. Epiphyllous liverworts are epiphytic on the leaf surface of other plants (from the Greek words *epi* and *phyllon*, which means "leaf").

In temperate rain forests, such as those of the Pacific northwest, ferns, mosses, liverworts, and lichens grow abundantly on tree bark.

Less obvious to the observer are microscopic algae that grow on the submerged leaves of water plants and other algae. Algal epiphytes (called periphyton), for example, are seen as a bright green, blue-green, or golden brown film on the submerged leaves of cattails (*Typha* spp.) and bulrush (*Shoenoplectus* spp.). Seaweeds (large, multicellular algae) often grow as epiphytes on other seaweeds or sea grasses.

Epiphytes, such as this bromeliad, grow on other plants. Their leaves often form a cup to collect and store rainwater.

EPIPHYTES IN DANGER

Collection of epiphytes, such as orchids, from their natural habitat has pushed some species almost to extinction. Even more tragic and destructive than overcollection is the systematic clearance of the rain forests to provide land for agriculture and mineral extraction. One felled tree results in the destruction of many epiphytes that rely on the living trunk and branches for growth and survival.

The abundant rainfall that characterizes the rain forests cannot sustain adequate regrowth because tropical soils are low in nutrients and poorly developed. Therefore, clearance results in a net loss of tropical forest and a corresponding loss of habitat for the epiphytes.

AT RISK

Epiphyte adaptations

The canopy, or uppermost layer of the forest, is often an entanglement of spreading branches and foliage and thus prevents much of the sunlight from reaching the plants below. Epiphytes growing on trees high in the canopy can absorb light and water more readily than plants on the dim forest floor.

Epiphytes have evolved numerous adaptations to survive on other plants. Some species produce long suspended roots that contain chlorophyll and can photosynthesize. They can also absorb water vapor. Other species have water-absorbing hairs or scales on their leaves or stems. The leaves may cluster in a tight spiral, forming a cup to collect and store rainwater.

E. SHUBERT

See also: FERNS AND FERN ALLIES; MOSSES AND LIVERWORTS; ORCHIDS; PLANT KINGDOM.

Further reading:

Benzing, D. H. 1990. *Vascular Epiphytes: General Biology and Related Biota*. Cambridge, U.K.: Cambridge University Press.

CONNECTIONS

● Epiphytes are not **PARASITES** because they do not take nourishment from their hosts but use them simply for support.

● Like **CACTI AND SUCCULENTS**, epiphytes have many adaptations for collecting and storing water.

ETHOLOGY

I n the struggle for survival, most animals use a series of complex modes of behavior to compete in finding food, escaping predators, and finding a mate. Scientists call the biological study of an animal's behavior in its natural habitats ethology.

The history of ethology

The founders of modern ethology, during the 1930s, were Austrian-born zoologist Konrad Lorenz (1903–1989) and Dutch zoologist Niko Tinbergen (1907–1988), who later received the Nobel Prize in medicine or physiology in 1973 for their work (there is no Nobel prize for biology). Lorenz and Tinbergen emphasized the study of animal behavior in relation to the animal's natural lifestyle and environment. This approach was very different from the one taken by comparative psychologists at the time, who examined a few species (mainly rats and pigeons) in laboratory experiments.

The comparative psychologists looked for general rules that applied to all other species. They focused on immediate (proximate) causes of behavior. In contrast, Tinbergen and Lorenz considered the adaptive significance and the evolution of behavior. They combined evolutionary (functional) explanations of behavior with causal explanations.

Functional and causal explanations

Ethologists make an important distinction between functional questions and causal questions. Functional questions concern the adaptive value of the behavior to the animal. This issue is the main area of concern for the field called behavioral ecology, the study of relationships between the behavior of a species and the ecological conditions under which it lives. However, causal explanations of behavior cover how behaviors work through physiological, neurological, and hormonal mechanisms.

These two approaches are quite distinct. For example, one could ask why a bird migrates. A functional answer could be that it migrates to reach areas where food is more abundant. A causal answer would be concerned with hormonal changes and how these changes might be affected by the seasons.

When scientists discuss the adaptive role or survival value of a behavior, they mean the acquisition of behavioral characteristics that make an organism better suited to its environment or way of life. This acquisition maximizes the organism's reproductive success (the number of its own and related offspring

Ethologists study the behavior of animals in relation to their environment. In studying an example such as these lions (Panthera leo) feeding on a kill, they might consider the differences in behavior between the males, females, and cubs.

CORE FACTS

- Ethologists study how animals behave in relation to their natural environments.
- Ethologists look at the adaptive role of behavior, the factors that cause a behavior, changes in behavior during an animal's development, and the evolutionary history of the behavior.
- Ethologists distinguish between functional and causal questions.

CONNECTIONS

● **PSYCHOLOGY** is the study of the mental processes behind human and animal behavior.

● A **BEHAVIOR** that gives an individual a competitive advantage is considered to be an **ADAPTATION**.

SOCIOBIOLOGY IN ACTION

In some species young birds born in one year do not breed in the next. Instead, they help their parents to care for the second year's brood. Similarly, adult birds that have lost their mates will sometimes help in the rearing of other birds' chicks. Biologists have observed this behavior among widely separated species, such as white-fronted bee-eaters in Africa, scrub jays in Florida, and acorn woodpeckers in the western United States. Sociobiologists want to discover how such behavior evolved. It seems that, in nests with helpers, a greater number of chicks survives, and this "helping" behavior serves to preserve the genes of the helpers.

A CLOSER LOOK

Dutch ethologist Niko Tinbergen was one of the founders of ethology. In 1973, with Konrad Lorenz and Karl von Frisch, he received a Nobel Prize in physiology or medicine for his work.

that survive to reproduce). Scientists note that individual animals display differences in behavior and that these differences are at least partly inherited.

An overview of current ethology

Gradually, the distinction between ethology and comparative psychology has been broken down. Earlier ethologists believed that much of an animal's behavior was preprogrammed genetically; comparative psychologists maintained that learning and experience were the major influences. In this "nature versus nurture" debate, behavioral studies have focused on the interaction of nature and nurture. Scientists are studying the interaction of heredity, physiology, and experience.

The 1975 publication of E.O. Wilson's book *Sociobiology* (the study of the biology of social behavior) did much to bring together evolutionary theory and behavioral studies (see the box at left). In recent years, theoretical models developed in economics and math have greatly influenced behavioral ecology. Economics and evolutionary theory rely on the notion that success (whether financial or reproductive) increases with efficiency. Economic models have been applied to studies of feeding behavior, and a branch of math called game theory can be used to predict how certain behaviors are adaptive and passed on to future generations.

C. CARBONE

See also: ALTRUISM; ANIMAL BEHAVIOR; SOCIOBIOLOGY; WILSON, EDWARD O.; ZOOLOGY.

Further reading:
Goodenough, J. et al. 1993. *Perspectives on Animal Behavior.* New York: John Wiley and Sons.
Manning, A., and M. S. Dawkins. 1998. *An Introduction to Animal Behavior.* Cambridge, U.K.: Cambridge University Press, 1998.

ANTHROPOMORPHISM

There is a natural tendency for people to interpret everything that happens from a human perspective, including animal behavior. Anthropomorphism is the attribution of human emotions and behavior to nonhuman things, such as animals. For example, when a pet dog crouches with its head down, after it has been scolded, it may be thought of as "feeling guilty."

Scientific views of the usefulness of such terms are mixed. Some ethologists believe that these terms encourage people to feel sympathy with animals, rather than seeing them as emotionless, purely instinctive creatures. This reaction may help prevent unnecessary animal exploitation and cruelty. Other ethologists, however, believe it is important that people should be able to respect animals on their own terms, without assigning them human qualities. Anthropomorphic terms, such as "selfish," "spiteful," and "sneaky," are also commonly used to describe the adaptive role of behavior

and can help to increase understanding of the complexity of that behavior. However, there is a risk that such human interpretations may be misleading and unproductive. Provocative terms have an added problem in that they extend people's own biases about human issues to those of animals. For example, the term *promiscuous* has been used to describe female mating behavior in chimpanzees. Such a term may cause people to focus on the misleading notion that female chimpanzees enjoy several mates, rather than on the adaptive role that promiscuous behavior plays in chimp society.

Although the use of anthropomorphism may hinder an unbiased scientific evaluation, it is impossible to avoid entirely the human perspective. Ethologists are human and have personal and political interests that may cause them to focus on certain aspects of behavior while ignoring others. Science, like the arts, is liable to be influenced by contemporary opinion.

A CLOSER LOOK

EUTHANASIA

Euthanasia is the practice of relieving incurable suffering by offering a gentle and painless death

Despite its merciful intentions, in virtually every country of the developed world, euthanasia is legally a crime. *Euthanasia* is defined as "bringing about a gentle and easy death, especially in the case of an incurable and painful disease," and it is most likely to be used in cases of terminal illness. Although illegal, this "mercy killing" is practiced everywhere to some extent, sometimes even without the knowledge or consent of the victim. The subject is extremely controversial, and it is argued that, if euthanasia were made legal, it would be open to abuse. Other than the state of Oregon, the only jurisdiction where, within certain constraints, a physician can terminate life without fear of being prosecuted is the Netherlands, which legalized euthanasia in December 2000.

Euthanasia can be described as voluntary or involuntary. In voluntary euthanasia the patient asks for his or her life to be ended. Another person, usually a physician, may give an overdose of sedative drugs or provide the patient with the means to bring about his or her own death. In involuntary euthanasia, the decision to end a person's life is taken by someone other than the patient. It may be done, for example, in the case of a newborn with multiple severe handicaps or a person suffering irreversible coma as a result of brain injury or disease.

Either form of euthanasia may be active or passive. Active means doing something directly to bring about a person's death; for example, a physician may inject a patient with a lethal overdose of a drug. Passive euthanasia is the failure to provide life-sustaining interventions for a terminally ill patient. Passive euthanasia may be either mercy killing, the ending of a person's life, or simply allowing the patient to die of natural disease progression. Active methods—commonly used in voluntary euthanasia—provoke the most controversy. They tend to be opposed by doctors, who point out that their prime responsibility is to protect the life of their patients, not to bring about their death.

When has euthanasia been used?

In Britain a report published in May 1994 stated that a third of physicians who had received requests

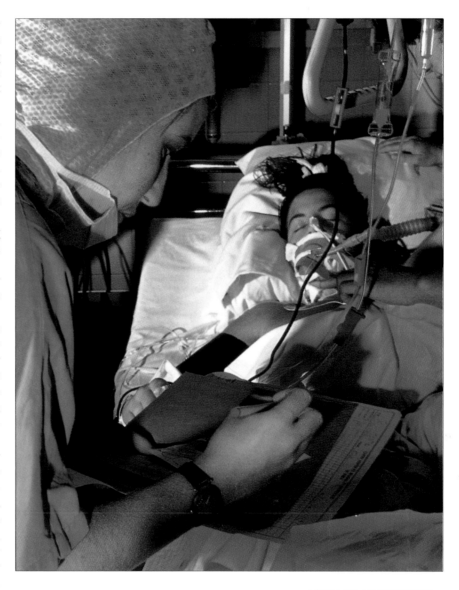

A patient on life-support equipment. Many people have expressed the wish that their lives should not be extended indefinitely by such means.

for euthanasia had taken active steps to end their patients' lives. Similarly, in Australia surveys of physicians and nurses in Victoria state revealed that both groups had practiced mercy killing.

One of the most memorable cases of physician-assisted suicide was the first of those involving Dr. Jack Kevorkian. In Michigan in 1990, Kevorkian, a retired pathologist, set up his "suicide machine"—a device for delivering drugs intravenously—so that a sufferer from Alzheimer's disease could kill herself. Over the next several years, Kevorkian assisted at least 130 other people to commit suicide. In 1998 he went beyond physician-assisted suicide to active euthanasia when he gave a lethal injection to a patient with Lou Gehrig's disease, a fatal neuromuscular disease. He was convicted of second-degree murder and sentenced to a 10- to 25-year prison sentence.

CORE FACTS

- Euthanasia is intended to bring about the gentle and easy death of a person suffering a painful and incurable disease or in an irreversible coma.
- Euthanasia is legal only in Oregon and the Netherlands. Elsewhere it is often secretly practiced by physicians and nurses.
- Opponents of euthanasia believe that its legalization would result in a general loss of respect for human life.

CONNECTIONS

● Legalization of euthanasia is a hotly debated topic in medical **BIOETHICS.**

● Some people argue that patients in the later stages of incurable diseases, such as **AIDS**, should be allowed to determine their own death.

● Doctors often use **LIFE-SUPPORT** equipment to keep patients alive.

In 1991 the *New England Journal of Medicine* published the testimony of a physician who had prescribed barbiturates to enable a patient with acute leukemia to end her own life. A jury refused to indict him. Also in 1991, the Los Angeles Hemlock Society published a guide to suicide, entitled *Final Exit*, by a British author who admitted involvement in the death of his first wife, terminally ill with cancer, in 1975. The book quickly became a bestseller.

The moral arguments

There are many sides to the euthanasia debate, which engages medical ethicists, physicians, philosophers, theologians, attorneys, pro-lifers, and right-to-die campaigners. A recurring theme is the "slippery slope" argument that, if active euthanasia was legalized, society would be moving toward making killing people more socially acceptable.

Opponents of active euthanasia make the point that there is a world of difference between letting a patient die of natural causes (for example, by not intervening and giving the patient medical treatment) and actively killing him or her. Others argue that morally what matters is the physician's intention. However, there is growing sympathy for passive euthanasia, reflected in various judgments in the United States courts. There has been an increase in cases brought by patients who have survived a catastrophic illness or accident only to be left with lives that they find intolerable.

A landmark judgment was given by a court in Atlanta, Georgia, in 1989. A formerly active 33-year-old man had been paralyzed from the neck down by a motorcycle accident four years previously. He asked that the respirator, which was keeping him alive, be disconnected. The judge ruled that a mentally competent person has the right to decide on the form of medical treatment he or she receives even if, as in this case, refusing treatment would result in death. In 1990 the United States Supreme Court ruled that a competent adult has a constitutional right to decline any and all unwanted medical interventions, including those that are potentially life prolonging. In 1997 the Supreme Court ruled there was no constitutional right to physician-assisted suicide. The Court indicated that the various states could authorize physician-assisted suicide or euthanasia. To date, Oregon is the only state to authorize physician-assisted suicide. That statute, adopted in a voter referendum, excludes any form of active euthanasia

In many countries the campaign to legalize euthanasia in general has been gaining in momentum, possibly prompted by factors such as the ravages of AIDS and the looming threat of Alzheimer's disease among rapidly aging populations (see AIDS; ALZHEIMER'S DISEASE). There is also growing disquiet at the extent to which modern life-support techniques can keep alive patients who are effectively beyond recovery to conscious activity. These are patients who, following catastrophic damage to the brain, are left in a persistent vegetative state, the so-called waking coma (see COMA; CONSCIOUSNESS). Such patients—up to 10,000 in the United States—never regain awareness but may survive in hospitals for many years. It was out of concern for these people and their families that the Appleton International Conference was convened in September 1992. Attended by specialists from nine countries, including the United States, it culminated in guidelines urging that such patients should be allowed to die.

Legal devices

Most people have a horror of incapacity, and it has been a major factor fueling demand for legal devices such as advance directives and living wills enabling mentally competent people to state in advance the circumstances under which they would not wish treatment to prolong life. Under the U.S. Patient Self-determination Act of 1991, hospitals and other healthcare providers are required to inform patients of state laws relating to these documents.

In some parts of the United States, there is also provision for nominating a healthcare proxy: a relative or friend to speak up for a patient who has become incapable of communicating his or her wishes. The point is to ensure patients are not subjected to further medical interventions when there is no hope of recovery.

P. PRATT

See also: ALZHEIMER'S DISEASE; COMA; CONSCIOUSNESS.

Further reading:
Burnell, G. 1993. *Final Choices: To Live or To Die in an Age of Medical Technology*. New York: Insight Books.
Keown, J. 1995. *Euthanasia Examined*. New York: Cambridge University Press.
Sheldon, T. 2001. Holland decriminalizes voluntary euthanasia. *British Medical Journal* **322**: 947–948.

THE NETHERLANDS EXPERIENCE

In December 2000, euthanasia was legalized in the Netherlands. Within certain boundaries, a physician can terminate a patient's life without fear of being prosecuted. Euthanasia is sanctioned on a right-to-die basis, so long as physicians comply with strict guidelines laid down by the Royal Dutch Medical Association. The patient must be the victim of unbearable suffering and must ask explicitly and repeatedly for his or her life to be ended.

A commission of inquiry appointed by the Dutch government published the results of its investigation into euthanasia and related topics in September 1991. This document revealed that nearly 2,700 cases of voluntary euthanasia/assisted suicide had occurred in the previous year. Most were cancer cases, but the most common reason for requesting euthanasia was that patients were tired of life and feared dependency and loss of dignity.

The commission estimated that more than 1,000 cases of euthanasia occurred annually in Holland without a specific request by the patient. These patients were unable to decide for themselves, owing to: reduced consciousness (54 percent of cases), permanent unconsciousness (31 percent), or dementia (8 percent). Under Dutch law, a physician who acts outside of the recognized guidelines faces prosecution for murder and a jail sentence.

A CLOSER LOOK

EVERGLADES

The Everglades are a unique habitat in southern Florida characterized by subtropical sawgrass marshlands

A channel through the Everglades in southern Florida. Concerted conservation efforts are now underway to protect and maintain the Everglades.

The Everglades are a wide area of subtropical wetlands in southern Florida, a habitat unlike that anywhere else in the United States. This rich habitat supports numerous species of fish, crustaceans, and reptiles, as well as more than 300 species of birds and around 30 species of mammals. Originally, the Everglades extended from Lake Okeechobee to the southern end of Florida, covering 13,000 square miles (33,700 km²). Now less than half of the original habitat is contained in the Everglades National Park at the southernmost end of Florida. Active steps are now being taken to preserve the Everglades, which once suffered from diminishing water supplies and pollution.

The Everglades climate is subtropical, with two distinct seasons: a rainy season that lasts from May to October and a dry season from November to April. Seventy percent of the region's rain falls during the rainy season, and the climate is warm and humid. This season is a productive time for the Everglades: a river only 6 inches (15 cm) deep but almost 50 miles (80 km) wide in places flows through the lush vegetation, bringing essential nutrients to boost plant growth, the plants in turn feeding the growing population of animal life.

During the winter dry season, the flow of water into the Everglades halts, and the marshes begin to dry up. One of the most famous animals of the everglades, the American alligator (*Alligator mississippiensis*), plays an important role at this time. The reptiles seek out dried-up water holes and dig down to find water, the result being the formation of pools called gator holes. Soon the only active life is found in and around these pools.

Plants grow on the banks, wading birds flock to the ponds to eat fish, and mammals come to the ponds to drink. Many of these creatures become prey for the waiting alligators. However, at the start of the next rainy season, the survivors are ready to spread out through the wet Everglades once again.

Hurricanes, which usually occur between August and October, are an important influence on life in the Everglades. They bring torrents of rain, which contribute significantly to the region's much-needed soaking. However, at the same time the hurricanes wreak havoc by uprooting trees and plants, destroying habitats, and killing the animals. In 1989, for example, Hurricane Andrew caused significant damage in the Everglades.

CORE FACTS
- The Everglades are a unique habitat in southern Florida.
- The subtropical climate has two distinct seasons: the rainy season lasts from May to October, and the dry season from November to April.
- Characteristic vegetation includes sawgrass and pine, cypress, and mangrove trees. The Everglades is home to many animals, including raccoons, opossums, and the Florida panther.
- People have drained much of the Everglades, and many species native to the area are endangered.

CONNECTIONS

● With its distinctive plant and animal life, the Everglades is unlike any other **BIOME AND HABITAT**.

● The Everglades lay atop a flat, shallow limestone bed. Limestone is a sedimentary rock composed mainly of calcium carbonate (CaCO₃). Although the underlying limestone is porous, it has been sealed by a thick layer of peat. Peat bogs are made of accumulated dead plants, **MOSSES** in particular. They grow at the rate of 1/25 inch (1 mm) per year.

● Some of the plants in the Everglades are **EPIPHYTES**, plants that grow on the trunks of other plants.

● **CONSERVATION** is an extremely important issue in the Everglades.

Plant and animal life

Along with the rainfall, the level of the land also determines how much water a plant will receive during the year. The Everglades are so broad and flat that small differences in elevation make a big difference. The lowest-lying parts of the Everglades are called wet prairie because they are under water most of the time. This wet prairie is covered with a thick mat of algae periphyton that live attached to underwater surfaces and are eaten by small fish. These fish are in turn eaten by reptiles such as turtles, mammals such as otters, and birds such as gallinules and herons.

Like most marshlands, the Everglades do not support the growth of many trees. U.S. swamplands, on the other hand, have many more trees than the Everglades. Sawgrass (a sedge, *Cladium jamaicensis*) is the Everglades' best-known feature. It grows to more than 11 feet (3.5 m) high and gets its name from the tiny sharp teeth along the leaf edges.

The Everglades, however, do support some pine, cypress, and mangrove trees. The pine forest there is noteworthy because it is host to over 30 types of plants that grow nowhere else in the world. Fires sweep through the vegetation periodically, revitalizing the soil and encouraging fresh plant growth. Animal life in the pine forests includes raccoons, opossums, and the endangered Florida panther (*Felis concolor coryi*).

Cypress trees (*Taxodium* spp.) tend to cluster around depressions in the ground where rich peat accumulates (formed from the partial disintegration of plant matter in wet places); the trees growing atop the peat form structures called cypress domes.

Mangrove trees grow along many seashores and where the water is brackish (slightly salty). Their roots extend into the swamp, trapping material that gradually clumps together to form dry land. These areas are vital to maintaining the Florida coastline against destructive hurricanes. These coastal swamps are home to a large number of fish and crustaceans, such as mullet, sharks, crabs, shrimp, and lobsters; large water birds, such as pelicans and spoonbills; reptiles, such as sea turtles; and mammals, such as manatees and porpoises.

Another well-known feature of the Everglades is its hammocks, or tree islands, on ground that is raised 1 foot (30 cm) or more above the surrounding area. This slight elevation is enough to ensure that the hammock is rarely if ever flooded, and thus, the trees are able to take root and flourish. Tropical hardwood trees such as mahogany (*Swietenia* spp.) and gumbo-limbo (*Bursera simaruba*) are most common. Colorful *Liguus* snails and orb weaver spiders make good use of these island refuges. The trees themselves are home for plants called epiphytes, which live on the trunk or branches of the tree to get sunlight that never reaches the ground because it is blocked by the tree's dense canopy of leaves (see EPIPHYTES). These epiphytes include orchids, ferns, and lichens.

Human impact

The Everglades have been a home to living organisms for thousands of years, but people have dramatically reshaped the habitat in the last 200 years.

The first human inhabitants of the region were Native Americans, principally the Calusa and the Tekesta. The Calusa called the Everglades by the name *Pa-hay-okee*, which means Grassy Water. Another native American group—the Seminoles—came from Georgia to the Everglades between 1835 and 1842. At that time, European settlers in the region thought of this area as nothing more than an ugly marsh. Their ideas changed in the middle of the 19th century, however, when hunters came to the region in search of alligators and plume birds, such as the roseate spoonbill (*Platalea ajaja*) and the snowy ibis (*Eudocimus albus*), for their exotic feathers, which were very fashionable for women's hats. As a result, vast numbers of these birds were hunted and killed.

From 1916 through 1928, workers completed a highway called the Tamiami Trail that sliced west through the Everglades from Miami to Naples. Hailed as a boon for the economic development of the region, the highway also made the marsh—and its endangered creatures—much more accessible and thus placed it in greater danger.

An even bigger problem for the wildlife of the Everglades has been the past attempts to drain the area to create dry land for farming and other uses. Efforts to drain the marshes began in 1881, but the turning point came in 1905, with the construction of a network of canals that carried water west into the Gulf of Mexico and east into the Atlantic Ocean. Farmers moved onto the newly reclaimed land south of Lake Okeechobee, raising cattle and planting a variety of agricultural crops, especially sugarcane.

By 2002, the Everglades had been reduced to less than half its original size. About a quarter has been

Epiphytes (orchids, ferns, and mosses) grow in the crooks of tree branches in the Everglades.

*The American crocodile (*Crocodylus acutus*) lives in the coastal waters of the Everglades. Much rarer than alligators, crocodiles can be distinguished by a tooth in the upper jaw that still shows when the mouth is closed.*

consumed by cities and towns; about the same area has been converted to farmland. What remains may gradually dry up as a result of residents' insistence on controlling the flow of water to prevent flooding. After hurricanes in 1926 and 1928 ruptured an earthen levee on the south side of Lake Okeechobee, killing thousands of people, the federal and state governments sought to prevent future floods by building a huge dike on the lake's southern shore. In 1947 another hurricane flooded the area, leading to the creation of the Central and Southern Florida Flood Control Project, masterminded by the Army Corps of Engineers. The result further altered the flow of water and nutrients through the region.

V. KIERNAN

See also: CONSERVATION; ENDANGERED SPECIES; POLLUTION; WETLANDS.

Further reading:
Blaustein, Daniel. 2000. *The Everglades and the Gulf Coast*. Tarrytown, New York: Marshall Cavendish.
McCally, David. 1999. *The Everglades: An Environmental History*. Gainsville, Fla.: University Press of Florida.

CONSERVING THE EVERGLADES

Concern over the environmental impact of people on the Everglades surfaced early. Legal protection for endangered species was first instituted during the late 19th century, and in 1947 the federal government designated part of the region the Everglades National Park. The park's aims are to help preserve the habitat and save endangered wildlife such as the Florida panther, the manatee, the green sea turtle, the loggerhead turtle, the snail kite, the peregrine falcon, and the cape sable sparrow, among others. In the 1980s scientists first demonstrated that water levels in the Everglades were dropping because of interference with natural patterns of water flow in the region. In addition, what water was there was found to be poisoned by runoff, such as phosphates from the sugarcane plantations. Phosphates promote the growth of cattails and other invaders that crowd out native Everglades plants. Such pest plants are a major problem for the park. They include melaleuca (*Melaleuca quinquenervia*), a rapidly growing tree introduced from Australia in 1906 as part of the effort to drain the swamps. Other troublesome exotics include the water hyacinth (*Eichhornia crassipes*), the Brazilian pepper (*Schinus terebinthifolius*), and the hydrilla (*Hydrilla verticillata*).

In 1988 the federal government sued the Florida state government for failing to ensure the park received clean water. A complicated legal wrangle began, involving the government and sugarcane growers. In 1993 all parties agreed to the Comprehensive Everglades Restoration Plan (CERP), an $8 billion program developed by the U.S. Army Corps of Engineers and the South Florida Water Management District, with federal and state agencies, Native American tribes, and the public. CERP will increase the amount of water running into the park and limit the amount of pollutants in the water. Under the plan growers must limit their phosphates runoff, and six artificial marshes must be built south of Lake Okeechobee to strain pollutants from the water before it enters the Everglades.

AT RISK

EVOLUTION

Evolution is genetic change that takes place over time within a group of organisms

*Opossums, like this Virginian opossum (*Didelphis virginiana*) survived the extinctions of the Cretaceous period, which saw the end of the dinosaurs, and still look much like their ancient ancestors.*

Fossils, whether or not they have living descendants, reflect evolutionary change. Most forms fit into existing taxonomic groups, suggesting common descent with modification.

The diversity of life

About 1.4 million species have been described, but it is estimated that this number is less than 10 percent of the total number in existence. Insects (900,000 described species) are by far the largest and most diverse group, accounting for more than half of the total number of known species. Angiosperms, which comprise the higher plants, number around 250,000 species. However, in terms of geological time, these numbers are insignificant. It is estimated that probably more than 99 percent of all species that ever lived on Earth are now extinct. About two billion species have probably evolved during the past 600 million years. Some species are not preserved (causing gaps in the fossil record), others are extinct or have evolved into other species, and a few survive in a form that has barely changed over hundreds of millions of years. For example, the horseshoe crab (*Limulus*) has changed little from its fossil ancestors that lived 500 million years ago; opossums, crocodilians, sharks, and coelacanths are also little altered.

Over time, organisms change and become better suited to their environment, a process called adaptation. Adaptation increases their potential for both survival and reproduction. Change occurs because certain traits are inheritable and can be passed from

Evolution can be discussed either in terms of the development of a species as it adapts to its surrounding environment over successive generations (microevolution) or according to the theory that life on Earth has gradually developed from simple to complex organisms over a four-billion-year history (macroevolution). The evidence that evolution has and is taking place comes from various sources including biogeography (the distribution of living organisms), comparative anatomy, embryology, biochemistry, paleontology, genetics, and molecular biology (see ANATOMY; BIOCHEMISTRY; BIOGEOGRAPHY; EMBRYO; GENETICS; PALEOBIOLOGY).

Scientists realized quite early on that living organisms differ in different climatic zones. However, they were unable to explain why similar climatic areas also have different flora and fauna or why, within these areas, organisms show broad similarities. Both observations can be explained by variation and natural selection, which gradually alter successive generations of living organisms.

Taxonomists use similarities and differences in morphology (comparative anatomy) to classify living organisms. They realized that, although structures such as limbs and wings are very different externally, their skeletal structure is the same (homologous). Such homologies could be explained if both birds and mammals had a common ancestor. Studies of the development of animal embryos supported this idea.

CONNECTIONS

● Living **FOSSILS**, such as the coelacanth and horseshoe crab, can provide clues about the process of evolution because they have remained mostly unchanged for millions of years.

● Genetic variation arises from **MUTATIONS**, which cause changes in **DNA**. Variation makes it possible for populations of organisms to evolve and become better suited to their environment (**ADAPTATION**).

CORE FACTS

■ Evolution explains how species and populations change. Over billions of years, life on Earth has progressed from simple to more complex organisms.

■ Natural selection acting on variation within a species results in evolution through adaptation and genetic change.

■ Neo-Darwinism, or the "synthetic theory of evolution," combined Darwin's theory of evolution by natural selection and Mendel's theory of heredity.

■ The development of molecular biology allows scientists to study genes and their constituent DNA to discover how organisms are related to one another.

■ Population genetics is the study of genetic variation within populations, including gene flow and genetic drift.

■ Two theories that attempt to explain emergent species are gradualism and punctuated equilibrium.

parent to offspring. Those traits that are advantageous allow a population to grow, while less favorable characteristics may result in extinction.

Evolution has no built-in purpose or direction—it is a matter of chance. Populations contain a variety of forms and have inheritable traits, which evolve through natural selection and thus gradually become better adapted to their environment. Although evolution is, overall, irreversible, sometimes small changes called reversals may occur within a species.

Early evolution

The question of when and how life originated is difficult to answer, but it is fundamental to the theory of evolution. The basic unit of life is the cell, which may have started and died out several times before becoming permanently established and able to replicate (multiply). Earth probably formed about 4.6 billion years ago, and it is thought that life followed soon after (around 4 billion years ago). The earliest evidence of life has been found in Greenland in rock that is 3.85 billion years old. In Australia there are fossils estimated to be 3.5 million years old that are similar to living cyanobacteria (plantlike photosynthetic bacteria).

There are many theories but no consensus concerning the origin of life on Earth. Chemical theories propose that life arose from organic molecules produced abiogenetically (not manufactured by organisms) and that a period of chemical evolution preceded the evolution of life. The most popular version of this theory, proposed in the 1920s, is called the Oparin-Haldane theory.

In 1953 U.S. chemists Stanley Miller and Harold Urey re-created what was thought to be the primitive atmosphere of Earth (water vapor, hydrogen, methane, and ammonia) in a sealed glass apparatus. They heated the mixture of gases to 182 °F (85 °C) and subjected it to an electrical discharge for about a week to simulate lightning.

The experiment generated four major types of organic molecules—amino acids (the building blocks of proteins), nucleotides (the building blocks of DNA), sugars, and fatty acids in their simplest form. All of these molecules are possible precursors to the more complex molecules that are essential for life (see CELL BIOLOGY; DNA; PROTEINS).

Some people think that life arose from the hydrothermal vents on Earth's deep ocean floor, which pump out warm water rich in minerals. Even today, there are bacteria that have evolved around such vents by adapting to the harsh conditions (see the box above).

Other theories suggest life is extraterrestrial in origin (see EXTRATERRESTRIAL LIFE). The theory of panspermia, for example, proposed by Swedish physicist and chemist Svante Arrhenius (1859–1927) in 1907, proposes that microorganisms, such as

An electron micrograph of blue-green algae, or cyanobacteria—thought to be some of the earliest known life-forms on Earth.

OTHER SITES OF EVOLUTION

All green plants, as well as certain algae, need sunlight to produce food (photosynthesis) and grow, the plants themselves being the primary food source of most organisms. However, in 1977, scientists researching the volcanic cracks (vents) in the crust of the Galapagos Rift in the Pacific Ocean discovered a new type of environment where organisms could convert chemicals into food using chemosynthesis. The ocean waters adjacent to the Galapagos Rift are close to freezing, but volcanic activity around the vents raises the water temperature surrounding the rift to around 632 °F (350 °C). Heat and hydrogen sulfide from the vents make this area a perfect spot for evolution of certain chemosynthetic bacteria that use the hydrogen sulfide for energy. These bacteria form the primary link in this deep ocean food chain. More than 295 new species have been discovered in the Galapagos Rift environment, including giant clams up to 1 foot (30 cm) long. There is also a red-colored worm, *Riftia pachyptila*, which lives in a self-made tube up to 25 feet (7.6 m) in length and about 1 inch (2.5 cm) in diameter. It has no mouth or digestive tract and presumably gains nourishment from bacteria living inside its cells. It is currently classified in a phylum on its own. Each member of this ecosystem has evolved and become better suited to its environment through adaptation. Their ancestors are not known, but they probably originated from other ocean organisms nearby. Perhaps similar organisms evolved early in Earth's history when there were more cracks in Earth's crust and volcanic activity was high. Some scientists speculate there may be similar life-forms elsewhere in the Solar System on a planet or satellite with unfrozen oceans and even volcanic activity (see EXTRATERRESTRIAL LIFE).

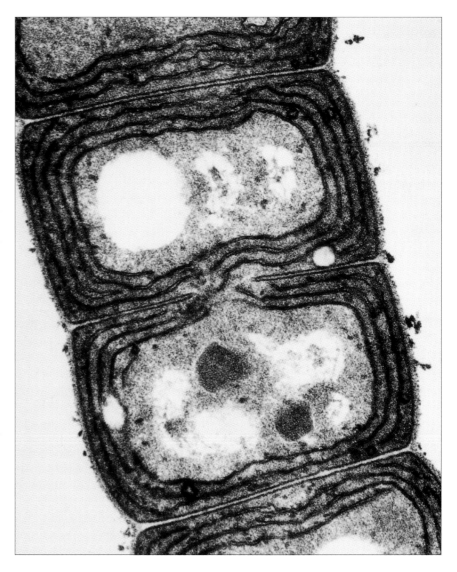

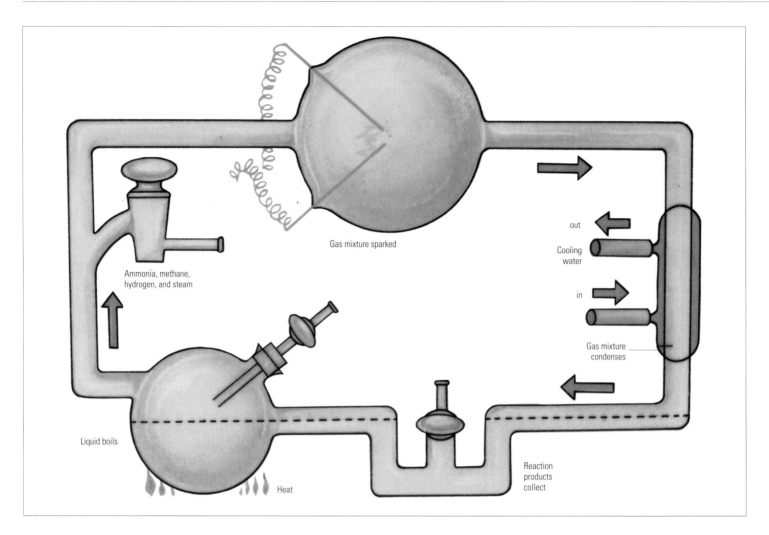

out

Cooling water

in

Gas mixture sparked

Gas mixture condenses

Ammonia, methane, hydrogen, and steam

Liquid boils

Heat

Reaction products collect

The type of apparatus that Stanley Miller and Harold Urey used in their experiments to recreate the conditions that characterized Earth's early atmosphere.

bacteria, drifted to Earth from space. However, it is unlikely that bacterial spores could survive exposure to cosmic radiation. Other scientists suggest that water, certain gases, and organic (carbon-containing) molecules, which are essential to life, arrived with comets and asteroids. This theory gained strength when, in 1986, spacecraft flying by Halley's Comet showed that the comet contained far more organic material than expected.

Early studies in evolution

Greek philosopher Anaximander (ca. 610–547 BCE) was probably the first person to introduce the idea of evolution (although he did not call it that) in his writing *On Nature*. He assumed that life started out as slime and eventually moved to drier places to develop. Another Greek philosopher, Aristotle (384–322 BCE), often referred to as the Father of Biology, taught that the form of natural objects is determined by their purpose: in other words, structure is determined by function (see ARISTOTLE).

Until the 19th century, it was generally thought that species were created miraculously. Even English naturalist Charles Darwin (1809–1882) was of this opinion before he traveled on the ship named *The Beagle*. Some naturalists believed in spontaneous generation, a theory that proposes living organisms suddenly develop from dead or decomposing matter. Italian scientist Lazarro Spallanzani (1729–1799) and, later, French chemist Louis

Pasteur (1822–1895) refuted this idea, by proving that life comes only from preexisting life (see BIOLOGY, HISTORY AND PHILOSOPHY OF; PASTEUR, LOUIS).

French naturalist Jean-Baptiste Lamarck (1744–1829) was the first to publish a reasoned theory of evolution (1809), although at that time it was called transformism. He suggested that favorable features, acquired during the lifetime of parents, could be passed on to their offspring. For example, giraffes that stretch up to eat from the higher branches of trees will have slightly longer necks. Any offspring of these giraffes will inherit these slightly longer necks. Although Lamarck's theory was discredited, he did recognize that today's giraffes have long necks and their ancestors had short necks. He knew nothing of genetics but attempted to explain how the change in neck length came about. He also set aside the idea of creationism (see the box on page 654). Lamarck recognized that animals changed over time and that these changes better adapted them to their environment.

Darwin and the theory of evolution

A unique system for classifying organisms developed by Swedish naturalist Carolus Linnaeus (1707–1778), the discovery of huge, extinct mammalian fossils by French anatomist Georges Cuvier (1769–1802), and the book *Zoonomia* written by Charles Darwin's grandfather, Erasmus Darwin (1731–1802) all helped Charles Darwin to formulate and explain his theory of evolution. However, there were two other publications that had a much greater influence on him. The first was *Principles of Geology* by English geologist Charles Lyell (1797–1875). Lyell estimated Earth to be many millions of years old. This estimate is significant because previously Earth was assumed to be only a few thousand years old, an insufficient time for the process of evolution to take place. Lyell also suggested that Earth has always undergone slow and steady change.

Darwin had a copy of *Principles of Geology* with him on *The Beagle*, and during the voyage he came to realize that species are not fixed entities but are continually changing in response to environmental pressures. He was not yet aware that natural selection was the driving force of evolution.

The second publication to influence Darwin was *An Essay on the Principle of Population* by English economist Thomas Malthus (1766–1834). Malthus argued that human populations always tend to outgrow their food supply, resulting in a "struggle for existence." This struggle caught Darwin's imagination. He saw it operating with much greater force among other animals because, unlike people, they have no control over their rate of reproduction.

In 1858, after 20 years' work, Darwin revealed his theory along with that of English naturalist Alfred Russel Wallace (see the box above right), and a full account of his theory of evolution by natural selection appeared the following year. The first edition of *On the Origin of Species by Means of Natural Selection* sold out in a single day (see DARWIN, CHARLES).

Darwin's theory is based on four premises. The first is that more individuals are produced than can survive. This premise leads to the second, that there must therefore be a struggle for existence. Third, individuals show variation, and those with advantageous features are more likely to survive in the struggle for existence (natural selection). Finally, if variation can be inherited, then those individuals with advantageous features will become more numerous in the population at the expense of those less well adapted (the principle of inheritance). Most important, Darwin's theory of evolution proposes that variation and evolution operate independently of one another.

Just before the publication of Darwin's book, an important discovery was made in a limestone quarry in Germany: the fossil bird Archaeopteryx was discovered. As it had feathered wings and reptilian teeth (see ARCHAEOPTERYX), it was thought to show a link between dinosaurs and modern birds. Such important evidence for evolution was all that English biologist Thomas Huxley (1825–1895) needed to convince the world of evolution. Huxley was a great supporter of Darwin's views and frequently spoke about them, notably tackling various religious figures and also Richard Owen (1804–1892), a famous anatomist of the time who held anti-Darwinian views. On reading Darwin's book, Huxley said, "How extremely stupid of me not to have thought of that." For his outspoken defense of Darwin, Huxley was often referred to as "Darwin's bulldog."

ALFRED RUSSEL WALLACE

Although Charles Darwin is popularly acknowledged as the originator of evolutionary theory, British traveler and naturalist Alfred Wallace (1823–1913) quite independently came to the same conclusions at the same time. In 1858 Wallace, then aged 35, was in Malaysia suffering with malaria. He wrote to Darwin telling him of his theory and enclosing his manuscript. The content was remarkably similar to that of Darwin's and even used identical terminology. Darwin was dumbfounded that his years of careful observations and work might come to nothing if he did not publish his ideas quickly. Within a fortnight, at a meeting of the Linnean Society in London, Darwin's outline of evolution was presented, followed by that of Wallace. A year later in 1859, Darwin's *On The Origin of Species by Means of Natural Selection* was published. Wallace also published various works on evolution and natural selection but was never quite convinced that evolution could account for the complexity of the human brain (thus, he was not completely divorcing himself from creationism). Wallace's most important work was *The Geographical Distribution of Animals*, published in 1876. In it Wallace attempts to separate (geographically) the characteristically Australian fauna from the Asian fauna. The geographic boundary between these types of animals, now explained by continental drift, is still called Wallace's line.

DISCOVERERS

EVOLUTION AND GENETICS

The work of Austrian botanist and monk Gregor Mendel (1822–1884) on variation and inheritance was first published in 1865, but it became well known and could be explained adequately only in the early 1900s (see MENDEL, GREGOR). Mendel's experiments on pea plants revealed much about how inheritance works. He concluded that all organisms have what he termed "particles of inheritance" (today called genes). The particles normally exist in pairs and are present in all breeding adults. In sexually reproducing organisms, the particle pairs split during gamete formation (first meiotic division) so that each ovum and sperm/pollen grain contains only one particle of each pair (an allele). The allele carries a version of the gene, for example, for tallness or shortness. Often one allele is dominant and the other recessive, but other conditions also exist. This is the genetic basis of variations on which selection processes act.

Some scientists theorize that life on Earth may have started many times and died out because of a bombardment of large asteroids and comets. This painting is of Halley's comet terrifying the citizens of Constantinople as it passed close by Earth.

CREATIONISM

Evolutionary theory is not accepted by creationists. Creationists believe that all forms of life are designed for a specific biological task and do not change over time owing to natural processes. All theories of creation seek to explain the variety and complexity of life on Earth as the work of the Creator. Until English naturalist Charles Darwin (1809–1882) published his theory of evolution in 1859, everyone, including Darwin at first, thought that structures such as the human eye could not arise by chance because they are so complicated. Creationists believed the eye had to be a product of conscious design by an all-powerful being. The creationist theory is impossible to test because it makes no predictions and cannot be contradicted because no one has complete knowledge of the Creator's plan.

A CLOSER LOOK

Three biologists, R. A. Fisher (1890–1962), J. B. S. Haldane (1892–1964), and Sewall Wright (1889–1988), demonstrated independently the link between Mendelian heredity and natural selection and therefore between genetics and evolutionary change. By 1950 Darwin's theory had been refined and developed and was now called the synthetic theory of evolution or neo-Darwinism.

Subsequent developments in molecular biology have further expanded scientists' knowledge of genetic change. Errors of DNA (deoxyribonucleic acid) replication (copying) and mutations occur, but these errors are passed on to the next generation only if the organism carrying the mutation survives to adulthood and breeds. Natural selection tends to eliminate unfit organisms, while those that are well adapted survive.

DNA and RNA

Over the last 25 years, molecular biologists have been able to study the rates at which genes change (see DNA; MOLECULAR BIOLOGY; RNA). Such studies have revealed that DNA molecules and their constituent genes give a good indication of evolutionary history and current trends in organisms. DNA and RNA (ribonucleic acid) polymers are likely to have played an important role in the early evolution of cellular life as carriers of information.

DNA plays an important role in the identification of relationships between organisms, a field of science called phylogenetics (see TAXONOMY). Until DNA could be isolated, relationships between organisms were based on anatomical evidence; sometimes, as with fossil material, this is still the only evidence available. (Although some fossils may contain DNA, for example, insects in amber and frozen material, usually only very small fragments of DNA are preserved and remain uncontaminated.)

DNA contains four molecular components called bases: C (cytosine), which always pairs with G (guanine), and A (adenine), which always pairs with T (thymine). Using a process called DNA hybridization, scientists mix single strands of DNA from two different species to see how similar they are (see DNA; GENETIC ENGINEERING). The more closely the two species are related, the more pairing there will be between their DNA strands.

Studies in molecular biology have also revealed that amino acids link to form proteins, based on instructions carried by DNA and RNA, and that cells can synthesize DNA and RNA with the aid of enzymes, which are themselves proteins (see ENZYMES). Genes are coded sequences of the DNA molecule in the chromosome, which themselves code for the precise sequence of amino acids within a protein. As mutations alter DNA base sequences, they produce changes in amino acid sequences, which result in new, modified proteins that can be traced over long periods of time.

Differences in the amino acid sequences can be counted for various species and compared with the approximate date that those same species separated from one another in the course of evolution. Geneticists studying particular groups of organisms have found that the number of differences in the amino acid sequences is proportional to the time that has passed since the species separated. This theory is called the molecular clock theory. As some molecules "keep better time" than others, any results must be substantiated using other evidence from the fossil record and elsewhere.

Mutations

Mutations are the source of all genetic variation. They are inheritable and can be harmful, beneficial, or neutral. Most mutations are detrimental because nonfunctional proteins are produced. Mutations are usually eliminated because the organism in which they occur usually fails to survive or to reproduce. The fitness (the ability of an individual to survive and spread its genotype to future generations) of that individual has been compromised in some way.

Neutral mutations are neither advantageous nor disadvantageous because they do not alter protein function or interfere with a process of natural selection. Mutations usually occur spontaneously but can be triggered by external environmental factors,

PUNCTUATED EQUILIBRIUM

The fossil record contains many examples of organisms that have remained virtually the same over millions of years, suggesting that evolution is not a continuous process. The idea that species evolve rapidly and then remain relatively unchanged over a long period (stasis) is called punctuated equilibrium. First put forward in the 1940s, this model of evolution was revised by two U.S. paleontologists, Niles Eldridge and Stephen Jay Gould in 1972. They proposed that when species are forming, they evolve rapidly, but once established, selection pressure is reduced, and biological change is minimal. No evolution occurs unless there is some further change, for example, in the environment, that triggers another speciation event. It is difficult to prove that evolution occurs in this way or in the more traditional way with gradual change (gradualism) leading to the formation of new species. It is possible that both types of evolution may occur but are dependent on circumstance.

EVOLUTION

including exposure to certain hazardous or toxic chemicals. The mutation rate in people is a subject of controversy. Some studies suggest that the rate of mutation is much higher than expected. Other studies suggest that some genes are more susceptible to mutation than others. It also appears that sperm carry more new mutations in its DNA than eggs do.

Population genetics

Modern evolutionary theory makes use of population genetics, the statistical study of heredity in populations rather than individuals. Developed during the 1930s and 1940s by a group of mathematicians and biologists working in Britain, population genetics is now one of the most mathematically sophisticated branches of biology.

The work involves measurement and extrapolation of the variation present in individuals of a sexually reproducing population and the effects of natural selection on that variation. The measurement of evolutionary change within a population is based on the Hardy-Weinberg law, proposed in 1906. The law demonstrates that allele frequencies (the ratio of homozygotes and heterozygotes for a given pair of alleles in a given population to the overall frequency of each allele) remain constant unless outside forces, such as mutation, act on them.

Within any population there is variation, and the total set of genes responsible for that variation is called the gene pool. There are five ways in which the gene pool can be altered—natural selection, mutation, gene flow, genetic drift, and nonrandom mating (positive assortive mating).
• Natural selection: Natural selection acts on the gene pool and may alter the frequency of the alleles and thus cause change in the population.

Favorable alleles increase in the population, while detrimental alleles tend to be lost. Surviving members of the population are better adapted to the environment in which they live. The resistance of cockroaches to various forms of insecticides provides an excellent example of the process of natural selection. All species of cockroaches are scavengers; they feed on garbage, dead insects, and human food, which they contaminate with their droppings. Industrial scientists have carried out an enormous amount of research—at great cost in terms of time and expense—to develop chemicals to control cockroaches.

Although some insecticides were initially effective, many cockroach species have developed high levels of resistance to the most widely used insecticides. The German cockroach (*Blatella germanica*), for example, has long been exposed to insecticides and, over many years, has developed resistance to nearly every type manufactured.

Natural selection can operate in three ways. If a particular trait increases fitness, then it will increase in the population at the expense of other traits, a process called directional selection. If natural selection operates against extreme forms in a population, intermediate forms will predominate through stabilizing selection. If extremes are selected at the expense of the intermediate forms, then selection is said to be disruptive and may eventually result in the formation of new species.
• Mutation: Mutations are inheritable changes caused by the alteration, insertion, or deletion of a base or bases in a DNA molecule. Mutation is the only source of variation for organisms that reproduce asexually (by binary fission; see CELL BIOLOGY). It is a random process that can occur through point

*A Mediterranean monk seal (*Monachus monachus*). Its streamlined body and flipperlike forelimbs are similar to those of other land animals that have adapted to aquatic environments.*

*A giant panda (*Ailuropoda melanoleuca*), gripping bamboo between its fingers and "thumb," a classic example of convergent evolution.*

from exclusion of others) because the gene pool is limited and inbreeding can occur. Cheetahs, for example, are all genetically very similar, evidence suggesting the population was reduced to a low level in the recent past (a genetic bottleneck).

• Nonrandom mating: In animals, sexual selection (traits concerned solely with increasing mating success) influences the gene pool because successful individuals produce many offspring, which inherit their genes, while unsuccessful individuals may not breed at all, and their genes are lost.

Choice of partner is not random: instead, males compete with each other for access to receptive females or females choose a partner based on male displays. Wapiti (*Cervus elaphus*), for example, fight during the breeding season (rut) for possession of females. Mature stags with the large antlers secure the biggest harems, whereas younger individuals may not breed at all. Male birds, such as the peacock (*Pavo cristatus*), display for females, the subsequent mating being a result of female choice. In the red-necked phalarope (*Phalaropus lobatus*), the roles are reversed. The females fight, and the males choose which one to mate with. Female reproductive success depends on maximizing the number of offspring, and so it is important to select the "best" male. Male reproductive success depends on the number of females they can inseminate.

Adaptation and evolution

All organisms are subject to natural selection. Within a species, a variation that gives some advantage to one individual over another increases that individual's chance of surviving and producing offspring. The feature therefore tends to increase in frequency. Organisms become better suited to their environment because of these features, or adaptations. Adaptations are the product of natural selection.

Some adaptations are unique. For example, the giant panda (*Ailuropoda melanoleuca*) has paws like a bear's but is capable of holding bamboo shoots, which are its main source of food. It can do so because a small bone in the wrist, called the radial sesamoid bone, and its associated muscles have been modified by natural selection to act as a false thumb.

Sometimes quite distantly related species show the same adaptations. These similarities, called analogues, are due to convergent evolution rather than inheritance from a common ancestor. Certain of the Australian fauna, commonly called marsupials, are very similar to placental mammals from other parts of the world. For example, the Australian wombat (*Vombatus* spp.) is similar to the groundhog (*Marmota*), which is a rodent, yet the wombat is more closely related to other marsupials—and the marmot is more closely related to other rodents than it is to the wombat.

Other organisms evolve and become less alike over time. This process is called divergent evolution. On the Galapagos Islands there are 13 species of finches (often called Darwin's finches), which are found nowhere else in the world, although there are

mutations on genes, chromosome inversions, translocations, and polyploidy (having more than two sets of the haploid number of chromosomes; see GENETICS). In people a mutant gene, called *HbS*, causes sickle-cell anemia. People with this gene produce hemoglobin that differs from normal hemoglobin by only one amino acid, but this difference is enough to alter the shape of the red blood cells so that they clump together and work less efficiently.

• Gene flow: Addition or loss of alleles in populations due to migration of individuals is called gene flow. If alleles are lost from one population, gene variation is reduced in that population. New alleles can also be gained from outside by immigration of individuals into new populations if these individuals mix and breed with members of their new group.

• Genetic drift: Genetic drift occurs in a population purely by chance, not through a selective process, and is the random change in allele frequency. Small populations are at greater risk of alleles being lost or fixed (complete dominance of one allele resulting

SPECIATION

If a group of animals or plants is isolated over many generations, it evolves and changes partly because the gene pool is restricted to the original breeding population (often a small founder population) and genetic variation is limited. Allopatric speciation occurs when these isolated individuals can no longer interbreed with the population from which they originated, even if the opportunity arises. On the Hawaiian islands, for example, there are over 800 species of drosophilid fly (genus *Drosophila*), and more than 95 percent are endemic to the island habitat in which they occur. Scientists think they all originated from a single pregnant female that was blown onto the oldest island, Kauai, in the north. Her offspring successfully colonized the island, diversifying into many different habitats, and then spread southward throughout the archipelago to Hawaii, although some would eventually recolonize the older islands. Females of these different *Drosophila* species are often very similar to each other, but the males can be markedly different, suggesting that differences in mating systems are of importance in the evolution of new species. As reproductive isolation is probably the most important factor in speciation, by evolving a different courtship display, a population of flies isolates itself from another despite other similarities. This phenomenon is particularly noticeable among sympatric species—those evolving in the same geographic area. Although these flies have been studied extensively over the last 40 years, there are still many new species to be described.

A CLOSER LOOK

places with similar habitats. These finches are descendants of birds that migrated to the Galapagos Islands from the mainland of South America. Over successive generations, the Galapagos Island finches have adapted to different niches, and their different diets have led to changes in the size and shape of their beaks. These birds are now considered to be different species. Some species of finches, such as *Camarhynchus parvulus*, are insectivorous; others, such as *Geospiza magnirostris*, eat seeds.

Coevolution (see COEVOLUTION) occurs when unrelated organisms evolve reciprocal adaptations through prolonged close interaction with one another. For example, the relationship between predator and prey is rather like an arms race. Other close relationships are associated with mimicry, that is, the close resemblance of one organism to another to the extent that a third organism cannot distinguish between them (see CAMOUFLAGE AND MIMICRY).

Adaptations within a single lineage (group of individuals descending from a common ancestor) that appear repeatedly over geological time are usually specializations that are selected for only under certain conditions. Once those conditions abate, the modified organisms die out, leaving the relatively unspecialized forms (basal stock) to continue the line. This type of evolution is called iterative evolution. To observe this type of evolution, there has to be an exceptionally good fossil record—as there is for planktonic foraminifera (chambered microscopic organisms), trilobites (a now extinct class of arthropods), and graptolites (an extinct marine group).

Speciation
New species are formed when an existing species gradually changes into another or splits into two or more new species that are isolated reproductively. Barriers such as mountains and rivers prevent contact between populations, which are then subject to different selection pressures and evolve differently. Other isolating mechanisms include incompatibility and timing of breeding season. Exceptions are called ring species because of their circular distribution pattern at the edges of two adjacent populations with a majority of members that usually do not interbreed. Such is the case with the herring gull (*Larus argentatus*) and the lesser black-headed gull (*L. fuscus*) of northern Europe: two species that are separated by a range (cline) of interbreeding forms.

*A herring gull (*Larus argentatus*) and its chick. This species and its close relative the lesser black-backed gull (*L. fuscus*) are examples of ring species.*

Two Royal albatrosses (Diomedia epomophora) and a chick at their nest in New Zealand. These birds are threatened with extinction.

Emergent species

Over geological time, species of many types of organisms have evolved and adapted to their environments. Some organisms have given rise to other species as they evolve, while others have remained unchanged for very long periods of time; most have become extinct. The first organisms were simple unicellular organisms, but by about 520 million years ago, representatives of most of the main animal groups, including brachiopods, echinoderms, and jawless fish (the first vertebrates), had evolved in what is called the Cambrian explosion. Over the next 400 million years, organisms passed through many stages and became increasingly complex. Put simply, fish gave rise to amphibians, amphibians gave rise to reptiles, and mammals evolved. Among plants, the ferns and then seed ferns evolved, followed by flowering plants. Hominids appeared only in the last five million years (see HUMAN EVOLUTION).

Evolutionary changes characterized by the branching of taxonomic groups is called cladogenesis. The speed at which these changes take place is unknown. Some scientists believe the rate of evolution varies with each species, so the changes can be slow or sudden. Change may depend on interspecific competition or the genetic constraints on variation (and therefore also on adaptation; see ADAPTATION; COMPETITION). Populations become separated and then follow different evolutionary paths, ending up genetically distinct from each other. There are two theories: that evolutionary change proceeds slowly (gradualism) or in rapid bursts (punctuated equilibrium; see the box on page 654).

Humans and evolution

As the human population increases and technology progresses, people have a greater impact on other species. Humans compete with other forms of life for space and resources, causing major changes in the environment and in the flora and fauna. Urban areas are places in which few other animals and plants can live successfully, a notable exception being rats (*Rattus* spp.). Industrial areas produce various types of pollution, which cause enormous problems even at some distance from the source. For example, acid rain caused by the emission of sulfur dioxide has killed populations of trees in the Adirondacks of New York. Air quality and visibility in the Grand Canyon is often affected by air pollution generated in Los Angeles. In rural areas, natural vegetation is removed, and fertilizers are used to improve crop production. In the 1950s and 1960s, the chemical DDT was used as an insecticide. It was banned in the United States in 1972, when scientists found it caused a severe decline in several bird species, including the osprey (see CARSON, RACHEL, LOUISE; DDT; ENVIRONMENTAL DISASTERS). DDT caused female birds to lay eggs with thin, fragile shells, resulting in many breakages during incubation and a considerable reduction in the number of hatchlings. Birds have long been studied to determine the effects of human activity on the environment. One major study concerns North American songbirds. Scientists are trying to determine if deforestation has affected the territories of songbirds. The results are inconclusive, but there are indications that the loss of songbird habitat has caused a decline in many songbird species.

Throughout history, the story is much the same; as people become established anywhere, so the natural flora and fauna decline. Wherever people traveled in the world, they took animals and plants with them for food and sport. In this way species were introduced to areas from which, under natural conditions, they were excluded by some type of barrier, such as an ocean or mountain. For example, although the horse (*Equus caballus*) evolved in the Americas, it became extinct there about 11,000 years ago (toward the end of the Pleistocene). It was reintroduced into the New World by Spanish explorers during the 16th century. In addition, the first settlers to arrive in North America were hunters. Over the next 100 years or so, the entire population of the passenger pigeon (*Ectopistes migratorius*) was wiped out. Demand for fur from Europe also caused several species to be hunted to near extinction, including the beaver (*Castor canadensis*), whose decline rivals that of the American buffalo (*Bison bison*).

People domesticated animals thousands of years ago. Practical breeding and then a knowledge of natural selection and heredity allowed them to "create" breeds of animals for food and as pets. This controlled breeding of animals and plants is called artificial selection (see SELECTIVE BREEDING). Cattle breeds, such as the Hereford, have been developed for beef, and others, such as the Holstein, for milk. Among dogs, individuals have been selected for qualities such as hunting, guarding, and herding; there are now over 400 breeds of dogs worldwide. One of the latest developments, genetic modification, is used mainly in plant crops (GM crops). It is a hotly debated topic at a time when other people are adopting an organic (natural) approach to farming (see GENETICALLY MODIFED FOODS).

The outcome of such extensive human interference with natural evolution is impossible to predict. Although the demands for cleaner air, better food, and renewable and alternative energy sources are mounting, the population is still growing. Technology may not always provide a solution. For example, over the last few years certain bacteria have evolved a resistance to the antibiotics used in the treatment of many illnesses (see BIOTECHNOLOGY). Several scientists predict that the next mass extinction on Earth will not be the result of environmental factors, such as an ice age, but of human actions.

KIM BRYAN

See also: ANATOMY; ARCHAEOPTERYX; ARISTOTLE; BIOCHEMISTRY; BIOGEOGRAPHY; BIOLOGY, HISTORY AND PHILOSOPHY OF; BIOTECHNOLOGY; CAMOUFLAGE AND MIMICRY; CARSON, RACHEL LOUISE; CELL BIOLOGY; COEVOLUTION; COMPETITION; CONVERGENT EVOLUTION; DARWIN, CHARLES; DDT; EMBRYO; ENVIRONMENTAL DISASTERS; ENZYMES; EXTINCTION; EXTRATERRESTRIAL LIFE; GENETICALLY MODIFIED FOOD; GENETIC ENGINEERING; GENETICS; HUMAN EVOLUTION; MENDEL, GREGOR; MOLECULAR BIOLOGY; NATURAL SELECTION; PALEOBIOLOGY; PASTEUR, LOUIS; PROTEINS; RNA; SELECTIVE

BREEDING; SEXUAL SELECTION; SPECIES; TAXONOMY.

Further reading:
Futuyma, D. 1998. *Evolutionary Biology.* Sunderland, Mass.: Sinauer.
Gould, Stephen J., ed. 2001. *The Book of Life: An Illustrated History of the Evolution of Life on Earth.* New York: W. W. Norton and Co.
Mayr, E. 2001. *What Evolution Is.* New York: Basic Books.
Osborne, R., and M. Benton. 1996. *The Viking Atlas of Evolution.* New York: Viking.
Patterson, C. 1999. *Evolution.* London: Natural History Museum.
Ruse, M., and E. O. Wilson. 2001. *The Evolution Wars: A Guide to the Debates.* Piscataway, N.J.: Rutgers University Press.
Zimmer, C., S. J. Gould, and R. Hutton. 2001. *Evolution: The Triumph of an Idea.* New York: HarperCollins.

The maidenhair tree, (Ginkgo biloba). Around 25 million years ago, several species of ginkgo trees flourished throughout North America, Europe, and Asia. Now only the maidenhair tree remains.

MASS EXTINCTIONS

There are several periods in Earth's history when large numbers of animals became extinct over a short period (geologically speaking). For example, it is estimated that about 240 million years ago at the end of the Permian period, approximately 96 percent of the existing marine organisms died. Such vast numbers cannot be explained by changes in genetic makeup or by a fall in birth rate. No one knows the cause of these massive extinctions, but there are many theories, including disease, climatic change, increased volcanic activity, and meteorite strikes. One of the most famous mass extinctions (called the KT event, or Cretaceous-Tertiary Mass Extinction event) occurred at the end of the Cretaceous period, about 65 million years ago, when more than half of all organisms died, including the dinosaurs. Present opinion favors a large meteorite strike because in 1990 a meteorite crater 94 miles (150 km) in diameter and with evidence of fallout was discovered at Chicxulub in Mexico. It is thought that the meteor caused clouds of dust to be thrown up into the atmosphere, blocking out much of the Sun's light. This situation could cause the atmosphere to cool or, if the dust clouds trapped the Sun's heat, to warm up. In either case, it caused climatic change that altered the global vegetation. This change in vegetation disrupted food chains around the world, with devastating effect (see EXTINCTION).

A CLOSER LOOK

EVOLUTIONARY PSYCHOLOGY

Evolutionary psychology uses the theory of evolution to understand human mental processes and behavior

According to the theory of evolution, animals have met the demands of living on Earth by evolving over millions of years. Peacocks have brightly colored tails that attract mates, polar bears have thick body fat that keep them warm in winter, and cheetahs have powerful back legs so they can easily catch their prey. Humans have evolved in the same way. For example, they have thumbs that grip things and hair that keeps them warm.

However, it is not just the human body that has evolved. Many psychologists believe the human mind and human behavior have also adapted during millions of years of life on Earth. Called evolutionary psychology, this belief has been used to explain everything from why children fight in school yards to why some people develop mental illnesses, such as depression and schizophrenia.

The evolving brain

The human brain is one of the most important parts of the human body. If the body has evolved to cope with life on Earth, the brain has probably evolved in a similar way and for similar reasons. Even the simplest study of the human brain reveals such is the case. Human brains are about four times the size of a chimpanzee's, for example. Most noticeably, humans have a much larger cerebral cortex (the twisted, walnutlike top and side surfaces of the brain). This size difference is consistent with people being by far the most intelligent creatures on the planet (see BRAIN; INTELLIGENCE; LEARNING).

However, evolutionary psychologists believe the structure of the brain has evolved in a much more detailed way and argue that this evolution has led to the development of a brain with many highly specialized "modules," responsible for such jobs as processing information from the senses, understanding language, and storing memories.

Traditional theories of psychology try to explain why people behave in the way they do at a particular moment in time or at a particular point in their lives. One example is a theory called behaviorism, which was very popular in the first half of the 20th century. Behaviorism explains behavior in terms of the good

Boys fighting in a school yard. Scientists called evolutionary psychologists believe that during millions of years on Earth, human minds and human behavior have adapted just as the human body has: this approach is called evolutionary psychology.

things (rewards) and bad things (punishments) that happen to animals and what they learn from these experiences during the course of their lives.

Evolutionary psychology takes a much longer term view. It tries to explain human behavior as not just a result of a lifetime of learning about the world but as a result of many generations of human evolution. Evolution occurs over a very long timescale (millions and millions of years), so in evolutionary terms people today are basically little different from those who lived by hunter-gathering (the method human ancestors used to collect their food) in the Pleistocene era (the period stretching from about

CORE FACTS

- Evolutionary psychology is based on the idea that peoples' brains and behavior (as well as their bodies) have evolved over millions of years.
- If evolutionary psychologists are correct, the brain has evolved into many specialized "modules."
- Evolutionary psychiatrists believe that mental illnesses, such as anxiety, depression, and eating disorders, occur when evolutionary changes to the brain or human behavior (adaptations) go wrong (become maladaptive).

CONNECTIONS

- Traditional theories of **PSYCHOLOGY** have had little to say about **EVOLUTION**.

- Some psychiatrists believe evolution could explain **EATING DISORDERS**.

1.6 million years ago to 11,000 years ago). Evolutionary psychology tends to focus on the types of problems human ancestors faced and how their brains evolved to meet those challenges, rather than on the problems people face in the modern world.

Social psychology

Much of psychology is concerned with how one person behaves in his or her immediate environment; by contrast, social psychology (which is closely related to sociology, or the study of human societies) looks at how people behave in groups of two or more. Evolutionary theory has much to say on this subject.

Many types of social behavior can be explained using the theory of evolution. From the point of view of passing on genes to future generations, it makes sense for people to look after their children, build homes or shelters, and cooperate in hunting for food throughout history. Other types of human behaviors can also be explained by thinking back to how people have survived over the millennia. To pass on their genes, a person must find a mate of the opposite sex, not just any mate but a mate best suited to helping him or her reproduce successfully.

Evolutionary psychologists have used ideas such as these to try to explain a wide range of different social behaviors. One example is aggression (behaving in a way likely to harm oneself or others). Animals often become aggressive when they compete for mates or when their territory is threatened. Selecting particularly aggressive mice and breeding them produces much more aggressive offspring than

selecting less aggressive mice and breeding those. This result suggests strongly that there is a genetic component to aggression.

Some psychologists argue that people originally developed aggressive behavior many thousands of years ago to help them pass on their genes and that if mice can pass on aggression from one generation to the next, so too can people. Other psychologists argue that such ideas are far too simple to explain human aggression. They point out that if aggression was simply built-in behavior, all people might be equally aggressive. However, different human cultures are aggressive to different extents, and the way children are brought up can greatly influence how aggressive they are as adults. Moreover, aggressive parents do not always have aggressive children.

Evolutionary ideas about social psychology are often linked with sociobiology, which was put forward in 1975 by U.S. biologist Edward O. Wilson (b. 1929). Wilson originally developed sociobiology to explain how ants behave in groups in their colonies, later extending the theory to social behavior in other animals (including people; see SOCIOBIOLOGY). Evolutionary psychology is a more recent theory, most concerned with why human brains and behavior have evolved in certain ways because of the need to pass on genes to future generations.

Cognitive psychology

Evolutionary psychologists believe different aspects of human behavior have evolved in quite separate ways. Human ancestors evolved with the ability to

A Kung bushman and his family sit by a fire near their traditional grass huts. In physical terms, people alive today are little different from the hunter-gatherers who lived thousands of years ago.

THE EVOLUTION OF LANGUAGE

The ability to communicate with other people using a complex written and spoken language is one of the things that distinguishes humans from other animals. Where did language come from? In the first half of the 20th century, a group of psychologists called behaviorists argued that language-processing abilities, along with other aspects of human behavior, were picked up entirely by trial and error during childhood. This view was challenged by influential U.S. linguist Noam Chomsky (b. 1928), who argued that the brain has a built-in mechanism for understanding the structure of language. Later, U.S. psychologist Steven Pinker (b. 1954) extended Chomsky's ideas by carrying out experiments to try to prove that children do indeed have a built-in language mechanism. Having confirmed that theory, he used evolutionary ideas to explain how the language mechanism (or "language instinct," as he called it) had arisen.

Not everyone supports evolutionary explanations of language, however. One difficulty with them is that they do not explain why, if language has advantages, so few other animals appear to use it. In addition, while evolutionary ideas explain how humans have come to understand language, they have less to say on the subject of how language is produced.

A CLOSER LOOK

Evolutionary psychologists believe the human brain has evolved to cope with life's challenges, just as the human body has.

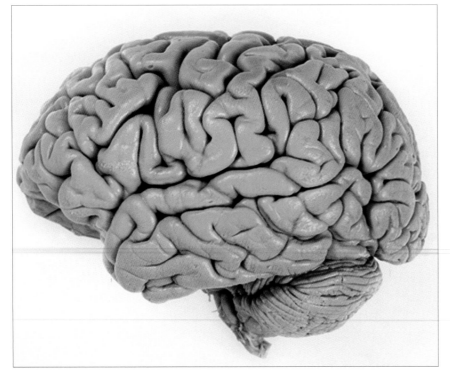

avoid predators, raise children, digest foods, and use language, but there is not necessarily any connection between these things (other than that they all help people to pass on their genes to future generations). According to evolutionary psychologists, the brain is not really a general-purpose device like a computer that can solve whatever problems it encounters, although it may seem that way from the outside. Rather, they claim it consists of hundreds or even thousands of "modules," each dedicated to a particular task, which can work together to solve problems as diverse as feeding a baby or understanding what a young child is saying. Just as a species of bird might gradually evolve larger wings, so

evolutionary psychologists believe the brain has eventually split into more and increasingly specialized modules—and for the same reason: because there is an evolutionary advantage in both cases.

The notion that the brain is built of specialized modules first appeared late in the 18th-century with a group of psychologists called phrenologists. They championed the idea that separate regions of the brain control things such as hope, love of parents and friends, and even criminal behavior. Moreover, the phrenologists claimed these parts of a person's character were closely related to the bumps on their skull. Most of these ideas had little scientific basis and soon fell into disfavor. Yet the idea that the brain contains at least some specialized areas and components became popular again during the 1980s.

Brain-scanning techniques, developed around this time, helped neuroscientists (people who study how the brain's structure is related to human behavior) to demonstrate that when specific parts of the brain become damaged, people can no longer do certain things. For example, a stroke (rupture or obstruction, often by a clot, of an artery of the brain) on the left side of the brain can leave people unable to speak or understand words. This result suggests very strongly that parts of the brain are dedicated to certain functions, such as understanding language, storing memories, and even recognizing faces.

One of the central issues in evolutionary psychology is to be able to explain why different cognitive (thinking) functions evolved in the human brain. Most cognitive psychologists believe consciousness (the way people see themselves as separate from the world and somehow controlling their own actions) to be the highest (most developed) cognitive function of all. Some cognitive psychologists think consciousness may have developed gradually as the brain evolved more and more specialized modules. All of these modules would eventually have needed some type of "brain supervisor" to manage communication between them and keep everything in check. Consciousness could have evolved in this way (see CONSCIOUSNESS).

Psychiatry

If evolutionary psychology can explain the good things about human behavior (such as why people look after children or speak languages), can it also explain the bad things (such as why people become mentally ill)? Some psychiatrists (doctors who specialize in treating mental illness) believe that it can. According to evolutionary psychiatrists, people become mentally ill because certain forms of human behavior that evolved to help human ancestors (adaptations) have gone wrong (become maladaptive) or are no longer appropriate in the modern world.

Some psychiatrists have tried to clarify how evolution could explain common forms of mental illness such as anxiety, mania, and depression (see MENTAL DISORDERS). Anxiety is an illness that occurs when someone fears or worries about things so much that it disrupts their everyday life (see ANXIETY). For human ancestors, being afraid served a useful purpose: fear helped them to avoid risks that could have cost them their lives. In the modern world, people have phobias (very strong fears) of things such as snakes and spiders (see PHOBIAS). Because snakes and spiders present little threat to most people, these fears only make sense if people try to understand them in terms of the threats human ancestors faced in the past.

Another type of mental illness, mania, makes people very confident, excited, and hyperactive. Evolution could have produced mania as a way of making human ancestors try much harder to achieve things. In moderation, it can be a good thing; taken to extremes, mania leads to bizarre behavior and makes it difficult for people to live in families or lead a normal life. Depression is another mental illness that might be explained using evolutionary theory. Virtually the opposite of people with mania, depressed people are very unhappy, lose interest in life, and may just want to sleep all day. However, evolution could have developed depression for a purpose: saving energy for things that really matter. In terms of survival and evolution, depression might be a tactic to ensure that "those who fight and run away, live to fight another day." Evolutionary psychiatrists have also tried to explain other forms of mental illness, including schizophrenia and eating disorders (see EATING DISORDERS; SCHIZOPHRENIA).

The value of evolutionary psychology

Evolutionary psychology offers a very different way of looking at human behavior from some other approaches to psychology because it tries to explain not just how people behave in the way they do but also why, in evolutionary terms. Although some of its explanations make a great deal of sense, not all psychologists agree with them.

One difficulty that critics often voice is that some of the ideas put forward by evolutionary psychologists are difficult to test experimentally, while some of their broader theories are unsupported by scientific data. Another problem is that evolutionary psychology is often identified with sociobiology. Although more respected now, the ideas behind sociobiology caused immense political controversy in the 1970s, when critics said it was "racist" and "sexist." The idea that behavior is substantially determined by natural selection has also proved controversial. Critics of evolutionary psychology argue that it devotes too much attention to natural selection at the expense of other factors that may influence the development of human brains and behavior.

Some of the arguments put forward by evolutionary psychologists agree with other forms of psychology. Thus, the suggestion that the brain has specialized modules agrees with the findings of modern neuroscience and the theories of cognitive psychology (see COGNITION; NEUROSCIENCE). However, the idea that the brain must have hundreds or even thousands of modules is less certain. Neuroscience and cognitive psychology suggest that the brain is made up of far fewer distinct modules.

An Argiope *spider. Some people are very frightened of spiders and snakes, a reaction that may relate back to the threats human ancestors faced in the past.*

In all, evolutionary psychology offers a new way of thinking about behavior not just at an isolated moment in the life of one person but at a particular point in the evolution of the human race. Evolution has brought new insight and understanding to many of the life sciences. Psychology, it seems, can also benefit from the same ideas.

C. WOODFORD

See also: ALTRUISM; ANXIETY; BRAIN; COGNITION; CONSCIOUSNESS; HUMAN EVOLUTION; INTELLIGENCE; LEARNING; MENTAL DISORDERS; NEUROSCIENCE; PHOBIAS; SCHIZOPHRENIA; SOCIOBIOLOGY.

Further reading

Badcock, Christopher. 2000. *Evolutionary Psychology: A Critical Introduction*. Cambridge, U.K.: Polity Press.
Buss, David. 1998. *Evolutionary Psychology: The New Science of the Mind*. Boston: Allyn and Bacon.
Buss, David. 1994. *Evolution of Desire: Strategies of Human Mating*. New York: Basic Books.
Evans, Dylan, and Oscar Zarate. 2000. *Introducing Evolutionary Psychology*. New York: Totem Books.
Pinker, Steven. 1997. *How the Mind Works*. New York: W. W. Norton.
Wright, Robert. 1994. *The Moral Animal*. New York: Vintage Books.

EXCRETORY SYSTEMS

Excretion is the process by which animals get rid of waste products from their cells

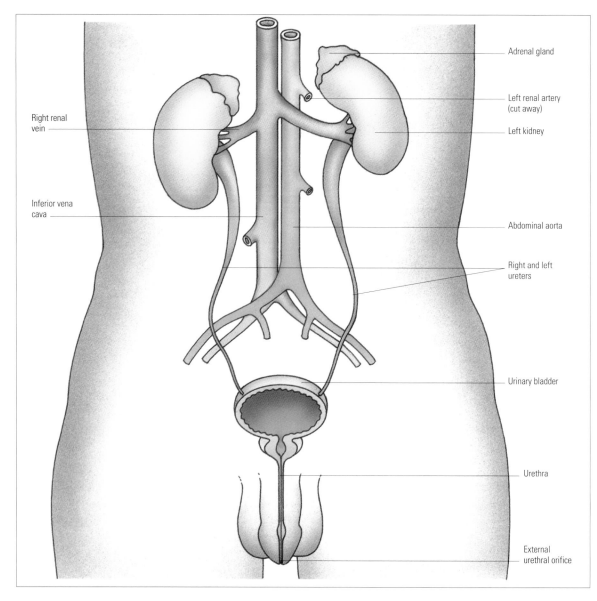

Adrenal gland

Left renal artery (cut away)

Left kidney

Right renal vein

Inferior vena cava

Abdominal aorta

Right and left ureters

Urinary bladder

Urethra

External urethral orifice

CONNECTIONS

● Excretory systems rid animals of the waste products of **METABOLISM**, the way in which living organisms obtain and use the **ENERGY** they need.

● The breakdown of **PROTEINS,** nucleic acids, and other nitrogen-containing compounds into nitrogenous wastes takes place in all tissues. In humans such wastes are converted by the **LIVER** to urea, which is excreted in the urine.

● The **NITROGEN CYCLE** is the circulation of nitrogen-containing molecules within **ECOSYSTEMS**. The excretion of nitrogenous wastes by animals plays a critical part in this process.

The human male excretory system, showing the kidneys, bladder, urethra, and ureters.

In the same way that waste products in a factory have to be removed or recycled, all animals, from the single-celled amoeba to the huge blue whale, have to dispose of wastes produced by their metabolic processes. Waste products that are not removed may become poisonous. Further, unless animal wastes are recycled by other organisms in their environment, they may build up and poison the surrounding ecosystem.

The elimination of waste products contributes toward keeping the chemical composition of the internal environment of the body relatively constant, a process called homeostasis (see HOMEOSTASIS). For example, the excretory system regulates the balance of substances that can make the body fluids acid or alkaline. Thus, excretion helps control the pH (a measure of acidity) of the body fluids. Excretion also controls osmotic pressure, which is the balance between dissolved substances and water in the body fluids.

The method an animal uses to dispose of metabolic waste products depends on its body structure and water availability in the environment in which it lives. For example, the desert-living camel must conserve as much water as possible; it excretes urine

CORE FACTS

■ The process by which animals get rid of waste products from the cells is called excretion.

■ Excretory systems contribute toward homeostasis, which keeps the internal environment of an animal's body relatively constant.

■ The main excretory organs are nephridia in most invertebrates, Malpighian tubules in insects, and kidneys in vertebrates.

■ Nitrogenous wastes (breakdown products of protein and nucleic acid metabolism) made by animals' cells are excreted as ammonia, urea, or uric acid.

that contains high concentrations of urea. Terrestrial insects, some reptiles, and birds excrete uric acid, which needs little water for its elimination. Freshwater fish lose most of their nitrogenous wastes through their gills as ammonia because water is freely available to them.

Excretory structures in different animals are varied in shape, size, number, function, and location. The four main types (the generalized excretory structures) are contractile vacuoles in protozoans, nephridia in most invertebrates, Malpighian tubules in insects, and kidneys in vertebrates. In addition, other organs such as gills, rectal glands, salt glands, lungs, skin, intestines, and the liver also play a role in the elimination of specific wastes.

Waste products

The major waste products eliminated by excretory systems are nitrogenous wastes. However, water, carbon dioxide, a variety of organic molecules, and feces also have to be removed from the body. Carbon dioxide (CO_2), the waste product of cellular respiration, is simply eliminated by diffusion from the surfaces of the gills, lungs, or other respiratory structures. The digestive wastes, feces, are not strictly excretory products because they have never been part of the body cells. The feces are disposed of through the anus, the opening at the end of the digestive system (see DIGESTIVE SYSTEMS), in a process called defecation. Feces often contain additional organic waste products, such as bile. In many organisms feces and waste products leave the body together via the anus.

Nitrogenous wastes contain nitrogen and are formed by the breakdown of amino acids, nucleic acids, and other nitrogen-containing molecules. During digestion, proteins are broken down into amino acids, many of which are used to produce energy by a process called deamination. First, ammonia is split off from the amino acid molecule. The remaining acid is then metabolized in the mitochondria to generate molecules of adenosine triphosphate (ATP), a source of energy for the cells.

Nitrogenous waste is generally eliminated as ammonia (NH_3), urea ($CO(NH_2)_2$), or uric acid ($C_5H_4N_3O_4$). In spiders and some other arthropod groups, this waste is eliminated mostly as guanine ($C_5H_5N_5O$), and in marine chondricthyean (cartilaginous) fish, as appreciable quantities of urea and trimethylamine oxide (TMAO), which is excreted in addition to ammonia (mainly via the gills). The form in which nitrogen is excreted depends very much on the habitat and life cycle of the organism.

Ammonia is the first nitrogenous waste formed during cellular metabolism. It is a small molecule, highly soluble in water and very toxic. It therefore has to be dissolved in large amounts of water before it can be disposed of. Aquatic animals, surrounded by plenty of water, can excrete ammonia directly into their surroundings across their gills or skin. However, most animals need to conserve water and cannot use large amounts of it to eliminate ammonia in their urine. In these animals, ammonia is converted to

urea, uric acid, or guanine, which are less toxic than ammonia and require smaller amounts of water for their disposal in the urine. Some of these animals also keep relatively high concentrations of urea and TMAO in their blood, raising its solute concentration and thus lowering the osmotic loss of water to the salty environment.

Urea lies between ammonia and uric acid in both its toxicity and its solubility in water. It is 100,000 times less toxic than ammonia and is used as a waste product by most adult amphibians and all mammals. Urea is formed in the liver in vertebrates by the combination of ammonia and carbon dioxide.

Uric acid is extremely insoluble in water, is not very toxic, and can be excreted as a semiliquid paste. These properties are useful for terrestrial organisms because uric acid does not need to be diluted with water before it is eliminated. Uric acid is excreted by land snails, insects, birds, and some reptiles. In birds it is mixed with feces from the digestive tract to produce a semiliquid paste. The urine produced by mammalian kidneys is a watery yellow liquid, consisting mainly of urea, some uric acid, and smaller quantities of organic acids and bases, chlorides, phosphates, and sulfates.

What determines the type of waste?

Whether an animal excretes urea or uric acid partly depends on whether it produces shelled eggs for reproduction. In animals such as mammals, in which the offspring develop internally, urea can be removed from the young through the mother's bloodstream in the placenta. Offspring that develop inside eggs cannot do so. Eggshells allow gases in and out but not liquids. An embryo producing urea inside an egg would be poisoned by its own waste. Instead, the embryo produces insoluble uric acid, a solid waste that is stored inside the egg and discarded with the eggshell when the animal hatches. Most animals can produce more than one type of nitrogenous waste. Crocodilians can produce uric acid and ammonia, whereas aquatic turtles excrete urea and ammonia.

Spiders excrete their nitrogenous waste as guanine, which is highly insoluble in water.

Some animals change the way they excrete nitrogenous wastes as they grow. For example, amphibians such as the bullfrog (*Rana catesbeiana*) excrete ammonia into the surrounding water when they are in their aquatic larval forms (tadpoles) and excrete urea as adults. Frogs and toads that remain fully aquatic, however, continue to produce ammonia, unless they are forced to live out of water. Tortoises can adapt to a dry environment by switching their normal production of urea to uric acid when water becomes limited.

PROTOZOAN EXCRETORY SYSTEMS

Aquatic animals with cell surfaces that are exposed directly to water, such as amoebas, do not need a separate excretory system. Waste products simply diffuse out of the cell. However, these animals must have some way of controlling the amount of water that enters or leaves the cell by osmosis.

The substances dissolved in the cells of freshwater protozoans make their body fluids more concentrated than the water surrounding them. Water therefore moves into the cells across the cell membrane through the process of osmosis, which powers the diffusion of water to make the concentrations of the solutions on each side of the membrane equal. However, the animal would swell and eventually burst if no steps were taken to counteract this influx of water. Consequently, freshwater protozoans have a structure called a contractile vacuole, which bails out excess water. This baglike structure is formed by a membrane, which is filled continuously with water by a series of small cytoplasmic canals that empty into it. When the contractile vacuole has taken up a certain amount of water, it connects to the surface of the cell membrane, where it joins its membrane to the cell membrane and expels the water to the outside. Fluid removed from contractile vacuoles contains urea, ammonia, carbon dioxide, and low concentrations of salts. These vacuoles can be thought of as rudimentary excretory structures.

Marine protozoans have less need for contractile vacuoles (although some species do have them) because their internal fluids have a similar concentration to the sea water around them (they are isosmotic) and not much water enters by osmosis.

INVERTEBRATE EXCRETORY SYSTEMS
Annelid worms

In larger invertebrates, such as annelid worms, most cells are not in contact with the environment, and they cannot rely on diffusion alone to eliminate wastes. True excretory organs are found only in animals with bilateral symmetry (the left and right sides of the body are mirror images of each other). The simplest type of excretory organ is called the nephridium (plural, nephridia), which is basically a tube. Nephridia develop from the surface of the body and grow inward. There are two main types of nephridia: the protonephridia present in flatworms and polychaete annelids (worms) and the metanephridia present in animals such as earthworms, which are more advanced annelids.

Flatworms are the simplest animals to possess excretory organs. They do not have a circulatory system, so waste products and excess fluids have to be collected from many points in the body. Most excretion of waste occurs directly through the gut and mouth. Nitrogenous waste, mainly ammonia, diffuses through the animal's surface. Flatworms also excrete excess water and some metabolic wastes using a system of protonephridia.

The protonephridia form a closed excretory system because the tubules are closed at one end. These closed ends are enlarged into bulblike structures called flame cells that contain one or more cilia (tiny hairs). They are called flame cells because the beating cilia resemble the flickering of a flame. Fluid from the body is sucked into the flame cells at the closed end of the tubule by the cilia's beating action. As the fluid moves slowly down along the tubule, certain substances are reabsorbed. The tubules open onto the body surface via nephridiopores, openings through which the remaining fluid is excreted.

Metanephridia form an open system, where both ends of the tubule are open. The internal opening contains cilia and is called the nephrostome. It opens into the coelom, or body cavity. Fluid and wastes from the coelom are conducted through the nephrostome, into the tubular metanephridium, and on to the outside. There is no filtration process; instead, fluid is swept into the tubules by the action of cilia. The metanephridia

The excretory organs of a typical flatworm. Flatworms are the simplest animals with a specialized excretory system.

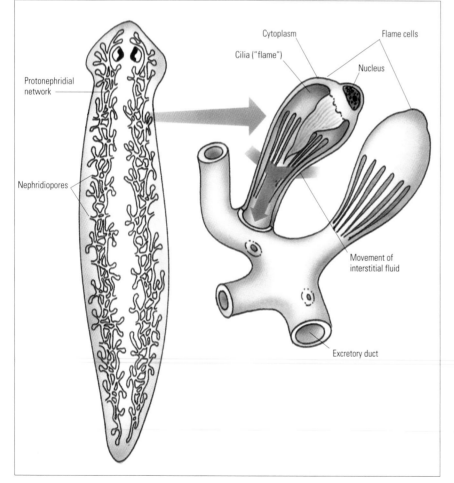

Cytoplasm
Flame cells
Cilia ("flame")
Nucleus
Protonephridial network
Nephridiopores
Movement of interstitial fluid
Excretory duct

EARTHWORMS

Earthworms are segmented annelids and have a body cavity (coelom). Their excretory organs are paired metanephridia. One pair is found in each body segment, except the first three and the last one. Protein breakdown and waste production occur in cells that lie in the body cavity attached to the gut walls. Ammonia and urea pass from them into the coelomic fluid and are swept up into the nephridia. Each nephridium occupies parts of two segments, with the nephrostome (or front end) lying in one segment and connecting with the main part of the tubule in the segment behind. Each tubule is looped to increase its surface area for reabsorbing useful salts. It ends in a bladderlike structure, which opens to the outside through an opening (nephridiopore). The earthworm's urine is dilute because the worm is in contact with fresh water in the soil and it must get rid of the water it gains by osmosis. The earthworm also excretes excess calcium through the calciferous glands in the esophagus. At least half of the earthworm's nitrogenous waste is secreted through the epidermis in mucus.

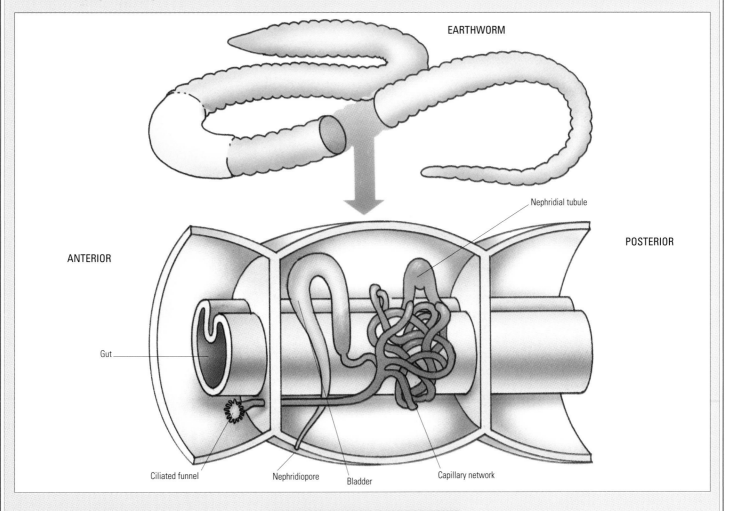

EARTHWORM

Nephridial tubule

POSTERIOR

ANTERIOR

Gut

Ciliated funnel   Nephridiopore   Bladder   Capillary network

A CLOSER LOOK

are surrounded by a network of blood vessels, which may reabsorb salts from the urine before it leaves the body at the nephridiopore.

Mollusks

Like other animals, mollusks use several methods of waste disposal. The choice of method often depends on where the animal lives. In water snails, ammonia diffuses from the blood across the molluscan gills (ctenidia) into the surrounding water.

Mollusks have one or two kidney tubules (or nephridia), formed from outgrowths of the coelom (coelomoducts). A typical kidney tubule has one end opening into the coelom (which contains the heart) and the other opening to the outside through a nephridiopore. In most species, fluid is collected in the tubules by ultrafiltration, the heart providing the necessary pressure for this process to occur. This ultra-filtration occurs in most mollusks directly across the heart muscle. (Ultrafiltration occurs where pressure forces fluid through a semipermeable membrane that witholds large molecules, such as proteins, but allows water and smaller molecules, such as salts, sugars, and amino acids, to pass.)

As with all ultrafiltration processes, there is no initial screening for waste products. Everything, except blood cells and large proteins, passes into the filtrate. During urine formation, useful materials are reabsorbed from the filtrate. When the animal has two kidneys, the substances reabsorbed from the left kidney may be different from those reabsorbed by the right.

This diagram shows an internal view of a typical insect excretory system, consisting of slender tubules, called Malpighian tubes, with blind ends that lie in the animal's body cavity.

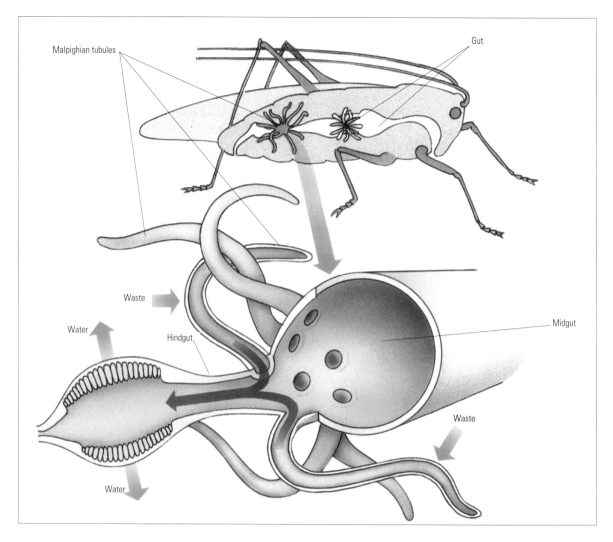

Malpighian tubules

Gut

Waste

Water

Hindgut

Midgut

Waste

Water

Crustaceans

Crustaceans use several methods to dispose of metabolic waste and maintain homeostasis. At the gills, the hard surface layer (cuticle) is extremely permeable, and ammonia is excreted across it by diffusion. Ammonia on the body surface seems to provide the conditions needed to convert carbon dioxide into calcium carbonate, which calcifies and strengthens the animals' exoskeleton. During molting, the exoskeleton is shed; some zoologists consider shedding to be a method of excretion. Some crustaceans store wastes, such as guanine, between their skin and exoskeleton and "excrete" it when they molt.

In crustaceans, most nitrogenous waste is secreted through the gills as ammonia or urea. Cells called nephrocytes and nephrophagocytes, present in the gills and in the bases of the legs, also take up excretory substances and store them in a crystalline or precipitated form.

Crustaceans have paired excretory organs in their heads, often at the base of their antennae, called antennal, or green, glands. They are made up of a long tubule folded back on itself. The lower part of the tubule is sometimes modified and enlarged to form a bladder for collecting and storing urine. Fluid from the blood is filtered into the gland, where its composition is adjusted by selective reabsorption and secretion. However, these organs are probably more important in maintaining the ionic balance and volume of body fluids than in excreting nitrogenous waste. They reabsorb calcium and potassium ions and glucose from the urine and secrete ions such as magnesium and sulfate into it. In marine crustaceans, such as lobsters, the urine has nearly the same salt concentration as the blood. In freshwater species it tends to be much more dilute.

Insects and spiders

Insects and spiders have a unique system of excretory organs called Malpighian tubules, which vary in number between species from 2 to over 100. The Malpighian tubules are tubular outgrowths of the

EVOLUTION OF THE VERTEBRATE EXCRETORY SYSTEM

Scientists studying the embryos of primitive vertebrates, such as dogfish, have shown that their excretory system develops from a series of tubules. Each tubule lies in a separate segment and opens into the body cavity. In the past these tubules may have opened separately to the outside. In more advanced vertebrates, the shape of these tubules changed to form the Bowman's capsule inside the kidney. As the vertebrates developed a single body cavity, the need for separate excretory organs in each segment was lost. Two kidneys were then developed to serve the whole body. However, each kidney has several lobes—probably the remnants of several segmental kidneys that have fused into a single organ.

EVOLUTION

digestive tract. They are closed at the other end, where they dangle in the fluids of the body cavity. Spiders and insects do not use a filtration system for excretion. Instead, as salts (mainly potassium and chloride ions) are secreted into the Malpighian tubes, an osmotic force that pulls water and wastes into the tubes is created; the resulting "urine" enters the gut. Specialized glands in the rectum then reabsorb most of the water and salts, leaving uric acid to be excreted. The uric acid and other wastes are excreted with the feces, which are almost dry.

This system is an important adaptation that makes insects excellent at conserving water. It is a major reason why insects have been so successful in colonizing terrestrial habitats.

VERTEBRATE EXCRETORY SYSTEMS

Vertebrates have adapted their excretion to allow them to live successfully in just about every type of habitat: in fresh water, sea water, and intertidal areas and on land, even in extreme environments such as deserts and the poles and at high altitudes. In the desert-dwelling kangaroo rat (*Dipodomys spectabilis*), for example, water conservation is vital to its survival. It loses little fluid in the urine and gets most of its water through the metabolism of its food. The kangaroo rat is so efficient in conserving water that it never needs to drink.

With the evolution of the body cavity and the circulatory system, the need for several excretory organs serving all parts of the body (as in annelid worms, for example) has gradually been lost. In most vertebrates, a single pair of kidneys fulfils the functions of filtration, reabsorption, and secretion. However, each kidney has several lobes, which are fused segmental kidneys. The initial blood plasma filtered into the tubules of the kidney contains all the substances carried by the plasma, except for the blood cells, platelets, and large proteins (see BLOOD). Reabsorption of useful materials such as glucose, amino acids, salts, and water takes place as the filtrate passes through the tubes of the kidney. Other substances, such as drugs and wastes, remain in the filtrate and may be secreted into the urine by the tubule. Urine enters the urinary bladder and is stored there for eventual excretion from the body.

All vertebrate kidneys are based on the nephron, although the structure and organization of the kidney varies between the groups. The nephron is a tubule in which filtration, reabsorption, and secretion of ions, molecules, and water take place in dif-

HOMEOSTASIS

Homeostasis is the process of maintaining a controlled and relatively constant internal environment in which the body cells can work efficiently. The excretory system of animals acts as a homeostatic mechanism to maintain relatively constant concentrations of water and salts in the body and to get rid of toxic waste (see HOMEOSTASIS). There are other processes that contribute to an organism's overall homeostasis: regulation of blood sugar concentration (see INSULIN); the uptake and distribution of oxygen to the cells and the elimination of carbon dioxide (see RESPIRATORY SYSTEMS); the defense of the body (see IMMUNE SYSTEMS); and the maintenance of a constant body temperature (see THERMOREGULATION).

ferent parts. In some marine bony fishes, the nephron is little more than a simple tube; in birds and mammals, a section called the loop of Henle makes the kidneys particularly efficient at producing concentrated urine. The loop of Henle is a long, fine tube that provides a large surface area for the reabsorption of large amounts of water and salts from the urine (see the box on page 672).

In some vertebrates, the skin, lungs or gills, and digestive system also contribute to maintaining fluid balance and removal of metabolic wastes. In some reptiles and marine birds, salt glands in various places in the head excrete salt that has entered the body with ingested sea water.

Fish

Vertebrate kidneys first evolved in freshwater fish. The body fluids of these fish are more concentrated than their environment, with the result that water constantly enters the body through osmosis. Freshwater fish are covered by scales and a mucous secretion, which reduces the passage of water into their bodies. However, water does enter through the gills by osmosis. In the kidneys urine is formed by filtration, and it is passed through the nephrons of the kidney with little reabsorption of water occurring. A very dilute and watery urine is produced. These fish excrete their nitrogenous waste as ammonia because the watery urine and external environment dilute it and make it harmless. Freshwater fish have the problem that they lose salts into the surrounding water, both by diffusion across the gills and, to a lesser extent, in their urine. Therefore, they have evolved cells in their gills that actively transport salt (mainly sodium and chloride ions) from the water into the blood as it flows through the gills (see (1) in the diagram below).

Osmoregulation in fish. Freshwater fish, marine bony fish, and sharks and rays adopt different excretory strategies depending, in part, on their external environment.

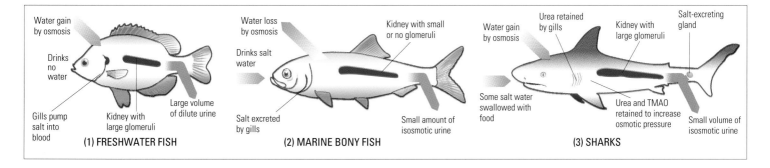

Water gain by osmosis

Drinks no water

Gills pump salt into blood

Kidney with large glomeruli

Large volume of dilute urine

(1) FRESHWATER FISH

Water loss by osmosis

Drinks salt water

Salt excreted by gills

Kidney with small or no glomeruli

Small amount of isosmotic urine

(2) MARINE BONY FISH

Water gain by osmosis

Some salt water swallowed with food

Urea retained by gills

Kidney with large glomeruli

Urea and TMAO retained to increase osmotic pressure

Salt-excreting gland

Small volume of isosmotic urine

(3) SHARKS

The desert-living kangaroo rat (Dipodomys spectabilis) produces highly concentrated urine to aid water conservation.

Marine fish are believed to have evolved from freshwater ancestors that went back to living in the sea. They have kept their body fluids less concentrated than sea water. Consequently, water is constantly leaving their bodies by osmosis. To counteract the risk of dehydration, many marine bony fish drink sea water. They keep the water and excrete the salt back into the sea by the action of specialized cells (chloride cells) in their gills. The kidneys excrete only a little isosmotic urine and some salts (2).

Most sharks and rays live in the sea and have the same problem of dehydration as other marine fish because their internal salt concentration is also low compared with that of sea water. To solve this problem, instead of pumping ions out of their bodies with their gills, sharks reabsorb urea from their urine and maintain a high concentration of urea in their blood and tissues; it may be 100 times the concentration found in mammals. Another nitrogenous waste, TMAO, is also used in this way. Therefore, the body fluids of sharks and rays have the same

osmotic concentration (isosmotic) as sea water does, and very little body water is lost to the sea through osmosis. They also have well-developed kidneys, which excrete a small volume of isosmotic urine and some of the excess salt (3).

Amphibians

Semiterrestrial and terrestrial amphibians (frogs and toads) excrete urea and cannot produce urine more concentrated than their blood. The outer skin of amphibians is permeable to water, however. Amphibians lose water on land by evaporation and take in water through osmosis when they are in water. When amphibians come on land, the rate of filtration in the kidneys is slowed down by restriction of the blood supply to them; this slowing lowers urine production and saves water. Hormones also make the bladder less permeable to water, allowing it to store dilute urine. Fully aquatic amphibians (newts) and larval frogs and toads (tadpoles) resemble freshwater fish in that they make and excrete ammonia as their nitrogenous waste.

Birds and reptiles

Most birds and reptiles produce uric acid and secrete it into their urine. In these animals urine is not stored in a bladder but passes straight to the cloaca, an area at the end of the digestive tract. From here it is excreted with the feces. Birds and reptiles living near the sea have salt glands near the nose or eye or, in the case of marine crocodiles, in their tongues to eliminate excess salt.

Terrestrial reptiles, like other land dwellers, have to conserve water. They reabsorb water in their kidney tubules. The urine of reptiles cannot be more concentrated than their blood, so this process is not very efficient. However, the uric acid precipitates in the cloaca, lowering the osmotic pressure of the fluid there and allowing water to be reabsorbed from the urine-feces mixture.

Mammals

Mammalian kidneys are very efficient at removing water from the filtrate and represent a huge leap forward in evolutionary development. Camel urine, for example, is eight times more concentrated than its blood, while that of desert rats and mice is 20 times as concentrated as their blood. (Birds are the only other vertebrates that can produce urine that is significantly more concentrated than their blood.)

Mammalian kidneys are so efficient because the functional unit of the kidney (the nephron) includes the loop of Henle, which is also present in some of the tubules of bird kidneys. The loop of Henle pumps salts (sodium and chloride ions) out of the urine (see the box on page 672), making the surrounding kidney tissues more salty. This process allows later reabsorption (and therefore conservation) of water from the urine flowing through the collecting duct by osmosis and also provides a large surface area for the reabsorption of water from the urine. The length of the loop of Henle is

EXCRETION IN PLANTS

Although plants have no specialized excretory system, they still produce waste products that need to be eliminated. At night plants produce carbon dioxide through respiration, which is lost through diffusion from the roots and leaves (see RESPIRATORY SYSTEMS). In sunshine the process of photosynthesis produces excess oxygen as a waste product (see PHOTOSYNTHESIS), which is also lost by diffusion.

Plants produce very few wastes because they make food only when they need it. Products such as tannins and silicates that are no longer needed can be stored in the fruits and leaves and are disposed of when these are shed.

proportional to the concentration of the urine it can produce. Desert animals, which produce concentrated urine, have very long loops of Henle.

THE HUMAN EXCRETORY SYSTEM

The human urinary system consists of a pair of kidneys, the bladder, and their connecting tubes. The kidneys are the size of small fists, shaped like lima beans, and lie on either side of the spine at the level of the lowest ribs. Urine is produced in the kidneys by filtration, secretion, and reabsorption. Leading from each kidney is a tube called the ureter, which transports the urine to the bladder by peristaltic contractions. Urine is pumped into the bladder until it has expanded enough to create the need to urinate. A single tube, the urethra, carries urine from the bladder to the outside. The urethra is longer in men than in women and in men also carries sperm during ejaculation (see REPRODUCTIVE SYSTEMS).

The functional unit of the kidney is the nephron, and there are about a million in each kidney. Each nephron consists of a U-shaped cup called a Bowman's capsule containing a bundle of blood capillaries called the glomerulus. The Bowman's capsule is attached to a long, narrow renal tubule, which is divided into several regions, each with a specialized function (see KIDNEYS). The end of the tube opens into a collecting duct, which carries urine away from the nephron into the ureter.

Formation of urine

Urine is formed by three major renal processes: ultrafiltration, secretion, and reabsorption. In humans the final urine can be as much as 4.2 times as concentrated as blood. Urine is yellow because it contains urochrome, which is produced when bile is broken down in the liver. The darkness of the yellow color depends on the amount of water in the urine: the less water the darker the color.

The ultrafiltration of blood that begins the process of urine formation takes place in the glomerulus and is powered by blood pressure. The filtrate, which contains water, salts, glucose, amino acids, urea, and other substances (blood cells and large proteins are left behind), then passes through the nephron (see KIDNEYS). Every 24 hours, 45 gallons (170 l) of water are filtered from the bloodstream into the renal tubules. Nearly all of this water is reabsorbed by the cells lining the tubules and returned to the blood. The average person eliminates about 3 pints (1.5 l) of water a day.

Not all the substances that need to be excreted are removed from the blood by ultrafiltration. Some substances remain in the blood after ultrafiltration has taken place and are secreted into the renal tubules from nearby capillaries. Potassium, urochrome, and ammonia are removed from the blood and added to the urine in this way. Secretion of acid (H^+, or protons) into the urine helps control the pH level (acidity) of the blood (see HOMEOSTASIS).

Substances in the filtrate that are still useful, such as amino acids, glucose, vitamins, and water, are reabsorbed from the tubules into the adjacent capillaries. The remaining water, urea, and other substances form the urine. The final adjustment in the concentration of the urine to be excreted occurs in the nephrons' collecting ducts. Because of the high salt reabsorption in preceding parts of the nephron, the urine is still quite dilute, and so further water can be reabsorbed. The amount of water conserved depends on the permeability of the walls of the collecting ducts, which is under hormonal control.

The role of hormones in osmoregulation

The human brain contains osmotic receptors, which constantly check the osmotic pressure of the blood. If the blood becomes too concentrated, because of dehydration or a salty meal, antidiuretic hormone (ADH) is released from the pituitary gland in the brain. ADH causes the collecting ducts to become more permeable to water by expanding water pores in their cell membranes. More water is then reabsorbed from the urine into the capillaries surrounding the collecting duct, leaving the salt

MARCELLO MALPIGHI

Marcello Malpighi (1628–1694) was one of the first scientists to study the microscopic structure of plants and animals. His studies began at the University of Bologna in Italy; he later moved to Messina, in Sicily, to become a professor of medicine. In 1661 Malpighi described the structure of the circulatory system. He also examined the liver, brain, spleen, and kidneys. He described the structure of the glomeruli in vertebrate kidneys and discovered the Malpighian tubules in insects.

DISCOVERERS

THE LOOP OF HENLE

Birds and mammals are able to excrete urine that is several times more concentrated than their blood plasma because of the evolution of a hairpin bend in the renal tubule called the loop of Henle (see diagram). The loop allows the filtrate to flow down into the medulla (middle part) of the kidney, where the tissue fluid gets progressively more concentrated (salty) with depth. The ascending and descending portions of the loop of Henle have different permeabilities to water and salts and so allow different substances to pass through them. The ascending limb pumps out salts, such as sodium chloride, into the fluid outside the cells in the medulla, making it very salty. This saltiness sets up an osmotic gradient between the tissue and the descending limb passing through it so that water diffuses out of the urine in the descending limb and into the kidney tissue, leaving a very much more concentrated urine inside the loop. As this urine passes up the ascending limb of the loop, its salts are pumped out into the surrounding tissue. So much salt is pumped out of the loop's ascending tubule that the urine leaving it is about one-third as salty as the blood, that is, it is very dilute. The process of concentrating the urine is performed by the nephron's collecting ducts, which carry the urine to the ureters. The ducts lie parallel to Henle's loop and pass down again through the medulla and its salty tissue fluid. As urine passes along the ducts, some of the urea is actively transported to the surrounding tissues to increase their saltiness. Also, if antidiuretic hormone is released from the pituitary, water leaves the collecting duct by osmosis into the medulla, concentrating the urine. It has been calculated that more than 99 percent of the fluid that filters into the nephron is reabsorbed.

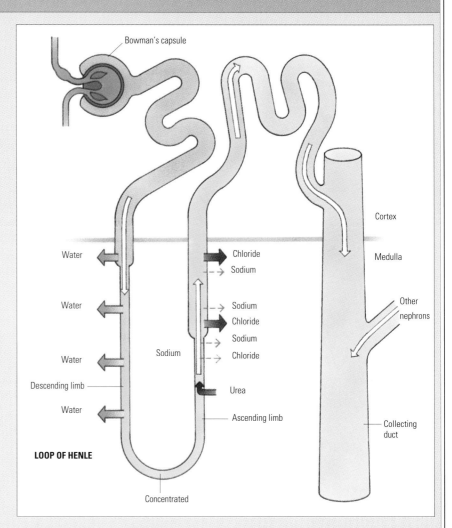

A CLOSER LOOK

behind in the nephron to be excreted in the final urine. Thus, the blood returns to its normal concentration. Conversely, when a lot of water has been taken into the body, levels of ADH decrease and the collecting ducts become less permeable to water.

The kidneys also maintain a constant concentration of salts in the blood. When the level of sodium ions drops too low, the adrenal gland increases its production of the hormone aldosterone. Aldosterone causes active reabsorption of sodium ions across two of the nephron segments and so decreases the amount of salt lost in the urine.

The skin as an excretory organ

Sweat, produced by glands in the skin, is a minor means of excreting waste substances from the body (see EXOCRINE GLANDS), although its main function is the control of body temperature. Sweat is a mixture of water, salts (mainly sodium chloride), urea, uric acid, ammonia, sugar, lactic and ascorbic acids, and amino acids. Humans lose about 2 pints (1 l) of sweat a day in temperate climates.

Kidney failure

Healthy kidneys are vital to life: total kidney failure is fatal unless dialysis or a transplant can be performed. Failure of the kidneys means they cannot remove soluble waste products from the body. Toxic wastes and water build up, and homeostasis is disrupted by the imbalance of the chemicals that the kidneys normally regulate. Kidney failure can be diagnosed from blood tests, urine examination, and kidney biopsy (examination of kidney tissue; see HISTOLOGY). Death usually results from a buildup of potassium, which is required by the body for cell function. The increased level stops the heart from contracting rhythmically.

J. STIRLING

See also: BLOOD; DIGESTIVE SYSTEMS; EXOCRINE GLANDS; HISTOLOGY; HOMEOSTASIS; IMMUNE SYSTEMS; INSULIN; KIDNEYS; PHOTOSYNTHESIS; REPRODUCTIVE SYSTEMS; THERMOREGULATION; UREA CYCLE.

Further reading:
Campbell, N., and J. Reece. 2002. *Biology*. San Francisco: Benjamin Cummings Publishers.

EXOCRINE GLANDS

Exocrine glands release secretions, usually through ducts, to the outer and inner surfaces of the body

The secretions of the exocrine glands can cool down a body, give nourishment, ward off attackers, and even attract the opposite sex. Sweat, poisons, milk, and pheromones are a few of the varied secretions of exocrine glands, secretory storage tanks that empty their contents onto the outermost layer of cells on the body's surface or the surface of the lining of body cavities deep within.

Embryology of exocrine glands

Exocrine glands grow out of the embryonic epithelium (epithelium is a continuous layer of cells covering an internal or external surface) and remain forever connected to the outer surfaces, usually through ducts. In the developing fetus, exocrine glands generally begin as ridges of epithelial cells that burrow into the underlying epithelial cell layers, creating a bud that then forms tubules or the more complex acini (sacs). At first, the tubes and other structures of the gland-to-be are solid; later, a lumen, or opening, begins to descend from the outer epithelial layer inward. The gland continues to grow until the lumen reaches the buds. Growth ceases, and the cells begin to enlarge and differentiate into the various gland structures.

TYPES OF EXOCRINE GLANDS
Oral exocrine glands

The names of oral exocrine glands, or salivary glands, refer to their location in the head or the area of the mouth into which they secrete: labial glands secrete into the mouth under the lips; molar glands are at the back of the mouth, near the molars; infraorbital glands originate near the eyes; palatal glands secrete on the palate (roof of the mouth); parotid glands originate near the ears, have ducts that pass under the skin of the cheek, and open into the mouth opposite the upper molars; inter-

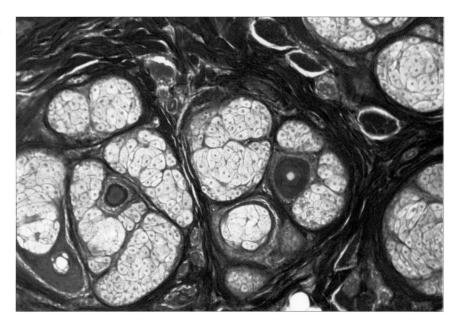

A transverse section through stained sebaceous glands in the human skin. These glands are associated with hair. They secrete an oily substance called sebum, which keeps the hair moist and waterproof.

maxillary (internasal) glands are situated in the upper jaw; and submandibular and sublingual glands secrete under the tongue.

The oral exocrine gland secretion with which people are most familiar is saliva. Saliva is a tasteless, odorless, slightly acidic (pH 6.8) cocktail of the secretions of all the oral glands, containing water, mucin (a glycoprotein, the main constituent of mucus), proteins, mineral salts, and the enzyme salivary amylase, which breaks down starches into water-soluble carbohydrates. Saliva also contains dead cells from the epithelium of the mouth, tongue, and tonsils.

The composition of saliva varies, depending on which glands are actively secreting and which type of cells make up the glands. The secretion of mucous cells is thick and sticky and is comprised mostly of mucin. Glands made of serous cells secrete a liquid that contains salts, protein, and salivary amylase but no mucin. Mixed glands make a little of both mucin and serous cells and therefore secrete a thick liquid mixture of mucin, salt, and salivary amylase. All oral exocrine glands are compound glands, with many branching ducts.

Saliva has a variety of important functions. The expression "mouth watering" indicates that the secretion of saliva in the mouth often occurs in response to the anticipation of a meal. Saliva does play an important role in digestion. It moistens the tongue and thus allows the taste buds to function and makes it easy for people to speak.

Saliva also facilitates swallowing and softens food. The detection of different foods in the mouth leads to a change in the oral gland secretions. Depending on the food present in the mouth, various glands may participate in the secretion, and each gland may vary its secretions.

CORE FACTS

- Exocrine glands are secretory cells that release their contents, usually via ducts, through the outermost layer of cells on the body's surface or cavity linings.
- There are simple and compound exocrine glands. Simple exocrine glands connect to surface cell layers with or without a branched duct. Compound exocrine glands look like inverted trees and reach the outer epithelium via branching ducts.
- Simple exocrine glands may be classified as coiled tubular, branched tubular, acinar, or branched acinar.
- Compound exocrine glands are classified as tubular, acinar, tubuloacinar, or saccular (larger acinar glands).
- There are many types of exocrine glands, including oral glands, such as salivary glands; sweat glands; sebaceous (oil) glands; mammary glands; and the pancreas.

CONNECTIONS

- The salivary glands and the pancreas secrete substances that play an important part in the functioning of **DIGESTIVE SYSTEMS**.

- Mammary glands provide **LACTATION** in **MAMMALS**.

- Exocrine glands can also secrete **PHEROMONES** for **COMMUNICATION**, sexual attraction, and **DEFENSE**.

CLASSIFICATION OF EXOCRINE GLANDS

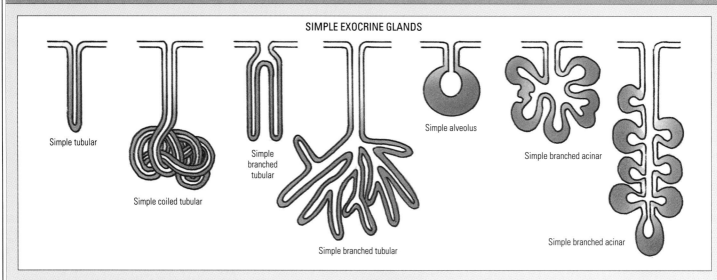

SIMPLE EXOCRINE GLANDS

Simple tubular

Simple coiled tubular

Simple branched tubular

Simple branched tubular

Simple alveolus

Simple branched acinar

Simple branched acinar

Unlike endocrine glands, which release hormones into the bloodstream to be carried away to remote parts of the body (see ENDOCRINE SYSTEMS), exocrine glands specialize in direct delivery. In their simplest form, exocrine glands connect to surface cell layers, with or without an unbranched duct. These glands are called simple exocrine glands. Simple tubular glands do not have a duct but instead open up onto the outermost epithelial layer. The intestinal glands, or "crypts" of Lieberkuhn, which secrete digestive juices into the large intestine of vertebrates, are an example.

Sweat glands are examples of simple coiled tubular glands, in which the inner part of the gland—the secretory portion—is in a coil that empties into a long duct leading to the skin surface. Simple branched tubular glands have a secretory portion, split into two or more branches and sometimes coils. Some exocrine glands of this type, those of the stomach, for example, have no duct. Others, in the tongue, esophagus, and large intestine, have a short duct.

When the secretory portion of an exocrine gland is a sphere or sac leading into a duct, the gland is called simple acinar. If the sac

(acinus) is divided into smaller sacs or if several small sacs line a duct, the gland is called simple branched acinar. Examples of these types of glands include sebaceous (oil) glands in the skin and the oil-secreting meibomian glands on the eyelids.

Compound exocrine glands resemble inverted trees, with glands emptying into branching ducts that get smaller as they reach the outer epithelium. They usually fall under the classifications tubular, acinar, tubuloacinar, or saccular glands. The terminal parts of compound tubular glands, like the pure mucus-secreting glands in the oral cavity, are coiled, branching tubules. The ends of compound acinar glands look like a cluster of eggs or spheres lined with budlike protrusions leading into ducts.

Compound tubuloacinar glands, such as the pancreas, are, as the name suggests, a cross between tubular and acinar glands— spheres attach to tubes leading into ducts. Finally, compound saccular glands are essentially compound acinar glands on a larger scale. Both the female mammary glands and the male prostate gland are examples of these types of glands.

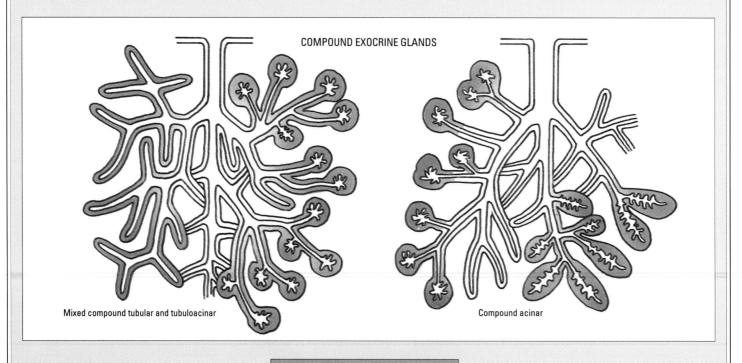

COMPOUND EXOCRINE GLANDS

Mixed compound tubular and tubuloacinar

Compound acinar

A CLOSER LOOK

Aquatic vertebrates do not need saliva to moisten their taste buds because they have adequate water in their mouths to begin with, and any digestive oral secretions would likely be washed away. The males of some catfish, however, do have oral secretions that help in their role as expectant parents. During the breeding season, these males carry fertilized eggs in skin folds in their mouths. The cells lining the skin folds constantly secrete fluid. Both the folds and the cells atrophy (wither away) after the eggs hatch.

Poisons are another type of oral secretion, exhibited by some land-dwelling vertebrates. In poisonous snakes, the poison gland, a palatal gland, opens into the base of certain fangs, and the poison goes into a tube in the tooth (see SNAKES). The two poisonous lizards, the gila monster (*Heloderma suspectum*) and the Mexican beaded lizard (*H. horridum*) have toxin-secreting glands under the tongue.

Invertebrates, insects especially, also produce oral secretions with a myriad of functions. The saliva of ticks, for example, contains the enzyme apyrase that prevents the blood of the host from clotting as the tick feeds. Many insect exocrine gland secretions are involved in chemical communication. The mandibular (jaw) exocrine glands of ants can emit an alarm secretion at the presence of an intruder. When major worker African weaver ants (*Oecophylla* spp.) are disturbed in their nest, for example, they emit a fragrant, musty odor that incites other worker ants to help defend the nest. The odor comes from a droplet of mandibular gland secretion, which diffuses into the air. The secretion of minor worker ants' mandibular glands, on the other hand, tells other minor workers to flee the site.

Certain stingless bees use their mandibular gland secretions to mark trails to nectar sources, by wiping their mandibles on rocks and plants along the way. Royal jelly, the substance that turns ordinary honey bee (*Apis mellifera*) larvae into queens, is a salivary secretion of nurse worker bees' hypopharyngeal (maxillary) and mandibular glands. In turn, the secretions of a queen bee's hypopharyngeal glands inhibits the development of the ovaries in worker bees.

Sudoriferous and sebaceous glands

Everyone is familiar with television commercials in which people are embarrassed because they have a body odor. People seem to spend a lot of effort ensuring that their sweat glands work as little as possible. It has been an uphill battle, considering that people have approximately two million sweat glands, secreting 1½ pints (850 ml) of sweat— a mixture of water (90 percent), urea, and other wastes—per day in a temperate climate.

Sweat has many useful purposes. Sweat glands essentially help to protect the body. When the weather is very hot, people perspire more, and the evaporation of sweat from the skin helps cool down the body. Sweat can also protect people against the buildup of waste products, frictional damage to the skin, and bacteria.

Human sweat glands are simple coiled tubular exocrine glands that lie deep beneath the skin's surface and open up on the skin surface as pores. They are derived from the epidermal ridges on the finger tips, palms, and soles of the feet during the fourth month of fetal development. Sweat glands are functional at seven months but are probably not used until after birth. Their activity is controlled by the hypothalamus at the base of the brain. Since the hypothalamus also responds to emotional stress, people are likely to "break out in a cold sweat" when frightened or nervous. When people apply antiperspirants, which contain

Many animals have sweat glands only in certain areas. The hippopotamus, for example, which spends most of its time with just its head above water, has sweat glands only in its ears.

aluminum chlorohydrate and other chemicals, they are helping to reduce the amount of sweat reaching the skin and to slow the growth of the bacteria associated with body odor. Roll-on antiperspirants are considered more effective than sprays or sticks because their liquid base helps aluminum chlorohydrate absorb into the skin more readily.

Some furry mammals have sweat glands only in their least furry regions: the feet of mice and cats and the lips of rabbits, for example. Other mammals lack sweat glands altogether. Cetaceans (whales and porpoises) have no sweat glands because their ocean habitat precludes cooling by evaporation; neither do pangolins, ant-eating mammals, which have a covering of horny scales.

Sebaceous glands arise from the outer epithelial sheath of hair follicles. The oil they secrete, called sebum, is usually secreted through the hair follicle. The shine created on brushed hair, comes from sebum coating the hairs. The meibomian glands, located just under the eyelashes, secrete onto the conjunctiva of the eye. The ceruminous glands in the ear canal secrete wax, which helps protect the sensitive tympanum (ear drum). Some sebaceous glands, in the lips, labia minora, and glans penis, are not associated with hairs.

The sebaceous glands normally secrete enough oil to keep the skin soft and lubricated. When they start overproducing oil, it clogs the pores and can cause the blackheads and pustules associated with acne. Acne, despite what many people think, is not a factor of poor grooming or eating junk food: most often, its cause is hereditary, combined with the onset of puberty. For mild cases, over-the-counter products containing benzoyl peroxide can help clear the skin. Many dermatologists now prescribe a cream or gel containing retinoic acid, a vitamin A derivative, for severe acne cases. Retinoic acid works by drying up the sebaceous glands in the skin.

Both sudoriferous and sebaceous glands can emit scents, useful for attracting the opposite sex or for defense. Anyone who has been sprayed by a skunk knows all too well the smell and sting of the secretions of its anal glands. Oil glands may have other uses. Birds, for example, have uropygial glands, located just above the base of the tail, which secrete an oil that is spread over the feathers during preening. The oil keeps the feathers waterproof, a condition that is especially important for waterfowl.

Mammary glands

Mammary glands are found only in mammals. They develop in both sexes from a longitudinal band of ectoderm formed early on in fetal development. The band, called a milk line, runs down the length of the embryo's body, between its budding limbs. Later patches of the milk line begin to thicken where nipple formation will eventually take place. The mammary gland buds then grow down into the dermis, forming milk ducts, which expand and eventually hollow out before birth. At this point the nipple is sunken into the skin.

Both females and males experience further mammary gland development early on in life. As they near sexual maturity, nipples form from the sunken spots, and in females, the ducts spread and branch. Owing to the change in hormones during pregnancy, the mammary glands develop acini, which grow and differentiate. After giving birth, a female's mammary glands will secrete a fluid called colostrum, which nourishes newborns until the milk begins to flow.

Why do people and primates have two nipples and other mammals several? The number and location of the nipples depends on typical numbers of young per pregnancy and the nature of the habitat. People have two nipples, located near the armpits, so they can protect the infants under the arms as they nurse. The same is true for nonhuman primates. Pigs, dogs, and other mammals develop long strips of nipples down either side of the underbelly because they have large litters.

Cetaceans (whales and dolphins) have two nipples near the groin so that the infants can nurse while the mother swims, feeds, and dives. Monotremes, (egg-laying mammals) such as the platypus (*Ornithorhynchus anatinus*), have mammary glands that resemble modified sweat glands. (Some

Three different ways of delivering milk from the mammary gland. In monotremes, such as the platypus, the milk emerges on tufts of hair. In the human nipple, the milk oozes from a number of narrow ducts. In ungulates such as the cow, the ducts discharge into a single larger sac called a cistern.

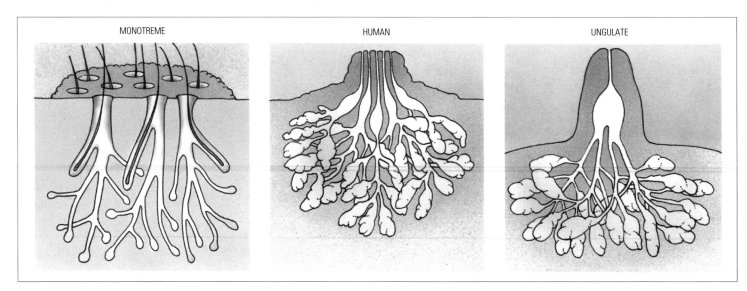

| MONOTREME | HUMAN | UNGULATE |

experts believe all mammary glands are modified sweat glands.) Young monotremes lap their milk from tufts of fur surrounding the nipples.

Pancreas

The pancreas is an unusual exocrine gland in that it secretes into the gut, not onto the skin surface. Thus, an apt description of the pancreas is "the salivary gland of the abdomen." It also has the distinction of being both an exocrine and an endocrine gland. It is made up of acini that secrete digestive enzymes into ductules (small ducts) leading to the duodenum, while, interspersed throughout the pancreas, the endocrine islets of Langerhans secrete the hormones insulin and glucagon into the blood.

Like other exocrine glands, which start as endodermal (innermost embryonic germ layer) buds that then burrow down into the underlying tissue layers, the pancreas arises from outpocketings of the endodermal lining of the embryonic gut on either side of the duodenum. One outpocketing becomes the dorsal pancreas, the other the ventral pancreas. These parts eventually fuse together.

The pancreas secretes its products in response to the presence of food. First, it secretes an alkaline fluid that neutralizes the chyme (acid-digested food) coming from the stomach and thus makes the pH optimal for the pancreatic enzymes—trypsin, chymotrypsin, carboxypeptidase, ribonuclease, deoxyribonuclease, pancreatic amylase, and pancreatic lipase—which are then secreted to carry out their role in the digestive process (see PANCREAS).

Specialized exocrine gland secretions

From insects to people, exocrine glands manufacture a whole range of secretions that are as varied as the structure of the glands themselves.

Some of the most interesting exocrine gland secretions occur in the insect world, especially among the social insects, which rely on exocrine chemicals for communication. Pheromones (see PHEROMONES) are used within a species to attract the opposite sex for mating, as an aid during courtship, to warn against danger, and to mark trails to food sources and territories. Insects are highly sensitive to the presence of pheromones and can detect them in the air even in minuscule quantities. Male silkworm moths (*Bombyx mori*), for example, get excited when exposed to just 0.000001 μg of the female sex pheromone bombykol.

Allomones are used by an insect when it interacts with other species. Defensive allomones are often kept in reservoirs and released when an insect is under attack. The insect may wipe them on the site of attack, ooze them out, or spray them on the attacker (see the box above). Appeasement substances are allomones that are used by some insects to forge symbiotic relationships. One type of beetle, for example, uses the secretions of its appeasement gland to get ants to carry it to the ants' nest, where the beetle then lives in comfort surrounded by sources of food.

HOT STUFF

In his writings Charles Darwin described his first-hand experience with defensive exocrine allomones. Apparently, while he was collecting beetle specimens, the naturalist found he did not have enough hands and, being a resourceful person, put one of the beetles into his mouth for safe-keeping. No sooner had he done so, than he heard a loud pop, followed by a painful burning sensation that filled his mouth. Needless to say, he let the beetle go. Experts believe that Darwin had experienced the wrath of the bombardier beetle (*Brachinus* spp.).

The bombardier beetle is a genius at chemical warfare. Using movable "turrets" on its rump, the beetle very accurately sprays superheated chemicals at its attacker. To store the explosive chemicals in its body without causing damage to itself, the beetle has two separate compartments in its gland reservoir; the inner compartment contains hydroquinones mixed with hydrogen peroxide, while the outer compartment is filled with enzymes (peroxidases and catalases). When the beetle is under attack, it releases the contents of the inner compartment, which flow into the outer compartment. The outer compartment enzymes oxidize the hydrogen peroxide to give water and oxygen and also oxidize the hydroquinones to give benzoquinone. The chemical reactions release gaseous oxygen and heat, and the mixture reaches a temperature of 212 °F (100 °C). The popping sound Darwin heard is caused by the gaseous oxygen acting as a propellant. The firing sound is discontinuous; scientists have recorded it at 500 to 1,000 pulses per second.

When a bombardier beetle is attacked by an ant, it can mix its chemicals, aim its turrets, and fire within 100 to 3,000 milliseconds. However, bombardier beetles are not completely impervious to attack. Some of their predators have developed ingenious ways to avoid getting sprayed by superhot chemicals. Blue jays (*Cyanocitta cristata*), for example, wipe the beetles on their feathers until the chemicals run dry. In addition, ants gang up on the beetles and force them to spray until the beetles use up their chemical defenses.

A CLOSER LOOK

Aquatic vertebrates, such as fish and amphibians, often have mucus-secreting exocrine glands in the skin. The glands may produce extra mucus to make the animal slippery when it is under attack. The mucus may also serve a more long-term purpose in protection, preventing the entrance of foreign molecules and bacteria into the body. Some fish also have poisonous spines for protection.

Terrestrial amphibians often secrete irritating alkaloids onto their skin. In some cases the alkaloids are highly poisonous, as in the case of the strawberry poison-dart frog (*Denrobates pumilio*). Lizards wipe the secretions of their exocrine vent glands on trees to attract insects. The glands on male lizards' hind limbs secrete a substance that hardens to create a spine for restraining females during copulation.

J. SCHULHOF

See also: DEFENSE MECHANISMS; ENDOCRINE SYSTEMS; PANCREAS; SNAKES.

Further reading:

Griffin, J. E., and S. R. Ojeda. 1996. *Textbook of Endocrine Physiology*. 3rd ed. Oxford: Oxford University Press.
Hickman, C. P., Jr, L. S. Roberts, and A. Larson. 2000. *Integrated Principles of Zoology*. 11th ed. New York: McGraw Hill.

EXTINCTION

Extinction is the total disappearance of a species

The dodo (Raphus cucullatus), once found on Mauritius, was extinct by the 1690s.

anagenesis, one taxonomic group replaces another, without any evolutionary branching. One type of extinction—called taxonomic, or phyletic, extinction—occurs when a species disappears through anagenesis (see EVOLUTION). In this type of extinction, the genetic heritage of the extinct species is passed on to its evolutionary descendants. In other types the genes of the extinct species are lost forever.

Loss of genetic material

This loss of genetic material—the reduction in biodiversity—most troubles conservationists and environmentalists, who seek to protect species endangered by human activities. Some scientists argue that extinction of any species is a loss in itself, and they believe that humanity does not have the right to extinguish any species.

Other scientists take a more practical line of argument, suggesting that plants and animals may have useful properties not known today and that humanity is denying itself enormously valuable products by driving species into extinction.

For example, nearly 2,000 different plants and animals produce substances that could prove to have cancer-fighting properties. Those living organisms that become extinct would take their medicinal properties with them. Similarly, plants that are unfamiliar to people could eventually prove to be valuable food crops—but not if they are driven into extinction first.

Extinction has been going on since life began; millions of species have died out over the ages, for a variety of reasons. Most of the species that have existed during the history of planet Earth—probably more than 99 percent—are now extinct. How do scientists define extinction? Here extinction is taken to mean the total disappearance of a species. Some people see it as the elimination of a particular species from the wild. By this definition, a creature that survives only in zoos or nature reserves could be considered extinct. Other scientists use the terms "regional extinction" and "local extinction" to refer to the elimination of a living organism from a specific geographical area but not from the planet as a whole.

Types of extinction

Because of the way organisms are interconnected with each other, the extinction of one species can lead to the extinction of another. For example, the saber-tooth tiger *Smilodon* may have become extinct because its prey, the mastodon, became extinct about 10,000 years ago. The extinction of a plant species can doom 20 to 30 other species of organisms that feed on the plant or depend on it for shelter.

New species are produced by evolutionary changes in existing species. In this process, called

Using fossils to map extinctions

Fossils, the preserved remains and traces of once-living organisms, are an important tool for scientists who study the progress of extinction through history (see FOSSILS). Strata, or layers, in Earth's crust represent different times in the planet's history. Fossils embedded in rock from the period in which they were formed provide paleontologists (scientists who investigate fossil remains) with the "fossil record." By studying the fossil record to see what fossils are present or missing at various times, scientists can determine when species became extinct. However, it is often impossible to discover the circumstances that caused the extinction.

CORE FACTS

- Extinction is the disappearance of a species.
- There are several types of extinction: taxonomic extinction, in which species disappear through evolution; mass extinction, where large numbers of species die out at the same time; and another type, in which the extinction of one species leads to the extinction of others.
- Human activities are causing the extinction of many living organisms.

Until the 19th century, few people suspected that the world's wildlife had ever included plants or animals that no longer existed. Fossils played a key role in convincing scientists of extinction. In 1876 French paleontologist Georges Cuvier (1769–1832) compared the skeletons of modern-day elephants with the recently discovered fossilized skeleton of the mammoth, which lived during the ice age. Cuvier showed that the skeletons were so different that the mammoth and elephant must be different species. In addition, the mammoth was so large that it could not be living undiscovered somewhere on Earth. Thus, he reasoned the mammoth must truly be extinct.

Mass extinction

At certain points in Earth's history, vast numbers of different species of living organisms around the world have died out within a relatively short period of time. (In geologic time, a short period of time can be 10 million years.) Scientists refer to this phenomenon as a mass extinction. Such an extinction could not possibly be due to genetic changes in the species involved.

From studies of the fossil record, scientists have identified a number of mass extinctions, including five in the last 500 million years. Species are continually becoming extinct, but in each of these mass extinctions, species suddenly started dropping much more rapidly than usual before eventually tapering off to a normal rate.

The earliest known mass extinction occurred about 650 million years ago, during the Precambrian period. At this time life was still in its early stages of evolution and consisted of large quantities of algae floating in Earth's primitive ocean. The fossil record reveals that about 70 percent of all algal species suddenly died. Some researchers suggest that the algae may not have been able to survive an intensive ice age that began at that time.

The most devastating mass extinction in Earth's history occurred between 255 million and 250 million years ago, at the end of the Permian period. This extinction, which stretched over some 10 million years (more than 100 times longer than humans have lived on Earth), killed 75 to 90 percent of all marine creatures and a large number of land species. Scientists have not agreed on a cause for this extinction, although some suspect that climate changes may have been to blame. Perhaps the best-known mass extinction occurred about 65 million years ago, at the end of the Cretaceous period, which also marked the end of the geological era called the Mesozoic and the start of the Cenozoic era. It was during this mass extinction that the dinosaurs died out; in addition, a wide variety of other ocean and land animals and plants died.

In 1980 U.S. researchers Luis (1911–1988) and Walter Alvarez (b. 1940) discovered that, at several different areas around the globe, the fossil record of this mass extinction reveals a layer of minerals containing the rare element iridium. The Alvarezes used this information as the basis for a dramatic theory. They suggested that an iridium-rich asteroid may have hit Earth at that time, throwing a vast cloud of dust into the atmosphere. The crash of the asteroid itself would not have caused a worldwide mass extinction, but the dense cloud produced by the impact would have cooled the atmosphere by blotting out sunlight for several years or warmed the atmosphere by trapping heat.

Either effect could have killed huge numbers of plants and the animals that depended on them for food. Since the theory was first proposed, other researchers have uncovered signs that the crater the asteroid made may lie off the coast of what is now Mexico's Yucatan peninsula.

This theory remains controversial. Some scientists have proposed other explanations for the iridium layer, such as the possibility that it was spewed into the air by volcanoes. Also, it is unclear whether an asteroid could have been responsible for the earlier mass extinctions because no extra iridium has been found in the fossil record for those times.

Other researchers think that mass extinction

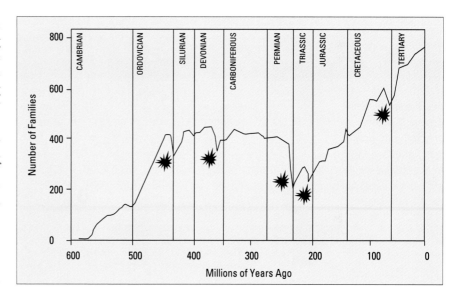

caused by asteroids might be quite common. Scientists have statistically analyzed recent mass extinctions and note that they have occurred in a regular pattern. Some scientists believe that this pattern suggests a periodic bombardment from space, by comets or asteroids.

Human influence

Like all other organisms, humans affect the environment in which they live. They feed on specific plants and animals, and human activity dramatically affects the ability of other organisms to live and function, making life more hospitable for some and less so for others. It is not surprising that people have driven many living organisms into extinction.

This state of affairs may not be a recent development. For example, more than half the world's species of large mammals, including the mammoth, the mastodon, and the woolly rhinoceros, began to die out at the end of the last ice age, around 11,000 years ago, in

This diagram shows the five mass extinctions that have taken place in the past 500 million years since the first known mass extinction of the Precambrian 650 million years ago. The data is based on families of marine organisms. A sixth major decline is in progress as a result of human activity.

According to biologist Edward O. Wilson, people are driving at least 27,000 species of living organisms to extinction every year by cutting down rain forests in the Amazon.

the geological period called the Late Pleistocene. Paul Martin of the University of Arizona has suggested that early humans hunted these animals into extinction, using primitive weapons that enabled them to hunt the large animals more efficiently. The objection to this argument is that the fossil record shows these species to have been widely distributed around the world, while humans were restricted to only a few areas.

Extinction has not abated as humans evolved. Humans have hunted some creatures into extinction and crowded others out of their natural habitats. At least 200 plant species native to the United States have become extinct within historical times, and about 20 percent of all bird species around the globe have also become extinct.

People may have caused as much extinction as did the mass destructions of the ancient past. U.S. biologist Edward O. Wilson estimates that the background extinction rate—the pace at which species become extinct in the absence of mass extinctions—is about one extinction per million species per year. In Amazonian rain forests alone, where the clearance of forests eliminates the homes of yet unidentified species, Wilson concludes that human activities are extinguishing species at a rate 1,000 to 10,000 times faster than this background rate. He estimates that by 2020, the world may have lost one fifth of its present species.

Pollution also plays a role in extinction, killing living organisms, and combined with other factors may drive species to the brink of extinction (see POLLUTION). For example, the bald eagle was

placed on the endangered species list primarily because of the effects of the pesticide dichloro-diphenyl-trichloroethane (DDT) on their eggs. Rachel Carson in her landmark 1962 book, *Silent Spring*, alerted people to the fact that DDT was causing birds to lay eggs so thin shelled that the chicks never hatched because the eggs cracked too soon. The use of DDT is now banned in the United States (see CARSON, RACHEL LOUISE; DDT; POLLUTION).

Scientists have also begun to realize that pollutants often contain environmental hormones — chemicals whose structures are similar to those of some animal hormones. If an animal absorbs such a pollutant, that chemical can cause problems with hormonally controlled systems in its body, such as the reproductive system. This disruption can lead to a wide array of birth defects in wildlife. Environmentalists are deeply concerned that this interference with animals' reproductive systems could lead to their extinction.

V. KIERNAN

See also: CARSON, RACHEL LOUISE; CONSERVATION; DDT; EVOLUTION; FOSSILS; POLLUTION; SPECIES; WILSON, EDWARD O.

Further reading:
Eldredge, N. 1991. *The Miner's Canary: Unraveling the Mysteries of Extinction*, New York: Prentice Hall Press.
Stearns, B. P., and S. C. Stearns. 2000. *Watching, from the Edge of Extinction*. New Haven, Conn.: Yale University Press.

EXTRATERRESTRIAL LIFE

Extraterrestrial life refers to those life-forms that may live outside Earth or its atmosphere

The possibility of life beyond Earth has fascinated philosophers, authors, and scientists for centuries, but only in the past few decades have people reached a point where they are scientifically capable of exploring other worlds in the Solar System, finding other systems of planets around stars other than the Sun, and attempting communication with possible extraterrestrial civilizations.

Requirements for life

Although alien organisms may be outwardly bizarre and totally different from anything on Earth, they would almost certainly be based on the same biochemistry. For this reason it is important to understand the basic conditions needed for life to begin and continue on Earth before one looks for the same conditions elsewhere.

The development of life requires energy and a medium (see ENERGY). Until recently biologists thought that the only source of energy could be light and heat from the Sun, perhaps aided by occasional bolts of lightning. Therefore, they assumed that life started on or near Earth's surface. Oceans and ponds would have provided the medium for life to evolve because, without some fluid in which chemicals can be dissolved, move around, and interact with each other, the development of complex chemical molecules would be impossible.

Another important requirement for life is an element capable of making multiple bonds with other atoms and producing very large molecules. This element, carbon, forms the basis of all known life. Carbon readily bonds with up to four other atoms, and if one of these is itself a carbon atom, it can create huge chains and extremely complex chemicals. Several other elements, such as silicon and germa-

A true-color composite image of Earth's western hemisphere taken by NASA's remote-sensing device, called MODIS.

nium, can form the same number of bonds as carbon, but carbon forms large molecules most easily. Carbon is also plentiful in the Universe (see CARBON CYCLE).

Pushing the limits

Given these requirements, it is possible to see why Earth is such a haven for life. The planet exists at just the right distance from the Sun to receive heat and light, and its temperature remains cool enough to retain liquid water on the surface. Earth's protective atmosphere also shields life from bombardment by harmful types of radiation such as X rays and ultraviolet light (see ULTRAVIOLET RADIATION; X RAYS).

If all life on Earth was dependent on sunlight and water, then Earth would be uniquely placed in the Solar System to develop life. However, recent discoveries have opened the door to other possibilities. Since the 1980s scientists have been coming to terms with the fact that life on Earth can exist without sunlight, flourishing in extreme conditions long thought to be completely inhospitable.

The most spectacular discoveries have been the life-forms that live around deep-sea volcanic vents where Earth's crust is separating (see OCEAN FLOOR). The organisms around these underwater oases, isolated in the midst of the frozen ocean depths, draw their nutrition from the hot chemical stew the vents spew from below Earth's crust.

Just as important has been the discovery of the "extremophiles" (from the Greek for "lovers of the extreme"). These tiny organisms, related to bacteria,

---

CORE FACTS

■ So far Earth is the only planet known to support life, but the prospects that life exists beyond Earth are improving.

■ The development of life requires energy, a medium such as water, and an element, such as carbon or silicon, capable of making multiple bonds with other atoms to produce very large molecules.

■ In the last 20 years scientists have discovered that some life-forms on Earth can exist without sunlight and in extreme conditions long thought to be completely unsuitable for life.

■ Astronomers and biologists, searching for life-forms elsewhere in the Solar System, are examining Mars, Venus, and the giant Galilean moons of Jupiter and other possible places.

■ Scientists have recently discovered dozens of planets beyond the Solar System and are evaluating the prospects for life on these worlds.

CONNECTIONS

● Early in its history, Venus experienced a greenhouse effect that caused **GLOBAL WARMING**.

● Harmful radiation such as **X RAYS** and **ULTRAVIOLET RADIATION** are prevented from reaching Earth by its **ATMOSPHERE**.

● Some life-forms that do not depend on the Sun for energy live around volcanic vents on the **OCEAN FLOOR,** where Earth's crust is pulling apart.

THE MILLER–UREY EXPERIMENT

The Miller-Urey experiment was an attempt to reproduce conditions on primordial (early) Earth in a glass vessel and see how far life would evolve. The experiment was devised in the 1950s by Stanley Miller and Harold Urey of the University of Chicago. They used a flask filled with gases to simulate their ideas of Earth's early atmosphere—methane, ammonia, water vapor, and hydrogen. Water was boiled and condensed to simulate evaporation and condensation in the early seas, and periodic high-voltage "lightning" sparks were passed through the gases. After just a few days, the artificial sea started to change color, showing that complex chemicals were forming. When the scientists analyzed these chemicals, they found they included amino acids (see AMINO ACIDS), the building blocks of proteins and a vital first step toward life (see EVOLUTION).

A CLOSER LOOK

flourish in environments that seem incapable of supporting life, such as temperatures close to or even above the boiling point of water or extremely acidic, alkali, or salty conditions. Some microorganisms can even survive by breaking down the sulfurous chemicals produced in volcanoes (see BACTERIA).

LIFE IN THE SOLAR SYSTEM

Armed with this new picture of life on Earth, astronomers and biologists have reassessed the prospects for life in the Solar System.

Martian microbes?

Mars has long been considered the prime candidate for life beyond Earth. Like Earth, Mars has four seasons and exhibits seasonal changes of color, once thought to be evidence of vegetation. In the late 19th century Italian astronomer Giovanni Schiaperelli (1835–1910)

A simulated view of Mars as it would be seen from the Mars Global Surveyor spacecraft. The search for water on the planet and with it possible forms of life was one of the main tasks of the NASA space probe Mars Odyssey 2001.

reported seeing a network of fine dark lines crisscrossing its surface, which he referred to as "canali." Some scientists speculated that these "canals" were evidence of an advanced civilization distributing water from the planet's polar ice caps into its red deserts.

These hopes were dashed in the 1960s when the first space probes to Mars sent back pictures of a dead world. No signs of life could be seen, not even primitive plants. The 1970s *Viking* missions to Mars took apparatus to test for living processes. Although these probes revealed abundant evidence for ancient water erosion, showing that Mars was once warmer and wetter, they found no indications of life.

Perceptions began to change once more in 1996, with the announcement by a team of National Aeronautics and Space Administration (NASA) scientists that they had found signs of fossilized life from Mars. The scientists studied a meteorite called ALH 84001, believed to have been blasted off the Martian surface millions of years ago and then hurled through space, landing about 13,000 years ago in Antarctica. The evidence for life in this meteorite was controversial and is still being investigated. Significantly, the researchers claimed to have detected chemicals that could have been produced only by the action of bacteria. The team also claimed to have found fossils of these Martians—tiny wormlike fossil nanobacteria, a thousand times smaller than Earth's bacteria.

Skeptics immediately raised three important objections: the existence of alternative mechanisms that could have generated the chemicals without the need for life; questioning whether the meteorite could have become contaminated on Earth; and raising concerns about the tiny size of the bacteria. Supporters of the claim countered by pointing to the recent discovery of very small extremophiles on Earth.

Meanwhile, results from the latest wave of space probes have bolstered further the prospects that life once existed and possibly even still exists on Mars. The orbiting *Mars Global Surveyor* has found strong evidence for liquid water existing just below the Martian surface and occasionally seeping out. The *Mars Odyssey* probe's first observations after its arrival in late 2001 detected extremely high levels of hydrogen in the Martian soil, suggesting that a widespread water table could lie just below the entire northern hemisphere.

Moons of Jupiter

Beyond the orbit of Mars, it is too cold for life to thrive if it depends only on the Sun. Nevertheless, in the interiors of certain remote worlds, scientists believe that biochemical processes could offer precious life-giving energy. The most enticing prospects for life come from the inner two of the four giant Galilean moons of Jupiter. Each the size of a small planet, Io and Europa are very different worlds with one important thing in common: Jupiter's immense tidal forces constantly wrench each of these moons this way and that, heating up the moons' interiors and making them both highly volcanic. Io is the most volcanic world in the Solar System. With all this energy being spurted into space, some scientists have speculated that Io could shelter extremophiles such as those that flourish around Earth's volcanoes. However, with its tenuous atmosphere it is probable that Io is too hostile even for those hardy organisms.

Europa, however, is a different story, and the best prospect for advanced life-forms beyond Earth. Here all the volcanic activity is locked away beneath an icy crust. The heat from Europa's volcanoes helps to warm the ice, almost certainly giving the moon an ocean 3,300 feet (1 km) deep, constantly fed with nutrients from the erupting volcanic vents. The icy crust above acts as a self-healing barrier against the hostile surface. Wherever this barrier cracks, water boils off into space until the gap rapidly freezes over; hence, Europa is covered in a network of fine cracks.

The outer Galilean moons—Ganymede and Callisto—are less enticing prospects for life, but there are hints that Callisto also has a subsurface ocean. How it would be heated is a mystery, however, because the satellite is too far away from Jupiter to benefit from tidal warming.

Finding life

Scientists still do not know whether life will evolve wherever the conditions are suitable. On Earth living organisms seem to exploit every possible niche, but will this postulate hold true on other worlds? There is simply no way of knowing because at present people have only one example of a living planet—Earth. However, investigations of Mars and Europa, planned to be launched within the next couple of decades, could expand this sample to three and thereby help answer some of these questions.

One controversial approach, the "panspermia" theory, sidesteps this issue, doing away with the need for life to evolve independently on different planets. According to this theory, the basics of life are carried through space, deep-frozen in comet ice, and occasionally crash to the surface of a hospitable planet. The idea that life or at least its building blocks might have evolved in deep space has been bolstered by the discovery of complex organic (carbon-based) molecules, such as sugars and alcohol, in interstellar dust clouds and also by the increasing evidence that much of Earth's water originated as comet ice.

LIFE BEYOND THE SOLAR SYSTEM

Earth's Sun is just one of a hundred billion stars in the Milky Way, so what are the chances for life evolving on the planets of other stars? How can people detect which stellar systems might have life, and will contact with other intelligences ever be made?

The Drake Equation

The answers to these questions depend on a long chain of what-ifs, summarized in an equation devised by U.S. astronomer Frank Drake (b. 1930), a pioneer of the organization Search for Extra-terrestrial Intelligence (SETI). Among the important queries Drake lists are:
• What proportion of stars are suitable for planets with life? Many types of stars are inhospitable for life

Jupiter (top center) and its four planet-size moons, called the Galilean satellites (relative size is not accurate, but relative positions are). Reddish Io (upper left) is nearest Jupiter; then Europa (center); Ganymede and Callisto (lower right). Io and Europa are highly volcanic, and some scientists believe they could harbor life in the form of extremophiles.

because not all are the same: small, faint stars do not produce enough heat and light, while massive, bright stars burn out in tens of millions years, far too quickly for life to evolve. Therefore, most scientists believe that only stars with size, brightness, and lifespan fairly similar to the Sun's, are likely to give rise to life.
• What proportion of sunlike stars have planets in the habitable zone around them?

For several decades, astronomers searched in vain for planets around other stars, but only since the 1990s have they known how to detect them. So far more than 50 extrasolar planets are known, but these are all giants like Jupiter, detectable because of their gravitational tugs on their stars. What is more, most of these systems are very different from Earth's, with the giant planets orbiting very close to their stars or in wildly eccentric ellipses. So far only one system comes close to looking like home. Earthlike planets at Earthlike distances are so far undetectable, although this situation will change in the next few years, and then astronomers should have a better idea of the odds.
• On what proportion of planets in the habitable zone around sunlike stars does life arise?

This is the biggest question of all and the most difficult to answer. The basic elements needed for life seem to be plentiful in the Universe, but things can still go wrong. For example, Venus, second planet from the Sun and Earth's near twin, became unhabitable early in its history when it suffered from a runaway greenhouse effect (see GLOBAL WARMING). Although astronomers are now developing techniques to measure the atmospheres of extrasolar planets, even if they find hospitable ones, there is no guarantee these planets will have life on them. The odds will change dramatically if scientists find that life has begun independently elsewhere in Earth's Solar System.

CARL SAGAN

Carl Sagan (1934–1996) was a planetary scientist who helped pioneer and promote the organization Search for Extraterrestrial Intelligence (SETI) and astronomy in general. He was one of the first people to apply scientific reasoning to the question of alien life. He studied the possibility of life on Saturn's moon Titan, in Jupiter's atmosphere, and elsewhere and investigated the origins of life on Earth. Sagan was also involved in many of NASA's space probes in the 1960s and 1970s and helped devise the various messages to other civilizations carried on the *Pioneer* and *Voyager* probes as they left the Solar System.

DISCOVERERS

What will aliens be like?

No one can predict what alien creatures might look like, although their biochemistry would probably be similar to that of life on Earth. Animal-like organisms would perhaps develop similar senses to those of humans, although their sense organs might be completely different. Aliens might also have some of the same "extra" senses known to exist in animals such as sharks and migrating birds.

Alien creatures are very unlikely to look like Earth animals. They would likely evolve to deal with the specific challenges of their world. For example, high or low gravity might produce squat or tall animals, respectively. In certain cases, one might speculate that similar conditions would lead to close resemblances to terrestrial beings. Animals that lived in an ocean, for example, would probably look like fish (just as whales do on Earth), and airborne animals would probably have a passing resemblance to birds.

Even if life does evolve on other worlds, what are the chances of it developing intelligence and becoming intelligent enough to make contact with people? To estimate the spread of civilizations, the Drake Equation contains a number of other factors, such as the time taken for life to evolve to intelligence and the chances of any intelligent life-form being wiped out by natural or self-inflicted disaster before they can develop the technology to communicate with other worlds. Although the Drake Equation is a useful tool for thinking about all the obstacles faced by a developing civilization, there is no way to estimate any of these factors except by guesswork. Optimists have used the equation to predict up to 10 billion mature civilizations in Earth's galaxy, while pessimists have used it to show that Earth's galaxy has just one such civilization—that of humans.

Finding aliens

The scale of the Universe, even Earth's small local corner of it, is so vast that light and radio signals take decades to pass between all but the closest stars. Extremely powerful transmitters and sensitive detectors are needed to have even a hope of contacting any neighbors. People have already transmitted their first message to the stars—beamed out from the giant Arecibo radio telescope in 1974—encoded in a series of on-off pulses that an intelligent alien could decode into a simple pictogram. The *Pioneer* and *Voyager* probes carried symbolic messages of friendship to possible civilizations they might encounter. However, the probes move very slowly through space—much, much slower than radio transmissions.

Although there are no current plans to send further messages, the discovery of an Earthlike planet orbiting a nearby star would almost certainly change this approach. In the meantime, astronomers sift through the observations of the world's radio telescopes looking for telltale signs of an artificial signal. So far, they have had no success, despite some false alarms and unidentified loose ends.

However, some SETI experts think scientists and astronomers may be looking in the wrong place. Like a car radio, their radio telescopes are limited to studying certain wavelengths, so they could be tuned to the wrong spot on the dial. Another way of finding aliens may be to look for the traces of any massive structure they have built. Super-advanced alien civilizations may have learned to manipulate space in ways people can only dream about, such as by building huge Dyson spheres (artificial structures enclosing stars to collect all their radiant energy) or even by colliding ancient, dying stars to generate new energy sources. Structures such as this would be detectable with normal optical telescopes, and some collided stars have been found, although in situations where they could have arisen naturally.

GILES SPARROW

See also: AMINO ACIDS; ARTIFICIAL LIFE; BACTERIA; BIOSPHERE; CARBON CYCLE; ENERGY; EVOLUTION; INTELLIGENCE; MOLECULAR BIOLOGY; PALEOBIOLOGY.

Further reading:

Dick, S. J. 2001. *Life on Other Worlds: The 20th Century Extraterrestrial Life Debate*. New York: Cambridge University Press.
Harrison, A. A. 1997. *After Contact: The Human Response to Extraterrestrial Life*. Cambridge, Mass.: Perseus Press.
Parker, B. R. 1998. *Alien Life: The Search for Extraterrestrials and Beyond*. Cambridge, Mass.: Perseus Press.
Shostak, S. 1998. *Sharing the Universe: Perspectives on Extraterrestrial Life*. Berkeley: Berkeley Hill Books.

EYES

For many species in the animal kingdom, sight is probably the most complex and important of all the senses. The organ of sight is the eye. Like other sensory organs, eyes have evolved from simple beginnings. The original seeing apparatus, developed by very early life-forms in the sea, was probably a patch of light-sensitive cells that could distinguish light from dark. These patches, or eyespots, are used by some invertebrates today. In planarian flatworms (*Dugesia*), the eyespots are bowl-shaped structures containing black pigment. This pigment shades clusters of light-sensitive cells from all light except that from light sources above or slightly to the front. As a result, flatworms can detect the direction of light and its intensity (see FLATWORMS).

Animals with eyespots can detect movement but are unable to see the objects that are moving. Image formation (vision) requires more complex eyes; eyespots are thought to have gradually evolved into true eyes—highly specialized sensory organs. They developed a lens that could concentrate light on a specific area of light-sensitive cells (photoreceptors), called a retina, to form an image. There are two main types of true eyes: the simple eye, present in all vertebrates and some invertebrates, and the compound eye of arthropods, such as crustaceans and insects.

THE SIMPLE EYE

Most simple eyes, including those of humans, work much as a camera does: they have a lens that can be focused for different distances and a retina at the back of the eye, which corresponds to the camera's film. Camera-like eyes form an upside-down image on the retina, but the brain corrects this topsy-turvy picture during its image processing so that animals with camera-like eyes perceive images the right way up.

A human eye is roughly spherical and is shaped by two pressurized chambers (the vitreous and aqueous humors; see the diagram on page 686), which are

The human eye (an example of a simple eye) is a camera-like organ with a single lens.

CORE FACTS

- Eyes are sensory organs that provide the brain with information to create images.
- There are two main types of eyes: simple eyes and compound eyes.
- Vertebrates, including humans, have simple, camera-like eyes with a single lens.
- The main parts of the mammalian eye are the lens, cornea, conjunctiva, iris, retina, and optic nerve.
- The sensory information collected by the eye is transmitted to the brain via the optic nerve. The visual cortex in the brain is mainly concerned with handling visual information.
- Arthropods have compound eyes with thousands of photoreceptors; other invertebrates have simple eyes.

filled with a clear jelly. The eyeball is surrounded by a tough outer layer, called the sclera—the white of the eye. It is further protected and lubricated by tears, a salty fluid produced by the lacrimal and Harderian glands in the upper eyelid. Attached to each eyeball are six small muscles that move it in synchrony with the other eyeball. Beneath the sclera is the choroid, which contains blood vessels that carry oxygen and nutrients to the eye and remove carbon dioxide and waste. The choroid is dark and prevents the light entering the eye from scattering and causing glare.

Light bounces off an object and enters the eyeball through a transparent front window, called the cornea, which is covered by the conjunctiva, a fine, transparent membrane that covers the surface of the eye and the inner surfaces of the eyelids. The cornea is composed mainly of densely interwoven, transparent collagen fibers and performs much of the initial focusing of the image. Behind the cornea is the aqueous humor, and behind this chamber is the iris, the colored portion of the eye. The iris is a ring of muscle with a hole through its middle (the pupil). In dim light, the iris relaxes and the pupil dilates to admit more light; in bright light, the iris tightens, the pupil contracts, and less light enters the eye.

Immediately behind the iris lies the lens. In birds and mammals, the lens can be focused with a circular, muscular ring called the ciliary muscle. When a person looks at something in the distance, the ciliary muscle is relaxed, and the lens is stretched flat by a ring of elastic ligaments: this process focuses the light from distant objects onto the retina.

When a person looks at something closer, as in reading, the ciliary muscle contracts, and the tension on the lens from the ligaments is removed. The lens then assumes its normal, nearly spherical shape, focusing light reflected from the page onto the retina. In reptiles, fish, and squid, focusing

CONNECTIONS

- **VISION** is the ability to sense with the eyes, which is called sight. In humans, light enters the eye and is absorbed by photoreceptor cells in the retina, which generate electrical impulses. These impulses travel along the optic nerves, conveying messages to the thalamus and visual cortex in the **BRAIN**.

- Some animals, such as **BIRDS OF PREY**, have excellent eyesight, so that they can spy their next meal from a long distance away while they are flying high up in the sky.

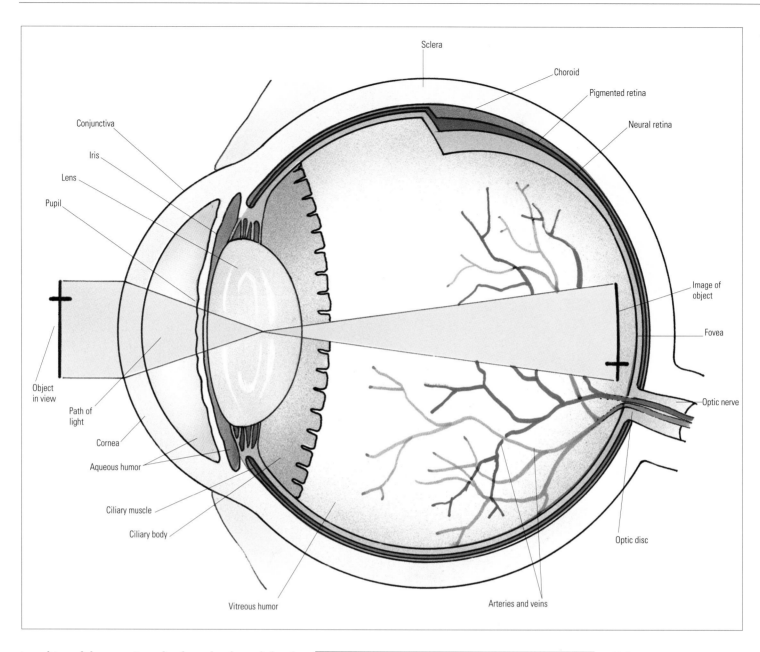

Sclera

Choroid

Pigmented retina

Neural retina

Conjunctiva

Iris

Lens

Pupil

Image of object

Fovea

Object in view

Path of light

Cornea

Aqueous humor

Ciliary muscle

Ciliary body

Optic nerve

Optic disc

Vitreous humor

Arteries and veins

is achieved by moving the lens back and forth within the eye with a series of muscles, instead of changing the shape of the lens.

The image, which is formed by the cornea and lens, falls onto the retina, a complex structure of photoreceptors and processing neurons on the back of the eye. There are two main types of photoreceptors in the retina—rods and cones—that make up the eye's visual "screen." A third type of photoreceptor, discovered at the beginning of the 21st century, appears to control the daily cycle of sleep and wakefulness. The retina requires a constant supply of oxygen and nutrients, and to meet this demand, it has many arteries and veins.

The human eye contains about 125 million rods and 6.5 million cones. The slender rods function best in dim light; they respond to a wide range of colors of light and thus allow people to detect shapes and movement at night. Nocturnal animals and those living in other low-light environments have mainly rods in their retinas. Cones, which are shorter and thicker, function best in bright light. They contain pigments that are most sensitive to

LIGHTING THE WAY

Bioluminescence—the ability of some organisms to generate their own light—is essential in the dark ocean depths. It is very common in cephalopods (octopuses and squid), the largest of which have bioluminescent markings around their eyes, and is created using an enzyme called luciferase, which is produced mostly by bacteria that exist in salt water. In many cases, bioluminescence is used as a form of identification between members of the same species. The patterns of bioluminescent light that organisms emit are to some extent comparable to the color markings of fish living nearer the ocean surface. In other cases, bioluminescence is used to attract prey or stun predators. Bioluminescence is not exclusive to deep-sea fish: it also occurs in the flashlight fish (*Anomalops katoptron*) of the Red Sea. In this species, a gland, present under the eyes, contains luminous bacteria. Bioluminescence also occurs in some algae and fungi and in insects such as fireflies (see BIOLUMINESCENCE).

Light enters the eye through the pupil, and is focused by the cornea and lens to produce an upside-down image of the object on the back of the retina.

blue, red, and green light. The different colored cones can respond to light within considerable ranges of wavelengths (colors), but they are named after the wavelength that their pigments respond to most strongly. If one or more types of cones are missing, partial or complete color blindness occurs. Many animals, such as cats, lack cones and so do not have color vision. A person can easily see a zebra in green grass, but to a lion's eye, the zebra's black-and-white stripes blend into the background.

The photoreceptors convert incoming light into nerve impulses. Several layers of processing neurons in the retina then encode this information in their own nerve impulses, which pass into the optic nerve and on to the brain. Where the optic nerve joins the retina, there are no rods or cones, so no image can be seen. This area is called the blind spot. Just above it is the fovea, where the photoreceptors are packed most densely; this is the area of greatest visual acuity (sharpest vision). Cones are most common in the fovea.

Each optic nerve contains about a million nerve fibers. Nerve impulses, transferring information about the color, shape, and motion of whatever comes into view, travel along the optic nerves to the vision centers in the rear of the brain's cerebral cortex. The two optic nerves (one from each eye) meet at the optic chiasma. Here about half of the nerve fibers from each eye cross over to join those of the other side so that each side of the brain receives signals from both eyes (see VISION).

Adaptations

Variations in the structure of the simple eye permit organisms to adapt to specific ways of living. For example, some predatory spiders and birds of prey possess a pit in the retina that works like the rear element of a telephoto lens to magnify the image. This focusing ability and acuity help them hunt. There are more photoreceptors per unit area in birds' retinas, especially in birds of prey, than in the retinas of any other animal. A hawk's vision, for example, is said to be eight times sharper than people's. Some birds of prey may have several foveas (areas of high visual acuity) in one eye, to provide excellent vision both straight ahead and downward.

Other variations of the simple eye are rarer. For example, a mollusk called the chambered nautilus has an eye that creates an inverted image without a lens, just as a pinhole camera does.

A protective device found in many birds, reptiles, amphibians, and some mammals is the nictitating membrane, or third eyelid. This translucent tissue can be drawn over the eyes to keep out harsh light, water, dust, and debris.

The location of the eyes on an animal's head is an indicator of its lifestyle. In predatory animals, the eyes are usually placed toward the front of the head so that their fields of vision overlap, giving greater depth perception (binocular vision). However, animals that are preyed on, such as deer and cattle, need to know what may be approaching them from behind. Therefore their eyes are positioned on the sides of the head, so they have a wide field of view but little binocular vision. Hippopotamus and crocodile eyes are elevated, so that these animals can see even when most of the head is underwater.

THE COMPOUND EYE

Most insects have three simple eyes but use another type of eye—a compound eye—for seeing. It is thought that in some insects, simple eyes stimulate the compound eyes and so quicken their response to changes in brightness. However, moths and bees do not use their simple eyes at all, and those eyes are covered with scales or hairs.

EYE DISORDERS AND DISEASES

Two out of five people in the United States need artificial aids to help them see well, most of them because their natural lenses are incapable of focusing light accurately on the retina. Eyeglasses and contact lenses are artificial lenses designed to correct focusing problems, the most common of which are hyperopia, myopia, and astigmatism.

Farsighted people have a problem focusing on objects that are close up: the condition is called hyperopia. One out of four people in the world have the opposite problem, myopia. They are nearsighted, which means they see close-up objects well, but not objects further away. While eyeglasses and contacts can correct hyperopia and myopia, new surgical procedures, called radial keratotomy and LASIK, are also effective treatments. They involve making incisions in the surface of the cornea to adjust its curvature, and thus its focusing power, to normal values. Another optical defect is astigmatism, where small abnormalities in the curvature of the cornea and/or lens cast an unevenly focused image on the retina. Astigmatism may now be corrected with contact lenses or glasses.

As people live longer, a larger proportion of the population are suffering from degenerative diseases of the eye. One of the most common eye problems are cataracts, where the lens grows cloudy and becomes opaque after a time, blurring and ultimately blocking the image cast by the lens on the retina. Cataracts cause blindness, but the defective natural lens

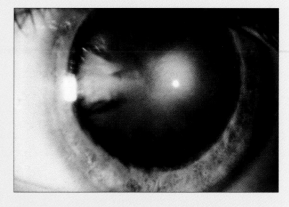

Cataracts (opaque areas of the lens) prevent light from reaching the retina, and can cause blindness.

can be removed surgically, and sight can be restored with an artificial lens.

In glaucoma, fluid builds up within the eyeball, creating excess pressure that reduces blood flow to the retina and may result in blindness. Sometimes the victim is alerted to the presence of glaucoma by eye pain, but often symptoms are not detected until vision has already been damaged.

Inherited (genetic) diseases can also severely damage vision. One of the best known is *retinitis pigmentosa*, which is characterized by progressive degeneration of the retina. More common in males, the condition usually begins with night blindness in adolescence and may lead to total blindness in later life.

Blindness does not necessarily mean total loss of vision. Many disorders impair vision without destroying it. Total or partial blindness due to infectious diseases and poor nutrition is common in developing countries, whereas in developed countries impaired vision is more often due to inherited defects.

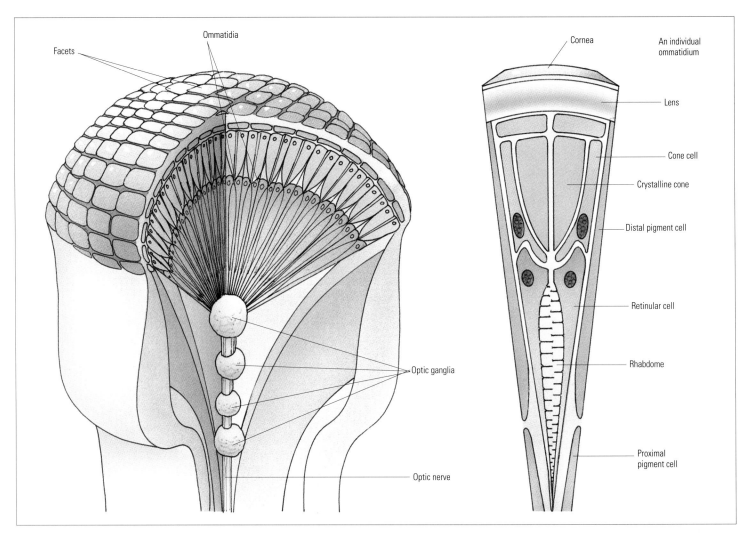

Facets
Ommatidia
Optic ganglia
Optic nerve

Cornea
An individual ommatidium
Lens
Cone cell
Crystalline cone
Distal pigment cell
Retinular cell
Rhabdome
Proximal pigment cell

Insects do most of their seeing with compound eyes, which are based on a completely different design. Instead of using the simple eye's single lens, which focuses light on numerous photoreceptors, the compound eye uses thousands of tiny lens facets, each focusing light on just a few photoreceptors. Each small group of lenses and photoreceptors is called an ommatidium. The image formed by compound eyes is right-side-up, but it is a mosaic picture because each ommatidium is oriented at a slightly different angle from the others. Each ommatidium has a light-sensitive central core, or rhabdome, which is surrounded by retinular cells that receive and transmit the sensory stimulus. Although compound eyes form coarse images, they enable insects to detect the slightest movement. Flies can detect flickers of up to 265 per second (the human eye detects only 45 to 53 flickers).

Compound eyes are also more sensitive to purple and ultraviolet (UV) light than simple eyes. Different flowers reflect purple and UV light differently, so two flowers that appear identical in color to people may appear quite different to insects.

There are two main types of compound eyes. Most are apposition eyes, in which each ommatidium is optically distinct from the others. These eyes exist in most primitive crustaceans, many crabs, and insects such as dragonflies, cockroaches, bees, and ants. Superposition eyes, in which the omma-

tidia cooperate optically, are more sensitive in low-light conditions. Moths, many types of flies, and beetles have superposition eyes. In some moths (as in some vertebrates), a reflecting layer of cells below the retina, called a tapetum, functions at night. In nocturnal species, the tapetum increases the eye's light-gathering capacity by reflecting light that has not been absorbed by the retina from the back of the eye back through the retina, and thus it has a second chance to stimulate the retina.

Diversity
Invertebrate seeing apparatus is much more diverse than that of vertebrates. It ranges from the primitive eyespot to the largest eye in the animal kingdom, that of the giant squid. In some invertebrates, such as jellyfish and starfish, the entire body is light-sensitive. Some organisms, such as arachnids and insects, have multiple compound and simple eyes. The cephalopods (octopus, squid, and cuttlefish) can see as well as or better than most vertebrates (see MOLLUSKS).

T. POWLEDGE

See also: BIOLUMINESCENCE; MOLLUSKS; VISION.

Further reading:
Rodieck, Robert W. 1998. *The First Steps in Seeing.* Sunderland, Mass.: Sinauer Associates.

The compound eye is made up of hundreds or thousands of ommatidia, each of which contains a lens and several photoreceptor cells.

FATS AND OILS

Fats and oils are organic compounds that act as energy stores in plants and animals

Fats and oils are organic (carbon-containing) compounds showing the same basic chemical structure and similar properties. They are important energy stores in both plants and animals, yielding more than twice as much energy per unit weight as carbohydrates. The oil inside seeds allows them to survive long periods of dormancy, while the layers of fat in polar bears allows them to survive the freezing temperatures of the Arctic environment.

Structure

Fats and oils are made of two basic units: glycerol and fatty acids. Glycerol is a three-carbon compound with three hydroxyl (OH) groups attached. Fatty acids have a long carbon chain (4 to 24 carbon atoms long) with a carboxyl group (COOH) at the end (see the box at right). Most fats and oils consist of three fatty acids attached to one glycerol molecule; thus, fats and oils are often called triglycerides. A simple triglyceride has three identical fatty acids; a mixed triglyceride has two or three different fatty acids. Most natural fats, including olive oil and butter, are made up of simple and mixed triglycerides and consist of fatty acids of varying chain length.

Saturated and unsaturated fatty acids

People often talk about saturated and unsaturated fats and oils, but what do these terms mean? The terms apply to the types of bonds in the fatty acid's long carbon chain. Each carbon atom can form four bonds with other atoms. Fatty acids containing only single bonds (when all of the carbon atoms are attached to two hydrogen and two carbon atoms) are saturated. If two of the hydrogen atoms are removed from adjacent carbons, the carbon-to-carbon link becomes a double bond. Fatty acids containing one or more double bonds are said to be unsaturated. Monounsaturated fatty acids contain only one double bond; polyunsaturated fats have more than one double bond.

Describing fatty acids

When chemists describe fatty acids, they use a shorthand notation that indicates first the number of carbon atoms, followed by a colon and the number of double bonds. Stearic acid is an important component of animal fat and some vegetable oils. It has 18 carbon atoms in its chain, and the carbon-carbon bonds are all single. The shorthand notation for stearic acid is 18:0. Oleic acid, the most common fatty acid, also has 18 carbon atoms but has a single double bond. It is present in nearly every vegetable and animal fat. The notation for oleic acid is 18:1.

Fatty acids with double bonds can be divided further into those with cis structures (in which the hydrogen groups lie on one side of the double bond and the carbon groups lie on the other side) and those with trans structures (in which the hydrogen groups

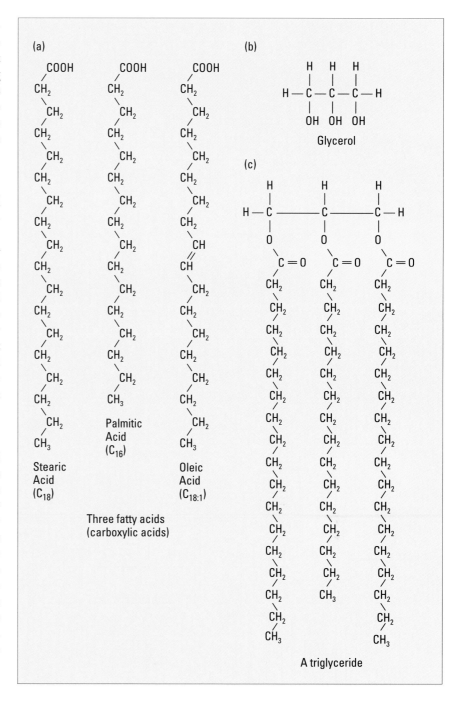

(a) Stearic Acid (C_{18}) — Palmitic Acid (C_{16}) — Oleic Acid ($C_{18:1}$). Three fatty acids (carboxylic acids)
(b) Glycerol
(c) A triglyceride

CORE FACTS

- Fats and oils are organic compounds made of a molecule of glycerol attached to fatty acids.
- Most fats and oils contain three fatty acids and are called triglycerides.
- Fats are solid at room temperature, while oils are liquid. Neither is soluble in water.
- Fats and oils are important energy stores in both animals and plants.

CONNECTIONS

- A layer of lipids, called the blood-brain barrier, surrounds and protects the **BRAIN**.

- In the **NERVOUS SYSTEM**, lipids insulate nerves and promote conduction.

Linolenic acid has cis double bonds (hydrogens on the same side of the bond); eleostearic acid has one cis and two trans double bonds (some hydrogens are on opposite sides).

EATING RIGHT

The U.S. Dietary Guidelines, issued by the U.S. Department of Agriculture and the Department of Health and Human Services, recommend that people consume no more than 30 percent of their total dietary calories as fat, with no more than 10 percent of those calories coming from saturated fat. The average diet of most Americans consists of about 40 to 45 percent of calories from fat. In contrast, fats may supply less than 5 percent of the energy consumed by people in some African and Asian countries.

Some studies that have examined the eating habits of large numbers of people have linked a high-fat diet (mainly triglycerides) with an increased risk of certain cancers, especially cancers of the colon, prostate, and breast. High-fat diets may also be linked to obesity and cardiovascular disease.

People who eat many specific saturated fatty acids (12 to 16 carbon atoms long) are more likely to develop clogged arteries and heart disease than people who eat fewer saturated fatty acids. However, stearic acid, an 18-carbon saturated fatty acid in animal fat, does not appear to be harmful. By reducing their intake of saturated fatty acids, people can lower their chances of developing heart disease. One way to cut down on saturated fatty acids is to eat monounsaturated and polyunsaturated fatty acids instead. Fish oils containing long chain (20- and 22-carbon) omega-3 polyunsaturated fatty acids may reduce triglyceride levels in the blood, so people who eat one or two servings of fish each week may lower their chances of developing heart disease. Some scientists believe that omega-3 fatty acids may also help to prevent the development of inflammatory diseases such as rheumatoid arthritis and asthma.

Because animal studies have shown that too much omega-6 polyunsaturated fatty acids, such as linoleic acid, may promote the development of some cancers, doctors recommend that no more than 10 percent of the total calories in the diet should be from omega-6 polyunsaturated fatty acids.

Important dietary saturated fatty acids and their sources

Lauric (12:0)	Coconut, palm kernel
Myristic (14:0)	Coconut, palm kernel, butter
Palmitic (16:0)	Palm, cocoa butter, butter, animal fat

Important dietary monounsaturated fatty acids and their sources

Oleic (18:1)	Olive, canola, peanut

Important dietary polyunsaturated fatty acids and their sources

Linoleic (18:2ω6)	Safflower, sunflower, soybean, corn
Linolenic (18:3ω3)	Canola, soybean
Eicosapentanoic (20:5ω3)	Fish oil
Docosahexanoic (22:6ω3)	Fish oil

lie on either side of the double bond). Most naturally occurring fatty acids are *cis*. This structure gives the molecule a pronounced kink; individual molecules are then unable to pack closely together, and thus, these fats are fluid. The trans form is linear; this structure allows the chains to pack tightly together and makes the fat more solid. Trans fatty acids are not commonly found in naturally occurring fats and oils, although some are found in milk and butter.

Polyunsaturated fats

The two main types of polyunsaturated fatty acids are classified by the location of the first double bond in the molecule. A common polyunsaturated fatty acid is linoleic acid, which has two double bonds. The first double bond is six carbon atoms from the omega end of the molecule; it is an omega-6 fatty acid. The omega end is the one with a methyl carbon group (CH_3) attached to it. The chemistry shorthand for linoleic acid is 18:2ω6 (ω is the Greek letter for omega). Another 18-carbon fatty acid, linolenic acid, has three double bonds; the first of these is located three carbon atoms from the omega end (18:3ω3), so linolenic acid is called an omega-3 fatty acid.

Scientific studies have shown that both omega-6 and omega-3 fatty acids are important in the diet and may play separate roles in the prevention of some diseases (see the box at left).

Fats, oils, lipids: what is the difference?

The term lipid is a general one referring to natural substances that are not soluble in water but are soluble in organic solvents, such as ether and chloroform. Common lipids include fats and oils, fatty acids, waxes, phospholipids, and cholesterol.

Although the distinction between fats and oils is somewhat vague, oils generally have a melting point below room temperature (cooking oil), while fats have a higher melting point and are solid at room temperature (butter). The melting point of fats and oils depends on the carbon chain length and the amount of unsaturation (double bonds) in the fatty acid chains. Triglycerides with a lot of unsaturated fatty acids are liquid at room temperature and so are considered oils; triglycerides with a lot of saturated fatty acids are solid at room temperature and are called fats. Vegetable oils tend to have a lot of unsaturated fatty acids, and animal fats tend to have more saturated fatty acids. Thus, people pour oil and vinegar on their salads but spread butter on bread (although butter left out of the refrigerator on a hot summer day may certainly become more pourable, and some oils become very thick if stored in the refrigerator).

Waxes, such as beeswax and carnauba wax, are related to fats and oils; they are esters of long-chain (16 or more carbon atoms) fatty acids and long-chain (16 or more carbon atoms) alcohols. They are excellent waterproofers. Phospholipids are triglyceride molecules with hydrophilic (water-loving) phosphoric acid groups substituted for one

Pure olive oil, extracted from the pulp and pits of the olives, is an important source of oleic acid.

or more of the fatty acid groups. They are made in the body and are important components of all cell membranes (see CELL BIOLOGY). Phospholipid molecules contain combinations of saturated and unsaturated fatty acids so that the membrane is fluid at normal cell temperature.

Cholesterol, a large alcohol containing four carbon rings, is not structurally related to fats and oils but is often combined with fatty acids in the body to make cholesterol esters. Cholesterol is an essential component of cell membranes and is also the precursor of several other compounds important to the body's function (see CHOLESTEROL). Plants contain similar compounds called phytosterols.

Functions of fats and oils

Fats and oils are an important form of stored energy for plants and animals. Cells free this energy by breaking down fatty acids into carbon dioxide and water. This process takes place primarily in the mitochondria. Triglycerides provide nine kilocalories of energy per gram, as compared with the four kilocalories per gram that carbohydrates provide. In addition, the body cannot store glycogen, which is the storage form of glucose, in the same amounts or for as long as it can store fat. If a person's intake of food or drink provides more carbohydrates than their body needs, they are converted to fat.

One can think of the body as a bank. Someone uses money from their checking account (the carbohydrate stores) for everyday purchases. If they deplete the money from their checking

USES OF FATS AND OILS

Many everyday products are made from fats and oils. The ancient Sumerians learned how to make soap more than 4,000 years ago by adding a strong alkali to an oil, still the first step in soap making (the alkali may be sodium hydroxide, for example). The most important fats used are tallow, from animal fat, and coconut oil. Soap molecules have long, hydrophobic (water-fearing) fatty acid tails and hydrophilic (water-loving) heads. In water, the molecules clump together around water-insoluble particles such as dirt or grease, with the hydrophobic tails in the center (see right).

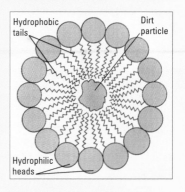

Then the water carries the particles away with the soap. Glycerol, a by-product of soap making, is used to make glycerin—the raw material of nitroglycerin, an important part of many explosive devices. Another form of nitroglycerin is nonexplosive and useful in treating the heart condition angina pectoris.

Cocoa butter and almond, olive, and palm oil are all widely used by the cosmetics and pharmaceutical industries in creams, ointments, and lotions. These industries have now begun to use microscopic spheres made of lipids, much like the basic structure of cell membranes, called liposomes. Liposomes can encapsulate moisturizers or fragrances in cosmetics. Pharmaceutical companies have begun testing drugs enclosed in liposomes, which can be designed to deliver the drug over a period of time or to target the drug to a certain part of the body.

Oils are essential in many liquid paints and varnishes to help them form hard, tough solids as they dry. The most widely used drying oils in the paint industry are linseed, dehydrated castor, soybean, and fish oils. In the past, animal and vegetable oils were used as lubricating oils in machinery, before being replaced largely by less expensive petroleum-derived mineral oils. Recent trends may bring the more environmentally friendly animal and vegetable oils back into wider use.

MAKING MARGARINE AND SHORTENING

Margarine was invented by a French chemist in the latter half of the 19th century. The French emperor Napoleon III offered a prize to anyone who could develop a good butter substitute. Hippolyte Mege-Mouries (1817–1880) made the first margarine from a component of rendered beef fat (called oleo oil; hence the older name, oleomargarine) and gave it a butter-like flavor by mixing it with skim milk and digesting the mixture with enzymes extracted from cow udders. Not a very healthy substitute for butter, but the original intent was to produce a less expensive product.

Margarine still costs less than butter, but most people now buy it for health reasons. Margarine is made with purified vegetable oils from soybeans, corn, cottonseeds, or other sources. The oils are usually blended together and then partially hydrogenated to make them semisolid. Hydrogenation solidifies oils by adding hydrogen atoms to the double bonds in the fatty acids, decreasing the amount of double bonds. The level of hydrogenation must be just right so that the margarine is spreadable at room temperature but melts quickly in the mouth. The hydrogenated oils are mixed with skim milk and other dairy ingredients to give them a sweet flavor. Food coloring, vitamin A, and agents that help the margarine keep its smooth texture and freshness are also added.

The process of hydrogenation produces trans fatty acids, as compared with the usual cis fatty acids. Although small amounts of trans fatty acids occur naturally in milk and butter, the increase in the use of tub margarines and their hydrogenated oils has resulted in an increase in trans fatty acids in the modern diet. Some scientists have wondered whether trans fatty acids might contribute to heart disease or cancer more than the cis forms of the same fatty acids. However, at present, all of the available data show that trans fatty acids are not more harmful than their cis counterparts.

account or if they need to make a large purchase, they can withdraw money from their savings (the fat stores). An obese person has accumulated a hefty savings account. Some organs, such as the liver and heart, require large amounts of energy to keep them working at their optimum rate, and more than half of this energy comes from fat. Hibernating animals live off their fat stores during the winter months, while warm-blooded Arctic and Antarctic animals, such as seals and walruses, also use fat, stored in fat cells (adipocytes), as an insulating layer.

Essential fatty acids

Linoleic and linolenic acids are two essential fatty acids that the body needs but cannot make. They must come from the diet; because these fatty acids are plentiful in chicken and in many plants, obtaining them is no problem. The body uses linoleic acid to make arachidonic acid, which is a building block for prostaglandins and thromboxanes. prostaglandins regulate hormones, cause smooth muscles to contract, and cause inflammation. Thromboxanes regulate the activities of blood platelets. Linolenic acid appears to be essential to the structure and function of cell membranes in the eye and the central nervous system.

S. LATTA

See also: CELL BIOLOGY; CHOLESTEROL; CONNECTIVE TISSUE; ENERGY; WAXES.

Further reading:

Chow, C. K. 1992. *Fatty Acids and Their Health Implications.* New York: Marcel Dekker.
Enig, M. G. 2000. *Know Your Fats: The Complete Primer for Understanding the Nutrition of Fats, Oils, and Cholesterol.* Bethesda Press Inc.
Erasmus, E. 1999. *Fats That Heal, Fats That Kill: The Complete Guide to Fats, Oils, Cholesterol and Human Health.* Vancouver, B.C.: Alive Books.

Warm-blooded animals in cold climates, such as the polar bear seen swimming above, have a thick layer of fat to keep them warm.

FEEDING

Feeding is the process in which living organisms obtain nourishment from other organisms

A male lion (Panthera leo) feeding on the carcass of a newly killed wildebeest on the African plains.

Some people are gourmands; they live to eat. This lifestyle does not exist in the wild. In nature organisms eat to live; they must take in just enough nourishment to survive and reproduce. Feeding is the process of obtaining nourishment: it involves finding, eating, and digesting food. Every living organism on Earth forms part of a food web of producers and consumers (see FOOD WEBS).

The most basic and earliest feeders are the single-celled organisms, such as bacteria and protozoans. Protozoans feed on bacteria, microscopic algae, or other protozoans, which they "swallow" whole, a process called phagocytosis. Amoebas are phagocytes. These gel-like protozoans move by creating false feet (pseudopods) that surge outward from the amoeba's body. When a pseudopod makes contact with a possible meal, the amoeba surrounds and traps the prey and then digests it alive.

From single-celled beginnings, animals evolved that ate plants, both in the sea and on land. Others evolved as hunters and flesh eaters. As millions of species evolved and adapted to changing ecosystems, feeding strategies became widely diverse.

Herbivores

Plant-eating animals are called herbivores. Eating plants has several advantages: in many ecosystems plants are abundant, they stay in one place, and their location is generally predictable. There are also disadvantages: the walls of plant cells are made of cellulose, a highly indigestible, rigid material. Herbivorous animals have specialized digestive systems and rely on bacteria in the gut to break down cellulose and release its energy. In addition, plant material generally contains little protein (seeds are an exception). Herbivores must spend a lot of time getting the nourishment they need, and while doing so, they are often vulnerable to predators.

Grazers

Many mammalian herbivores, such as cattle, sheep, horses, and rabbits, have adapted to feeding on grasses. Grasses are particularly popular and, when young, contain a relative abundance of proteins in additon to carbohydrates. Some hooved mammals, such as horses, have sharp incisors, so they can cut through tough grass stems. Cattle twist grass stems around their tongues and rip them free. Sheep eat grass much as cattle do, but their split upper lips

CORE FACTS

- Feeding is the way in which organisms obtain nourishment from other organisms.
- The term covers the processes of finding, eating, and digesting food.
- Organisms may be phagocytes, herbivores, carnivores, scavengers, parasites, omnivores, or filter feeders.
- An animal's anatomy, behavioral traits, and physiology dictate how it obtains food, what food it eats, and how it digests it.

CONNECTIONS

● Much of the daily activity of life-forms is devoted to feeding, and evidence supporting Charles **DARWIN**'s theories have been found by observing adaptations and specializations that improve a species' feeding strategies.

● In **SYMBIOSIS**, two organisms have a mutually beneficial relationship. For example, some birds hitch a ride with large herbivores, and feed off the blood-sucking parasites that infest the animal hide.

● Food is broken down inside cells to provide **ENERGY** and the raw materials for growth and repair.

Domestic cattle are typical grazing herbivores, feeding on grass. Although grass is one of the most nutritious of plant foods, grazing animals require complex digestive systems to process the food they take in (cows have stomachs with four chambers) and rely on bacteria within their stomachs to help them break down the cellulose in the cell walls of grass.

Grass and leaves are the most obvious plant foods. In harsh climates, animals look for varied forms of nourishment, which also minimizes competition. Grouse feed on the buds and shoots of heather plants. Boars, warthogs, and baboons dig beneath plants to gather the nutrient-rich roots, tubers, or bulbs. Some primates, such as the white-eared marmoset (*Callithrix argentata*), scrape away outer bark with their teeth and lick sweet sap with their tongue. Insects, such as aphids, also eat plant sap and are sometimes so expert at getting it that they are considered pests that destroy crops.

Other herbivores are adapted to eating seeds or fruit. Many species of birds, from sparrows to parrots, have beaks that enable them to eat the seeds or nuts of grasses, herbs, shrubs, and trees. Bears, raccoons, monkeys, and toucans eat fruit, which is high in sugar and therefore rich in energy. Bees, bats, and hummingbirds that sip flower nectar are also classed as herbivores.

Carnivores

An animal that has taken energy from plants is itself an abundant energy source: its meat is highly nutritious and full of protein. So a whole range of carnivores has adapted to exploit other animals as food sources. These adaptations are as varied as the animal species preyed on.

For example, big cats, such as tigers, have become very specialized hunting machines. Their front-facing eyes give them excellent depth perception, which enables them to judge precisely the location of prey. They are capable of sudden bursts of speed to get to their victim. Their long, sharp claws help them catch and hold prey. Their immensely strong jaws can clamp around the prey's throat, snapping its neck and killing it instantly, or strangling it slowly. Like most predatory mammals, including wolves and dogs, these large cats have fangs for ripping flesh, while their back teeth are sharply pointed for shredding and slicing flesh (see CATS).

Big cats have adapted to kill other large animals, often after a vigorous struggle. Other carnivores are adapted to catch different prey. Among mammals, for example, anteaters have very long, sticky tongues to seek out and collect swarming ants. Among birds, oystercatchers have specialized bills for dealing with oysters, mussels, and limpets. Herons have long, sharp bills for spearing fish or frogs. Raptors—birds of prey such as eagles, hawks, and owls—seize prey in their strong claws and rip open and shred the flesh with their hooked beaks (see BIRDS OF PREY).

Sedentary hunters

Some carnivores simply wait for prey to come to them. In the insect world, for example, the long arms of the preying mantis enable it to reach out swiftly to seize its insect prey, and many spiders guard their webs and wait for prey to land. Chameleons sit quietly camouflaged on tree branches waiting for a bug to pass by. Their

enable them to feed on very short grasses close to the ground. Some rodents, such as prairie dogs, have sharp incisors to bite through grass blades. Rabbits also have incisors, but these teeth gnaw the grass instead of cut it. To compensate for the heavy wear on these teeth, they grow continuously during the animal's life (see TEETH).

All mammalian grasseaters have strong, fairly flat-topped back teeth. These grinding teeth pulverize grass and its cellulose (see CELLULOSE) to release nutritious substances from inside the plant cells.

Browsers

Browsers are herbivores, such as deer. They eat leaves and other plant parts and come in all shapes and sizes. For example, West African duikers (*Cephalopus* spp.) are like miniature antelopes, just 10 inches (26 cm) high. They eat the leaves of one type of tiny forest bush. Giraffes have adapted to feeding on the topmost leaves of trees in the savanna. These adaptations enable animal species to exploit a food source with little competition.

In rain forests, where most greenery towers hundreds of yards above the ground, arboreal (tree-living) monkeys rip leaves off the trees with their hands, and sloths and countless species of insects feast on the abundance of leaves in the rain forest canopy (see INSECTS; TROPICAL RAIN FOREST BIOMES).

independently roving eyes can scan 180 degrees. When an insect is sighted, a chameleon shoots out its sticky-tipped tongue (fully half the length of its body) and snares and hauls in the meal—all in 40 milliseconds. Ant lions are insects that bury themselves in holes in the sand. The sloping sides of the hole prevent ants that fall in from clambering up the sliding sand; thus, they become trapped inside. The ant lion senses the movement and flicks sand at the ants to knock them down into its grasp.

Scavengers

Some animals wait for other carnivores to make a kill or locate animals that have died from other reasons and then move in to eat. These scavengers require various skills. They must locate dead meat quickly: vultures, for example, flying high above the plains, have excellent eyesight. They also need to be able to use the parts of a carcass that other animals leave behind. For example, some vultures have strong beaks that are able to break open bones and devour the nutritious marrow inside.

Parasites

Parasites live in or on another animal and feed on the host's food or its body (see PARASITES). Some parasites, such as tapeworms, may spend their whole lives in the gut of another animal; others may be parasitic for only part of their lives. Most parasites do not kill their hosts. Animals, including people, live with lice as permanent residents on their skin sucking their blood. Some animals are parasitoids and are fatal to their hosts. There are species of wasps that lay eggs in live caterpillars, for example. The wasp larvae grow by eating the caterpillar alive from the inside out.

Omnivores

Omnivores, such as humans and apes, can exploit almost any food source (including both plants and animals) and are highly adaptable to changing conditions. Bears are also omnivores, eating a varied diet of berries, meat, fish, and just about anything they can find (including garbage). Raccoons are omnivorous and are adaptable feeders, and thus, they have adapted well to human encroachment on their natural habitat.

Filter feeders

The oceans, particularly coastal regions, are teeming with minute organisms, both plant and animal, that float in the water. Many marine animals have adapted to feed on this microscopic bounty. These animals include barnacles, which filter their food out of the water. When feeding, the barnacles use kicking actions of their modified legs. They use these feathery body appendages to sweep small zooplankton and bacteria from the water.

Some waterfowl, such as shoveler ducks (*Anas clypeata*), filter minute plants from the water with their beaks, which contain a type of sieve. Another filter feeder is the flamingo, which submerges its

large beak in the water with its head upside down. It then sweeps its head from side to side, pumping water through a sievelike structure in its upper jaw. Finally, its tongue presses out the water, leaving behind a mouthful of tiny animals and plants.

Baleen whales are also masters of filter feeding. These toothless whales filter krill (planktonic crustaceans and larvae), their principal food, from ocean water through two dense rows of plates suspended from their jaw. The hundreds of plates are rimmed with overlapping hairs that form a mat. The whales take in water by opening the mouth and then force it out through the mat and the plates, the krill being trapped inside.

Carnivorous plants

Some plants must supplement the food produced by photosynthesis because they live in environments such as bogs and moorlands, where the soil lacks nitrogen. These carnivorous plants use

Baleen whales feeding on small marine crustaceans called krill. These whales lack teeth but have a baleen—two rows of horny plates attached along the upper jaw—which they use to filter out planktonic crustaceans and larvae from large quantities of seawater.

AMPHIBIOUS ALTERATIONS

Some animals change their diet at different stages in their life cycle. Frogs are a good example. When tadpoles emerge from their eggs, they are totally aquatic: they breathe through gills and have a tail for swimming. Tadpoles are herbivores, adapted to eat aquatic vegetation and algae. They have a beaklike mouth for scraping algae off rocks, and many tadpoles are filterfeeders.

As tadpoles grow, they metamorphose (change shape). The tadpole becomes a frog, an amphibious animal adapted to living in water and on land. Adult frogs are insect-eating carnivores. As the tadpole metamorphoses into an adult frog, its beakish mouth becomes the familiar wide frog's mouth. The frog develops a long, sticky tongue, which it flicks out to catch its insect prey. A frog's tongue is attached to the front of its mouth, not the back. When prey is caught, the tongue flips the insect toward the back of the mouth, where it is swallowed.

animals as a source of nitrogen (see CARNIVOROUS PLANTS). Carnivorous plants have developed various ways to catch their prey. For example, the Venus's-flytrap (*Dionaea muscipula*) capture's insects by using a hinged trap, which snaps shut on the victim. Other plants, such as sundews (*Drosera* spp.), secrete a sticky liquid to trap small insects.

Feeding adaptations

How an animal species obtains food and what types of food it eats are inherited along with its anatomy and physiology—the form of its body and the way its body works. Thus, deer have bodies, teeth, and digestive systems adapted to browsing, chewing, and digesting leaves. A tiger takes energy from the body of another animal, and it is totally unsuited to getting nourishment from plants. In addition, theories exist to account for the prevalence of host-specific herbivorous insects, which themselves account for much of the world's existing biodiversity.

The golden-winged sunbird (Nectarinia reichenovi) fiercely defends its feeding territories to have access to the nectar that forms the major part of its diet.

The Galapagos finches studied by Charles Darwin provide a classic example (see DARWIN, CHARLES; NATURAL SELECTION). Although only one seed-eating finch species is thought to have reached the isolated Galapagos Islands many thousands of years ago, the variety of food available on the islands provided the opportunity for diversification. New species arose, as some finches developed large, powerful beaks able to crack open nuts, and others evolved thin beaks for catching and eating insects.

Whatever the feeding strategy a species has evolved, it faces a trade-off between the energy value of the food it eats and the amount of energy it must expend to obtain it. To survive, the animal must take in more energy than it uses. Penguins may travel for days before they find shoals of highly nutritious fish. Herbivores generally do not have to go so far to find their food, but because it contains fewer calories than carnivores' food, they have to spend more time and therefore energy eating and digesting their food to survive. Elephants usually spend at least 12 hours every day finding and eating the 100 pounds (45 kg) of food each adult needs.

The golden-winged sunbird (*Nectarinia reichenowi*) feeds on the nectar of certain flowers. A sunbird may defend a rich patch of blooming flowers against all other birds that try to feed there. Fighting or chasing away other birds takes a lot of energy. However, sunbirds that defend nectar-rich territories save energy in the long run because they do not have to fly from one flower patch to another looking for nectar.

Animals have evolved to make the best use of the available food sources. However, competition for survival is still literally a matter of life and death. The young, the old, and the sick are most likely to fail to find enough food to meet their energy needs, and their deaths keep animal populations in check.

The deaths of both plants and animals also provide food for other organisms, apart from being a vital food source for scavengers. When life began on Earth, so did death. Among the earliest organisms to evolve were probably bacteria that fed on the dead. Saprobes, or saprophytes, break down the tissues of dead organisms. The bacteria break down dead cells, releasing the nutrients into the environment. This decaying process makes substances available to other organisms. Saprophytic bacteria and fungi are invaluable recyclers of the materials that support life.

N. GOLDSTEIN

See also: BIRDS OF PREY; CARNIVOROUS PLANTS; CATS; CELLULOSE; DIGESTIVE SYSTEMS; FOOD WEBS; INSECTS; NATURAL SELECTION; NUTRITION; PARASITES; TEETH; TROPICAL RAIN FOREST BIOMES.

Further reading:

Robbins, C. T. 1993. *Wildlife Feeding and Nutrition.* 2nd ed. San Diego: Academic Press.
Schwenk, Kurt, ed. 2000. *Feeding: Form, Function, and Evolution in Tetrapod Vertebrates.* New York: Academic Press.

FEET

Feet are body structures used by animals for movement, defense, and feeding

With their variety of uses, feet are important and versatile body structures in the animal kingdom. They have several different forms and functions. For humans, feet represent stability and movement; for other animals, feet are also a means of feeding, tasting, and even smelling.

The vertebrate foot

In vertebrates the foot is defined as the part of the leg below the ankle joint on which the body stands and moves. The Greek word for foot is *podos*; many words referring to feet, such as *podiatry* (medical care of the foot), contain the root word *pod*.

In mammals the foot consists of the ankle bones, metatarsals, and digits. These parts of the foot can be compared to the human hand because hands are modified feet. The ankle bones correspond to the wrist, the metatarsals to the palm, and the digits to the fingers and thumb, the big toe being the thumb (see HANDS).

The foot of an adult human has 26 bones, 19 muscles, and about 30 joints and acts as a supple shock absorber when the heel hits the ground. The foot also acts as a strong lever to push the body forward from the toes when walking. Humans have an arch on the soles of the feet that provides a degree of leverage.

The feet of mammals vary greatly, and their size and shape depend largely on how much the mammal climbs, walks, or runs. Different mammals walk on different parts of their feet, and they can be placed into three groups according to which parts they walk on. To visualize the differences, place the palm of the hand down on a table.

Monkeys, humans, bears, apes, and some other animals walk with all three parts of their foot in contact with the ground. This is the position of the hand when the fingers, palm, and wrist all touch the table. However, rabbits, rodents, dogs, and cats walk only on their digits, with all or most of the digits touching the ground. This is the position of the hand when the palm is raised off the table with the fingers still on the table. These animals usually move more quickly, more quietly, and more nimbly than the first group of animals.

The third group, the fastest animals of all, includes hoofed animals (ungulates) such as horses, goats, deer, and antelope. They run on only the tips of one or two digits. If the hand is raised even farther, so that just the tip of the middle finger touches the table, this represents the horse's foot. The horse has a single hoof; the other digits (fingers and thumb) have disappeared or been reduced through evolution. Goats, deer, and sheep have retained the equivalent of the middle finger and the ring finger. These animals have a cloven hoof, which is really two separate digits (toes).

Most birds' feet possess four digits, although there are some that have only two or three digits. In four-toed birds, the three front toes usually point forward, while the rear toe, which corresponds to the big toe of the human foot, points backward.

Many birds' feet are adapted for perching. The tendons that bend the toes are arranged so that when a bird alights on a branch, the weight of the bird bends the leg, and the toes flex and grasp the perch. Perching birds can sleep while sitting on a branch. The more deeply they sleep, the less likely they are to fall off, as a relaxed bird puts more weight on its legs, causing its leg joints to bend even further and their toes to grip even tighter.

Opposable toes

Like the thumbs of human hands, the big toes of some primates, such as lemurs, monkeys, and apes,

Feet come in various shapes and sizes, and different animals walk on different parts of their foot.

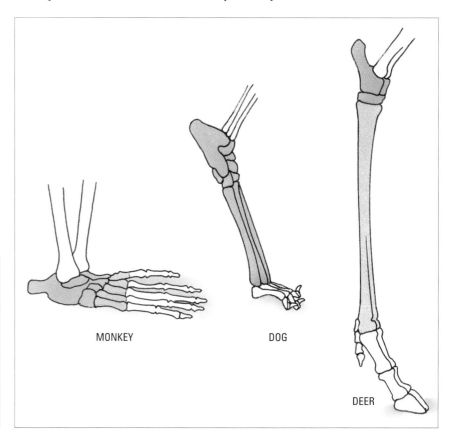

MONKEY DOG

DEER

CORE FACTS

■ Feet have a variety of uses, including movement, feeding, digging, fighting, and as sensory organs.

■ The vertebrate foot is the part of the leg below the ankle joint, on which the body stands and moves.

■ Invertebrates have different types of feet. Gastropods have a large muscular foot; bivalves have a bladelike foot. The foot of cephalopods surrounds the animal's head, forming tentacles.

are opposable. The human hand is unusual because it has an opposable thumb, that is, the thumb is able to touch the tips of all the other digits on the hand. This ability gives the human hand great precision and strength for gripping. The human foot, however, has lost its ability to grip. It has no opposable toe and possesses very short, parallel toes.

However, people can still learn to use their feet for grasping. In the 1960s, for example, a drug called thalidomide was given to pregnant women to relieve nausea. The drug caused a birth defect, called phocomelia, in which babies were born with short arms and fused fingers. These children learned to perform many tasks, such as feeding themselves, writing, and painting, using their feet in place of their hands.

The rear toe of some birds is also opposable, although it lacks the precise movement of the human thumb. Birds, such as woodpeckers, have a fourth toe that can be bent sideways to make the foot more flexible. This movement allows the woodpeckers to cling to the side of tree trunks as well as to perch on branches.

Some parrots have two outer toes that point backward and grip in the opposite direction of their two forward-pointing toes. These parrots are the most dextrous of all birds because the layout of their feet enables them to use the feet like human hands, holding and manipulating objects close to their bill. This adaptation is absent in species of parrots that feed solely on the ground.

Fish hawks, also called ospreys (*Pandion haliaetus*), have the typical bird foot, with three front toes and one rear toe. However, one of the front toes is reversible; it can also point backward. This mobility, combined with strong feet and tiny spikes on the underside of the toes, allows the fish hawk to keep hold of its slippery prey.

Many flightless flat-footed birds, such as ostriches (*Struthio camelus*) and emus (*Dromaius novaehollandiae*), have lost their opposable rear toe and have only two or three front toes. This arrangement gives their feet a hooflike appearance and enables the birds to escape danger by running more quickly. They may reach speeds of around 30 miles per hour (50 km/h).

Defensive feet

While most animals use their feet for walking and running, some animals also use their feet for fighting. Common cassowaries (*Casuarius casuarius*), large ostrichlike Australian birds, have powerful legs and feet with sharp claws on their inner toe, which, like ostrich feet, can deliver a fatal kick. Several hoofed animals, including moose and donkeys, also strike out with their front feet. Mules and horses, however, are well known for kicking out with their hind feet.

Some slugs (snail-like gastropod mollusks that lack a shell) have developed another use for their feet when they are attacked. They can self-amputate the

hind part of the foot, leaving it wriggling on the ground to distract a predator while they escape (see also the box below).

Gripping

Feet that do not have opposable toes may have other adaptations to allow them to grip tightly. The underside of a starfish, for example, contains hundreds of tiny tube feet, called podia, which grip the bottom with their tips and pull the animal along. The foot

Owls' feet possess sharp claws, so the bird can catch, kill, and carry prey.

OTHER TYPES OF FEET

Invertebrate feet are very different from those of vertebrates. The feet of mollusks such as gastropods, bivalves, and cephalopods come in different forms. Gastropod means "bellyfooted" and refers to the broad, flat, muscular foot of animals such as snails and slugs. The foot moves by a series of waves that proceed from the back to the front of the foot. In some species, tiny beating hairs called cilia propel the animal on a layer of slime, which is secreted at the front of the foot. Bivalves are mollusks with two shells, such as clams and oysters. The pointed, bladelike foot of these animals sticks out between the two shells into the sand or mud, where it swells at its end to get a grip. Foot muscles then pull the shell forward or down so that the clam can dig. Cephalopods ("head-footed" animals) include squid and octopuses. Their foot surrounds the head and forms arms or tentacles, which have suckers to grip the surface. The most primitive type of foot known is a pseudopod ("false foot"); it is not an organ but a temporary feature of some protozoans such as amoebas. The cytoplasm of the amoeba streams in one direction, forming a bulge, or pseudopod, in the cell membrane, which anchors against the substrate. The organism then moves, as its remaining cytoplasm flows into the pseudopod.

of some bivalve mollusks secretes threads that harden on contact with water, forming a glue. In this way, the gripping foot anchors the animal to one site so that it is not washed away by the current.

Some animals produce glue so they can move on sloping surfaces. Tree frogs (family Hylidae), for example, have large pads on the end of their toes that secrete a thin adhesive fluid. At any one time, one set of feet sticks to the surface of trees, while the other set of feet moves forward.

Houseflies (*Musca* spp. and *Fannia* spp.) use two mechanisms to move on difficult surfaces: their curved claws cling to rough surfaces, and hairs on their feet secrete a sticky substance for clinging to smooth surfaces. These mechanisms are so effective that flies are able to walk upside down (see FLIES). Some geckos (lizards) use tiny hairs on their toes to literally stick themselves to a wall or ceiling as they walk.

Most substances that are secreted from feet permit animals to stick to a surface, but snails secrete a slippery carpet of slime to lubricate the ground underneath them. This slime reduces the friction that is created as the snails slither along.

Communication
Flies, moths, and butterflies can taste and smell through sensory organs on their feet. Spiders' feet are equipped to detect vibrations, and the spiders can tell if vibrations in their webs are made by struggling prey, the wind, or a predator. Some male spiders can find a mate by following the vibrations in their webs sent out by the females. Crabs and most other crustaceans can also taste with their feet.

Bannertail kangaroo rats (*Dipodomys spectabilis*) also communicate with their feet. They signal to their neighbors and defend their territories by drumming their feet on the ground. Each rat has a particular drumming tone, and some can produce blaring sounds. Many other animals use stamping on the ground to communicate aggression or, in the case of dogs, willingness to play.

Adaptations
The outside toes of the feet of kingfishers (in the family Alcedinidae) are fused, to give them strength for digging. These birds excavate tunnels in earthen banks, where they lay their eggs. Spadefoot toads (family Pelobantidae) get their name from a broad, sharp, horny "spade" on the inside of their hind feet, which they use to dig a burrow.

Wallace's flying frog (*Rhacophorus sygropalmetus*) has large, fully webbed feet, and the tips of its digits are expanded to provide a large surface area so that the frog can parachute from one tree to another. The toes of many aquatic birds, such as ducks and geese, are also webbed; this feature enables them to paddle. Many swimming mammals, such as otters, muskrats, and beavers, share this trait.

The seal's hand and foot bones are modified to form large, spreading flippers. The back limbs do most of the swimming, while the front flippers are used for steering. Although they do not look like hands or feet, the seal's flippers still have the five digits that are typical of many mammals. Dolphins and whales have lost all parts of their hind legs except the pelvic bones (and these are very small) and use their tails for swimming.

M. ALLEN

See also: ANATOMY; DARWIN, CHARLES; EVOLUTION; FLIES; HANDS; PERCHING BIRDS; SKELETAL SYSTEMS.

Further reading:
Kent, G. C. 2000. *Comparative Anatomy of the Vertebrates*. Burr Ridge, Ill.: WCB-McGraw-Hill.
Schmidt-Nielsen, Knut. 1997. *Animal Physiology*. New York: Cambridge University Press.
Vonhoff, J., and J. Kozak. 2000. *Fixing Your Feet: Prevention and Treatments for Athletes*. Fremont, Calif.: Footwork Publications.

FOOT DISORDERS

Tight shoes can cause several foot disorders. Bunions are painful swellings at the base of the big toe. They occur when the big toe is pushed inward in the direction of the second toe. The joint at the base of the big toe sticks out, and a small sac of fluid, called a bursa, develops over the joint and becomes swollen, inflamed, and painful as it rubs against the shoe.

Corns are the most common skin problem on the feet. They are small, cone-shaped areas of thickened skin, often found between the toes. A hard corn shows that the skin is being rubbed. Verrucae are plantar warts found on the sole (the plantar surface of the foot); they are sometimes misnamed plantar's warts. Like warts found on other parts of the body, these verrucae are caused by viruses and are easily spread by close contact with the infected area. Although many verrucae clear up on their own, some may need to be removed using chemicals or laser treatment. Athlete's foot is a fungal infection that causes itchy, irritating patches of skin between the toes. It can be treated with antifungal lotions or tablets. Clubfoot is a congenital deformity that affects more boys than girls. The foot curls under and inward, so the child walks on the top and outside edge of the foot. Clubfoot is treated with plaster casts or surgery.

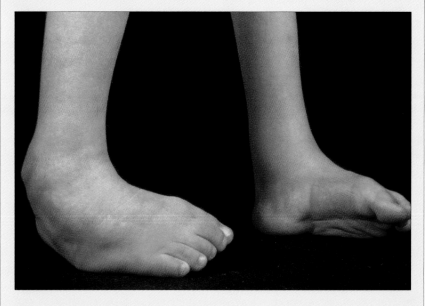

Clubfoot is a genetic disorder in which babies are born with twisted feet.

FERMENTATION

Fermentation is the process by which cells metabolize carbohydrates or other substances in the absence of oxygen

Brewers of beer and bakers of bread have used fermentation since ancient times, but it was not until the 19th century that French biochemist Louis Pasteur (1822–1895), the Father of Microbiology, proved that fermentation was due to the activities of living cells.

Fermentation is the process that some cells use to metabolize carbohydrates or other organic substances in the absence of oxygen. Scientists have harnessed this ability to help manufacture products from antibiotics to sausages. In biotechnology, fermentation describes any process in which microorganisms are used on an industrial scale (see BIOTECHNOLOGY). Oxygen is often supplied to encourage the organism to multiply faster.

CORE FACTS

- Fermentation is a process employed by certain cells to metabolize carbohydrates in the absence of oxygen.
- Cells that grow in the absence of oxygen are called anaerobes. Some anaerobes can also utilize oxygen; others are able only to tolerate it.
- Fermenting cells generate energy by a series of oxidation-reduction reactions.
- Fermentation is used widely in the food industries and also in biotechnology.

Life without oxygen

Most cells require oxygen to live; they are called aerobes. Aerobes generate energy using an oxygen-dependent process called aerobic respiration. Other cells can grow only in the absence of oxygen; they are called obligate anaerobes. These cells are wholly dependent on fermentation to generate the energy they need. Other cells can grow and respire aerobically in the presence of oxygen but switch to fermentation when oxygen is not available; these cells are called facultative anaerobes. A fourth category of cells can grow in the presence of oxygen but will, nevertheless, generate energy through fermentation. They are called aerotolerant organisms.

Clostridia bacteria, including the species that cause tetanus and botulism, are obligate anaerobes. Most types of yeasts, including those used in baking and brewing, are facultative anaerobes. Lactic acid bacteria, which are widely used to make cheese and other fermented dairy products, are aerotolerant organisms.

Oxidation reduction

The fermenting cell generates energy through a series of oxidation-reduction reactions, in which compounds either give up or receive electrons. A compound that gives up electrons is said to be oxidized. The electron acceptor, a substance that

Cheese is made by fermenting milk with lactic acid bacteria; different species make different kinds of cheese.

accepts the electrons, is described as reduced. The electron transfer is accompanied by a release of energy. The electron can be thought of as the baton in a relay race, and the organic compounds as the runners. The first runner, the fastest, hands the baton to the second runner, who is not quite as fast. In chemical terms, the first "runner" becomes oxidized and the second "runner," now holding the baton, is reduced. Because the second runner is not quite as fast as the first, there is a difference in energy in the race. The second runner hands the baton to a third runner, who is a little slower than the second, in a similar oxidation-reduction reaction. With relay runners, all of this energy is lost, but in chemical oxidation-reduction reactions some of the energy is conserved within a variety of

CONNECTIONS

● Fermentation can cause food spoilage, but it can also be important in **FOOD PRESERVATION**.

● Fermentation of vegetable matter is the main chemical reaction at work in composting, the production of natural **FERTILIZERS**. Fermentation also plays a part in making silage as animal feed.

compounds in the form of high-energy phosphate bonds. The most common high-energy compound is adenosine triphosphate (ATP; see ENERGY).

Glucose fermentation

A typical fermentation reaction is the conversion of glucose to ethanol and carbon dioxide, with the generation of two molecules of ATP. This reaction, alcoholic fermentation, is used by many yeasts.

Each step requires a specific enzyme (see ENZYMES) to catalyze the reaction, and each must occur in order. Several important changes happen along the way. The first part of the biochemical pathway breaks down glucose (a sugar molecule containing six carbon atoms) into two three-carbon molecules. With the help of the enzyme hexokinase, a molecule of ATP donates a phosphate to glucose to form glucose-6-phosphate and leaves adenosine

---

FERMENTED FOODS

A relaxed picnic on a warm summer's day might include a loaf of bread, some cheese, salami, crunchy dill pickles, and a jug of wine or cold bottle of beer, followed by chocolate cake. Aside from sharing space in a picnic basket, these foods have something else in common: their manufacture involves fermentation.

The ancient Egyptians discovered that if they allowed bread dough (without added yeast) to stand for several hours, the resulting loaf had a lighter texture and better flavor than dough that was baked immediately. They did not know it, but their bread was leavened by carbon dioxide gas, from the fermentation of sugars by bacteria and yeasts that had happened to float in on the breeze. Most yeasted breads are now made with added baker's yeast (Saccharomyces cerevisiae), mixed with a small concentration of lactic acid bacteria. These ferment sugars contained in the flour, as well as any added by the baker, to produce carbon dioxide, organic esters and acids, alcohols, and carbonyl compounds. These fermentation products contribute to that wonderful smell and taste of freshly baked bread.

Beer, along with bread, is one of the oldest fermented foods known to humans. The Egyptians made a fermented drink from barley and other grains at least 6,000 years ago. Barley, sprouted and dried to produce malt (which contains the sugar maltose), is still used to make beer; in some cases, unmalted grains such as rice or corn are also used. The beer maker adds a culture of pure yeast to a malt-containing preparation called wort; the malt and other grains provide the yeast with fermentable carbohydrates and amino acids. The primary products are ethanol and carbon dioxide.

The Egyptians and other peoples did not know about the yeasts that naturally grew on grape skins, but they did know that if they let grape juice sit for a time in pots, modern they could make wine. Wine-makers sometimes use yeast cultures, as well as the grape's own yeasts. Grape juice also contains lactic acid bacteria, which use fermentation to convert malic acid to lactic acid and carbon dioxide. This process makes the wine less acidic and, at the same time, less likely to be spoiled by other microorganisms.

The type and quality of wine depend on the composition of the grape juice used to make the wine, which in turn depends on the variety of grape, climate, time of harvesting, and soil composition. The yeast strain used to carry out the fermentation is also important to the final taste of the wine. The fizz in good-quality sparkling wines comes from a second fermentation that occurs when cultured yeast and sugar are added to the wine after it has been bottled.

Cottage cheese, mild cheddar cheese, and strong Limburger cheese begin with bacteria fermenting lactose in warmed milk. The principal bacteria used in cheese fermentation—the lactic acid streptococci—were first isolated from sour milk by English surgeon Joseph Lister (1827–1912) in 1878. In the late19th century cheese makers began using purified bacteria cultures. Before then, they relied on the bacteria that were naturally present in the environment. During the initial fermentation process, the bacteria convert the lactose in the milk to lactic acid, carbon dioxide, and other fermentation products that contribute to the taste of the cheese.

The ancient Greeks learned that they could preserve meat by salting, curing, and drying it. Thus, the sausage was born. The fermentation products, lactic and acetic acids, give sausages—salami, for example—their characteristic "tangy" taste. Fresh meat naturally contains several species of lactic acid bacteria, so sausage makers sometimes do not add starter cultures of these bacteria. Although freshly slaughtered meat contains some glucose (from the breakdown of muscle glycogen), sausage makers add a mixture of rapidly and slowly fermentable carbohydrates to the ground meat. Next, removing oxygen from the mixture, allows lactic acid bacteria to flourish, crowding out other amino acid-fermenting bacteria that spoil meat. Other components of sausage, such as fat, curing agents (such as nitrate or nitrite, which inhibits the growth of spoilage organisms), and spices, contribute to the flavor.

Lactic acid fermentation, or pickling, is an ancient method of preserving vegetables—commonly, cucumbers, olives, and cabbage (sauerkraut). To make dill pickles, cucumbers are soaked in a salt and water solution with dill weed and spices. There are many bacteria, yeasts, and molds in the initial brine, but as fermentation products make the solution more acidic, the fermenting organisms' lactic acid and other bacteria, as well as fermenting yeasts, soon crowd out any spoilage organisms.

Even the cocoa beans used to make the chocolate cake in the picnic basket are fermented. Just after harvesting, the beans are heaped on plantain leaves or in large boxes and left to ferment for several days. Naturally occurring yeasts and lactic and acetic acid bacteria ferment carbohydrates to produce ethanol, lactic acid, and acetic acid. At the end of fermentation, the beans are dried, washed, and prepared for roasting. Fermentation is thought to be essential to the development of true chocolate flavor.

Many other foods are fermented. Yogurt and buttermilk are familiar examples; they originate from the fermented milk products made over the centuries in the Middle East, Africa, and Europe. People in Asian countries have long made fermented foods from soybeans, sometimes mixed with grains: soy sauce, miso, and tempeh, for example. Cassava, a starchy root, is fermented in many African countries. Fermented cereal grains are the basis for many African foods and alcoholic drinks.

Why are so many foods fermented? In many cases, fermentation is a method of preserving food. This process is especially important to people who have no refrigerators or freezers. It makes some foods edible (olives picked right from the tree taste terrible). Without fermentation bread would be flat and beer would be unknown. Fermentation is something of an art because the maker of fermented foods must ensure that desirable organisms carry out their jobs while preventing contaminating organisms from producing fermented products that ruin the taste of the food or are even toxic.

A CLOSER LOOK

INDUSTRIAL FERMENTATION

Fermenting bacteria and yeast can produce many of the same products that are more commonly derived from petrochemicals. Concern for the environment and the need to conserve natural resources has led many scientists to investigate harnessing the tiny organisms to produce industrial quantities of these products. Many of the processes are still too expensive to compete with cheaper petroleum-based products, however.

Some gasoline formulations, especially in the midwestern United States, contain 10 percent ethanol, derived from the fermentation of corn starch (which has first been converted to sugar) by yeasts. Scientists continue to search for new yeast strains that are more tolerant to ethanol because ethanol production is limited by the amount of alcohol the yeasts can tolerate (the ethanol they produce eventually becomes so concentrated that it kills the yeast cells).

Some clostridia bacteria produce acetone and butanol as a result of sugar or starch fermentation. This became the major process for the industrial production of acetone and butanol during World War I (1914–1918; see the box on page 703). Acetone-butanol fermentation was phased out as petrochemical processes became cheaper. Concerns about depleting nonrenewable resources have renewed interest in using clostridia to produce acetone and butanol for industry. Although fermentation is still too costly to replace petrochemicals as a source of acetone and butanol, scientists are trying to develop genetically engineered clostridia to make them produce the products more efficiently. Some scientists are studying ways to make the process even cheaper by using waste products (potato pulp or sugar beet pulp) as the energy source for the bacteria.

Methanobacteria, believed to be some of the most ancient microorganisms, produce methane gas from carbon dioxide. Methane is the major component of natural gas, used as a source of energy. Scientists are again trying to produce genetically engineered strains to speed up methane production because the bacteria work slowly. Scientists are also studying the ways in which microbes ferment waste products from the food-processing and paper-making industries. Making these fermentations economically feasible would yield a double bonus: the microbes gobble up polluting waste, while making useful products such as ethanol, methane, acetone, and butanol.

All of these fermentation methods are anaerobic, but many large-scale biotechnology processes employ fermentation in which a supply of air or oxygen is necessary. Among many products produced by this means are antibiotics, citric acid, and a range of enzymes and amino acids.

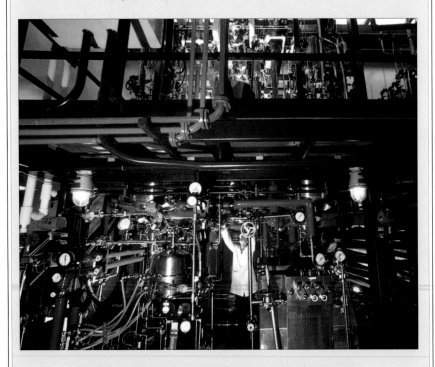

SCIENCE AND SOCIETY

diphosphate (ADP). A second enzyme, glucose phosphate isomerase, shuffles two groups of atoms to convert glucose-6-phosphate to fructose-6-phosphate. A second ATP molecule also donates phosphate, with the aid of the enzyme phospho-fructokinase, to form fructose-1,6-bisphosphate. A fourth enzyme, called aldolase, splits the molecule into two three-carbon molecules: glyceraldehyde-3-phosphate and dihydroxy-acetone phosphate. The latter molecule is converted to glyceraldehyde-3-phosphate by an isomerase.

There are now two glyceraldehyde-3-phosphate molecules. So far, there have been no oxidation-reduction reactions, and energy has been lost. However, the glyceraldehyde-3-phosphate molecules are ready to make up for the lost energy and generate more as well.

With the help of the enzyme PGAL-dehydrogenase, the two molecules of glyceraldehyde-3-phosphate each give two electrons to the coenzyme NAD^+, which is converted to NADH (this is the first oxidation-reduction step).

At the same time, the two molecules each take up inorganic phosphate to become 2,3-bisphosphoglycerate molecules. The second phosphate bonds are also high-energy bonds, and so one phosphate from each molecule can be transferred to a molecule of ADP, the result being in two molecules of phosphoglycerate and two molecules of ATP.

The enzyme enolase then removes a molecule of water from each phosphoglycerate molecule, forming phosphoenolpyruvate. Now the phosphate bond is again a high-energy bond, and two more molecules of ADP accept the phosphate groups. The result: two molecules of pyruvate and two more molecules of ATP. These first two stages of glucose fermentation, the conversion of glucose to pyruvate, are called glycolysis.

The cell is not done. Because it has only a limited supply of the coenzyme NAD^+, it must oxidize the NADH used earlier back to NAD^+. Pyruvate decarboxylase removes a carbon dioxide molecule from each pyruvate molecule, resulting in the formation of two molecules of acetaldehyde and two molecules of carbon dioxide. With the enzyme alcohol dehydrogenase, two NADH molecules transfer two electrons each to the acetaldehyde molecules to yield two molecules of ethanol and two molecules of NAD^+.

The ultimate products of glucose fermentation are two molecules of ATP (four molecules of ATP were produced, but two were used at the beginning), two molecules of ethanol, and two molecules of carbon dioxide (CO_2). For the cell, the crucial product is the energy-carrier ATP; the cell excretes the rest as waste products.

Ethanol and CO_2 are anything but waste products for the brewer and the baker, however. Ethanol is the crucial product in alcoholic beverages, and carbon dioxide makes bread dough rise. The total amount of energy released in the process of glucose fermentation is 57 kilocalories per mole of glucose;

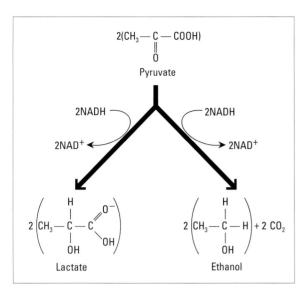

$$2(CH_3 - \overset{\overset{\displaystyle O}{\|}}{C} - COOH)$$

Pyruvate

2NADH → ← 2NADH

2NAD⁺ ← → 2NAD⁺

$$2\left(CH_3 - \overset{\overset{\displaystyle H}{|}}{\underset{\underset{\displaystyle OH}{|}}{C}} - C\overset{\displaystyle O^-}{\underset{\displaystyle OH}{}}\right)$$

Lactate

$$2\left(CH_3 - \overset{\overset{\displaystyle H}{|}}{\underset{\underset{\displaystyle OH}{|}}{C}} - H\right) + 2\ CO_2$$

Ethanol

The second stage of fermentation, which results in the production of lactate and ethanol, regenerates NAD.

14.8 of those kilocalories are stored in the high-energy bonds of ATP, and the rest is lost as heat. Aerobic respiration, in contrast, is a much more efficient process: it can produce as much as 38 ATP molecules from each glucose molecule.

A second fermentation pathway occurs in muscle cells, particularly during physical activity, when there is a high demand for energy and a shortage of oxygen. The enzyme lactate dehydrogenase catalyzes the reduction of pyruvate by NADH, yielding NAD^+ and lactic acid (lactate). Lactic acid build up in the tissues results in a feeling of stiffness after exercise.

Variations on a theme

The variations on the theme of glucose fermentation range as widely as the organisms that carry out fermentation. Some fermentations are important in the food industry; others can be used to produce industrial chemicals. A large number of organisms convert sugars to pyruvate, but from this point the fate of the pyruvate can be very different. Many lactic bacteria reduce pyruvate to lactic acid; others convert half of the glucose molecule to lactic acid and half to ethanol and carbon dioxide. Enteric bacteria—a family that includes *Escherichia coli*, which lives in the human intestinal tract, as well as disease-causing organisms such as *Salmonella* and *Shigella*—form acetic, lactic, and succinic acids, as well as ethanol, carbon dioxide, and hydrogen.

Other organisms ferment amino acids. The bacteria that cause tetanus, gas gangrene, and botulism (*Clostridium tetani*, *C. perfringens*, and *C. botulinum*, respectively) ferment amino acids. Many of the products of amino acid fermentation smell terrible, thus the foul odor associated with these infections. More pleasant products of amino acid fermentation are found in wines and cheeses.

Bacteria in the colon ferment glucose to a variety of acids, ethanol, and hydrogen, carbon dioxide, and methane gases. Intestinal gas accumulates when bacteria in the colon produce more gas than the intestine can absorb. This also occurs when people eat foods such as legumes, that contain carbohydrates that cannot be absorbed by the intestine but can be metabolized by bacteria.

S. LATTA

See also: ANTIBIOTICS; ANTIMICROBIALS; ATP PRODUCTION; BACTERIA; BIOTECHNOLOGY; CARBOHYDRATES; CELL BIOLOGY; ENERGY; ENZYMES; KREBS CYCLE; METABOLISM.

Further reading:
Brock, T. D. 1994. *Biology of Microorganisms*. 7th ed. Englewood Cliffs, N.J.: Prentice-Hall.
Platt, G. C. 2002. *Fermented Foods of the World*. Boca Raton, Fla.: CRC Press.

CHAIM WEIZMANN

During World War I (1914–1918), the British were desperately short of the chemicals acetone and butanol. Acetone was needed as a solvent for nitrocellulose to make the smokeless explosive cordite, while butanol was required for the manufacture of synthetic rubber. By 1915 a young scientist named Chaim Weizmann, working in Manchester, England, had developed an anaerobic fermentation process, using the bacterium *Clostridium acetobutylicum*, which would produce 12 tons (11 tonnes) of acetone and 24 tons (22 tonnes) of butanol from 100 tons (91 tonnes) of molasses or grain.

Weizmann discovered that the strains of *C. acetobutylicum* that gave the highest yield produced spores that were particularly resistant to heat. He therefore subjected his cultures to sudden heatshocks of 212 °F (100 °C), and isolated the survivors. Breweries in Britain and Canada were quickly converted to the new fermentation process. In 1948 Chaim Weizmann, who had long been a dedicated Zionist, became the first president of the new state of Israel.

Members of the World Zionist Delegation who met in 1921, including mathematician Albert Einstein (second left) and biochemist Chaim Weizmann (second right).

DISCOVERERS

FERNS AND FERN ALLIES

Ferns are an ancient group of nonflowering plants that reproduce by spores rather than seeds

A walk through the forest at the right time of the year is certain to uncover a familiar carpet of ferns in some cool shady spots. At one time the ancestors and relatives of today's ferns and fern allies (horsetails, club mosses, and fork-ferns) covered much of the world. They are an ancient group of nonflowering, vascular (they have a specialized conducting system), leafy plants generally called the pteridophytes (from the Greek words *pteris*, "fern", and *phyton,* "plant"). Ferns have been an important part of Earth's vegetation for millions of years. They flourish in moist habitats and dominated the vast swamp forests that covered much of Earth's surface during the Carboniferous period (360 to 290 million years ago), when treelike club mosses and horsetails grew to over 100 feet (30 m) tall. Remains of these species form the world's great coal beds. There are now few surviving fern allies, mostly small and inconspicuous plants, but ferns are still quite common in many parts of the world.

Life cycle

Like most plants, ferns and fern allies alternate their reproductive generations: there is an asexual phase called a sporophyte and a sexual phase called a gametophyte (see the diagram opposite). The sporophyte is a diploid plant (it has two sets of

Tree ferns can reproduce vegetatively to form shoots on the trunk or at the base.

CORE FACTS

- Unlike other vascular plants that reproduce by seed, ferns reproduce by spores.
- Ferns and fern allies alternate their generations, having asexual sporophyte and sexual gametophyte plants.
- In some species of ferns and fern allies, the gametophyte is unable to photosynthesize and must form a symbiotic relationship with a fungus to obtain food.

EVOLUTION OF FERNS AND FERN ALLIES

The origin and relationships of the ferns and their allies are uncertain and remain controversial. The first vascular plants are known from the Silurian period (440 to 408 million years ago) and are thought to have arisen from an ancient group of green algae. These early vascular plants are placed in three extinct divisions: the Rhyniophyta, Zosterophyllophyta, and Trimerophyta.

The fork-ferns were once considered to be the most primitive of the living Pteridophytes (ferns) and were grouped together with the extinct plants into the division Psilotophyta (with a single family, Psilotaceae).

However, other work has questioned whether *Psilotum* and *Tmesipteris* (the two genera of the Psilotaceae) are after all closely related to these extinct plant groups, and their origin is now uncertain.

Club mosses and horsetails are known from fossils from the Devonian period (408 to 360 million years ago). Scientists believe that the club mosses originated from members of the Zosterophyllophyta, but no fossil horsetails are known that indicate their origin. Ferns are known from fossils going back to the Carboniferous period (360 to 290 million years ago). However, their origins are also uncertain.

EVOLUTION

CONNECTIONS

● **REPRODUCTION** in ferns is different from that in many other plants.

● Ferns and fern allies are distinguished by the differences in their **LEAVES AND LEAF STRUCTURE.**

chromosomes, 2*n*) and produces spores that form the gametophyte. It may also reproduce by vegetative reproduction (see the box on page 706). The gametophyte plant is haploid (it has a single set of chromosomes, *n*) and produces sperm and eggs. A zygote is formed when an egg is fertilized and it then grows into the sporophyte, the dominant and familiar stage in the life cycle of ferns and their allies. The gametophyte and the sporophyte are usually free living.

In some species the gametophyte is green and photosynthetic and lives on the soil surface; in others it is colorless and lives underground. Subterranean gametophytes cannot photosynthesize, so they obtain food by forming a symbiotic (mutually beneficial) relationship with a fungus. The gametophyte may live for many years as a tiny, inconspicuous plant; for many species, this stage has never been seen in nature.

The gametophyte grows and produces sex organs on its surface. The female sex organs are called archegonia (singular, archegonium) and contain one egg each. The male sex organs are called antheridia (singular, antheridium) and each contains many sperm. The sperm have long, whiplike extensions called flagellae, which help them move. The gametophyte is often covered by a thin film of moisture. Once shed, the sperm swim over the gametophyte in the surface film of moisture to reach another gametophyte, enter an archegonium, and fertilize the egg. A zygote with two sets of chromosomes is formed and develops into a sporophyte. Initially the sporophyte grows attached to the gametophyte, but its growth soon overwhelms the gametophyte, which dies. The sporophyte then forms roots, rhizomes, and new leaves.

Classification and description of groups

Ferns and fern allies have differently structured leaves. Fern allies have small or straplike leaves with a single midvein. Ferns have large, well-developed leaves, called fronds, which contain highly branched leaf veins. In addition, the sporangia (the spore-bearing structures) of fern allies are present on specially modified leaves called sporophylls, whereas they are present on the lower surface of ordinary leaves in the case of ferns.

Different classification schemes have been proposed for the ferns and their allies. Many scientists once placed fork-ferns, club mosses, horsetails, and ferns in a single division (phylum), Pteridophyta, which was divided into four classes, one for each of these groups. Now most scientists place fork-ferns, club mosses, horsetails, and ferns in separate divisions.

This diagram of the life cycle of the fern illustrates the alternation of generations between the asexual and the sexual stage.

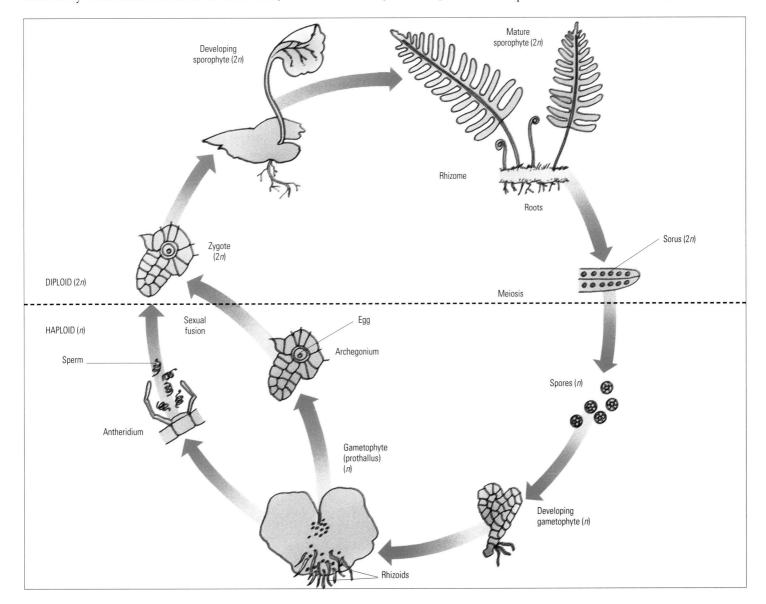

FERNS AND PEOPLE

Ferns are grown worldwide in gardens and as house plants. As well as being decorative, many ferns are edible and have medicinal properties.

The fiddleheads (young fronds) of many ferns are eaten either raw or cooked while they are tender. In North America, the coiled fronds of some species of ferns are regarded as a great delicacy, for example, fronds of *Matteuccia struthiopteris*, *Osmunda cinnamomea*, and *Onoclea sensibilis*. The fronds of a few species, including *Pellaea ornithopus*, are used to make a tea substitute.

Many species of ferns have been used in herbal medicine for centuries. Taken internally, infusions made from various species of ferns have been used as a cure against parasitic worms, asthma, rheumatism and for their diuretic properties. Applied externally as a paste or poultice, they have been used to treat wounds, bruises, burns, sprains, bites, and stings.

However, some ferns have harmful properties. Bracken (*Pteridium aquilinum*) and some species of horsetail are poisonous to livestock. Bracken is also known to be carcinogenic (cancer causing) if eaten by people.

SCIENCE AND SOCIETY

Fork-ferns

Fork-ferns usually grow hanging on tree trunks or in rock crevices (see EPIPHYTES). However, some terrestrials may also grow erect on the forest floor. Fork-ferns grow in tropical regions, Australia, and the Pacific.

The sporophyte of the fork-ferns is a small, herbaceous plant. It lacks roots but has an underground stem (rhizome) that bears rootlike structures called rhizoids. Fork-ferns are divided into two genera: *Psilotum* and *Tmesipteris*. The aerial stems of *Psilotum* are branched, flattened, and photosynthetic. They have either very small leaves or none at all. The stems of *Tmesipteris* are usually unbranched and nonphotosynthetic. Instead they bear small, green, photosynthetic leaves that are spirally arranged along the stem.

VEGETATIVE REPRODUCTION IN FERNS

Although ferns reproduce by spores, which are important for colonizing new territories, many also reproduce vegetatively in a variety of ways. Some produce miniature plantlets on their fronds. Some of these plantlets do not develop fronds or roots while still attached to the parent plant (for example, *Tectaria gemmifera*). However, when mature, they fall off, develop roots and fronds, and grow into new plants. In other species the plantlets form fronds and may have roots while still attached to the parent plant. They remain thus until the parent frond touches the ground and begins to die. In some ferns these plantlets are found near the tips of the fronds (for example, *Polystichum lentum* and *Asplenium paleaceum*). In other species they are scattered along the midrib (for example, *Polystichum setiferum*) or over the whole surface of the frond (for example, *Asplenium bulbiferum*). Certain ferns, such as *Asplenium rhizophyllum*, which is often called the walking fern, have long, straplike leaves that can develop new plantlets at their leaf tips where they touch the ground.

Many species of ferns can reproduce by a process called stolon proliferation. Stolons are stems that grow either underground or along the surface of the soil, which can root and produce plants at intervals along their length.

Some tree ferns (*Cyathea* and *Dicksonia* spp.) can produce small shoots either on the trunk itself or around the base. These shoots usually lack roots and have only a couple of small fronds. They remain dormant until the parent tree fern dies, when the shoots start to grow.

The spores will not germinate unless they are buried, after which they develop into an underground gametophyte. This gametophyte becomes a tubular, colorless structure covered with rhizoids. It is unable to photosynthesize and must become infected with a fungus in order to grow.

Club mosses

This division contains the largest group of surviving fern allies, with more than 1,000 species in three familes: *Lycopodiaceae*, *Selaginellaceae*, and *Isoetaceae*.

Club mosses are mostly terrestrial and have roots, stems, and leaves, although many species of *Lycopodium* and *Selaginella* are creepers or epiphytes and thus grow on trees and rocks. *Isoetes* are grasslike plants, which grow in marshy or swampy habitats. They are widely distributed, particularly in the tropics. The living species of club mosses are small plants, but some fossil members were as large as trees, growing to over 100 feet (30 m) high (*Lepidodendron* spp.).

Horsetails

This division contains 15 living species in a single genus, *Equisetum*, believed to be one of the oldest living genera of vascular plants. Living horsetails are relatively small, herbaceous plants, but some of the extinct members of this division were large trees up to 100 feet (30 m) high.

Horsetails are widely distributed throughout the Northern Hemisphere. Most species live in wet or damp habitats, alongside rivers, streams, and ditches. The sporophyte has a highly branched underground rhizome, which produces roots and aerial stems. In living horsetails these stems grow up to about 3 feet (90 cm) high. The aerial stems are tubular, hollow, and often ribbed. They form distinct segments, called internodes, joined together at regular intervals at nodes. Small, nonphotosynthetic, scalelike leaves are found in a circle around each node. Thin side branches are usually also sited at each node; these branches and the main stem are green and photosynthetic.

The aerial stems are either sterile or fertile because they either lack or bear spores, respectively. Spores develop in sporangia, which are found on specialized scalelike leaves called sporophylls. The sporophylls are clustered together to form a conelike structure (strobilus) at the end of a fertile stem.

Spores germinate on the soil surface and grow into a gametophyte, which is a small, inconspicuous, straplike green plant, up to $1\frac{1}{5}$ inches (3 cm) in diameter. This plant is photosynthetic and is anchored to the ground by rhizoids.

Ferns

There are estimated to be at least 8,500 species of living ferns, more of which are continually being discovered. Most ferns live in the shaded damp forests of the temperate and tropical zones and are particularly abundant in tropical rain forests. Some ferns are climbing vines, some are epiphytes growing on the

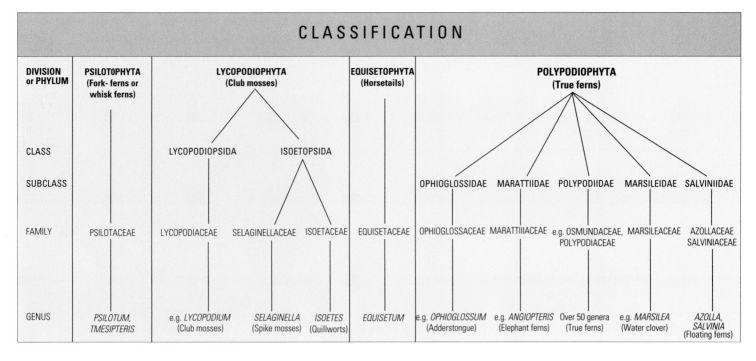

CLASSIFICATION

DIVISION or PHYLUM	PSILOTOPHYTA (Fork-ferns or whisk ferns)	LYCOPODIOPHYTA (Club mosses)			EQUISETOPHYTA (Horsetails)	POLYPODIOPHYTA (True ferns)				
CLASS		LYCOPODIOPSIDA	ISOETOPSIDA							
SUBCLASS						OPHIOGLOSSIDAE	MARATTIIDAE	POLYPODIIDAE	MARSILEIDAE	SALVINIIDAE
FAMILY	PSILOTACEAE	LYCOPODIACEAE	SELAGINELLACEAE	ISOETACEAE	EQUISETACEAE	OPHIOGLOSSACEAE	MARATTIIACEAE	e.g. OSMUNDACEAE, POLYPODIACEAE	MARSILEACEAE	AZOLLACEAE SALVINIACEAE
GENUS	*PSILOTUM, TMESIPTERIS*	e.g. *LYCOPODIUM* (Club mosses)	*SELAGINELLA* (Spike mosses)	*ISOETES* (Quillworts)	*EQUISETUM*	e.g. *OPHIOGLOSSUM* (Adderstongue)	e.g. *ANGIOPTERIS* (Elephant ferns)	Over 50 genera (True ferns)	e.g. *MARSILEA* (Water clover)	*AZOLLA, SALVINIA* (Floating ferns)

trunks and branches of trees, and some are aquatic plants, floating on water (for example, *Salvinia* spp. and *Azolla* spp.). Classification of the ferns is controversial. One possible classification arranges them in five subclasses: Ophioglossidae, Marattiidae, Polypodiidae, Marsileidae, and Salviniidae. The Ophioglossidae are small, simple plants consisting of an underground rhizome with rootlets and, in most species, producing a single frond. Unlike other ferns, the young fronds are not coiled in the bud. The single frond is divided into a sterile and a fertile section. The sterile portion is green and photosynthetic, and the fertile portion bears sporangia clustered into a spike. Once they become buried, the spores germinate to form gametophytes, which cannot develop unless they are infected with a fungus.

The Marattiidae are mostly large ferns of tropical forests. In some species the rhizome forms a small trunk. In most species the fronds are highly divided and are often very large; in the elephant fern, *Angiopteris*, they may grow to over 26 feet (8 m) long. Sporangia are grouped together into structures called sori, which are found on the underside of the leaves. The spores germinate on the soil surface to form the gametophyte, which is anchored to the soil by rhizoids. The gametophyte may live for up to six years and can grow to over 2 inches (5 cm) long.

Most ferns belong to the extremely large and diverse subclass called the Polypodiidae. These ferns range in size from the tiny filmy ferns that grow to ²⁄₂₅ to ³⁄₂₅ inch (2 to 3 mm) to large tree ferns growing 30 to 90 feet (10 to 25 m) high.

Pests and predators

Ferns have few parasites or predators. Snails, slugs, and insects often attack the young, uncurling fronds, called fiddleheads, but fully grown fronds seem to be rarely eaten. This fact suggests that ferns contain unpalatable or toxic substances.

K. McCALLUM

See also: ALGAE; ANGIOSPERMS; EPIPHYTES; FERTILIZATION.

Further reading:

Cobb, B., and L. L. Foster, 1999. *A Field Guide to Ferns And Their Related Families: Northeastern and Central North America.* Boston: Houghton Mifflin.
Rickard, M. 2000. *The Plant Finder's Guide to Garden Ferns.* Portland, Oreg.: Timber Press.

The wood horsetail (Equisetum sylvaticum) in its fertile stage, clearly showing the strobili, or cones, with sporophylls bearing the sporangia that contain the spores.

FERTILITY

A characteristic of all living creatures on Earth is the ability to produce offspring. For microbial life, reproduction is a simple process of binary fission triggered by chemical and physical changes in a single parent. Reproduction is more complex for sexually reproducing organisms, and the ability to produce offspring is the outcome of an intricate series of biological changes in both parents that determine fertility.

Most men and women are fertile: that is, they are able to produce offspring through sexual intercourse. About 80 percent of couples who engage in regular sexual intercourse will conceive a child within a year; another 5 percent will take longer. This high probability of pregnancy is remarkable considering the many factors needed to ensure that a baby is produced. To conceive a child, both parents must meet certain fertility requirements.

A man must be able to generate an adequate amount of semen (more than 2 ml). At least 60 percent of the sperm it contains must be motile (able to move spontaneously), and at least 60 percent must be normal in size and shape. In addition, the man must have an adequate sex drive and the potency to obtain and maintain an erection and so release sperm into the woman's vagina.

The woman also must have healthy functioning organs so that she produces normal ova (eggs) on a regular basis and is able to maintain a pregnancy to the full term. A woman's sex drive also helps to encourage sexual intercourse, particularly during her most fertile periods.

Humans first become capable of reproduction after puberty (see ADOLESCENCE), which occurs in most girls between the ages of 11 and 13 years and in boys from ages 13 to 15 years. During puberty, the hypothalamus in the brain starts to secrete a substance called gonadotropin-releasing hormone (GnRH). GnRH causes the formation of two further hormones in the pituitary gland: follicle-stimulating hormone (FSH) and luteinizing hormone (LH).

In men the same quantities of GnRH, FSH, and LH are produced every day. These hormones in turn trigger production of a constant supply of

Howard and Georgeanna Jones, directors of the Jones Institute in Norfolk, VA, with two babies conceived by in vitro fertilization at the institute.

testosterone (male sex hormone). Testosterone powers the male sex drive and causes the formation of sperm. Testosterone is formed mainly in the testes but is also secreted by the adrenal cortex (see ENDOCRINE SYSTEMS).

Women undergo regular cyclical fluctuations in hormone levels (see MENSTRUAL CYCLE). Alterations in hormone concentrations stimulate the production of an egg (ovum) and induce an intricate series of changes in the reproductive system to establish the proper internal environment for the fertilization, implantation, and development of the egg.

CORE FACTS

- The ability to produce offspring is the outcome of an intricate series of biological processes in both parents.
- About 80 percent of human couples who have regular sexual intercourse will conceive a child within a year.
- Between 10 and 15 percent of couples are considered infertile.
- IVF, embryo transplant, and surrogate motherhood are ways to provide a child for infertile couples.

CONNECTIONS

- **HORMONES** secreted by the **ENDOCRINE SYSTEM** affect fertility.

- In captive breeding programs to protect **ENDANGERED SPECIES,** the animals can have problems with fertility.

The effects of age

Fertility in women declines with age. At the time of a female child's birth, all the ova she will carry in her life are already present in a rudimentary form in her ovaries. After age 35, fewer ova are released, making it increasingly difficult for most women to conceive. Pregnancy does not become completely impossible for women until they complete menopause (after which no more ova are released), generally between the late 40s and the mid-50s.

Men are biologically capable of fathering children well into later life. However, a man's sex drive declines with increasing age. As a result, men tend to engage in sexual intercourse less frequently, and they may have more difficulty obtaining and maintaining an erection. Both of these factors reduce male fertility.

Fertility rates

When it comes to human populations, overall fertility is affected by social as well as biological factors. There are many different ways of measuring fertility among men and women in various population groups. The total fertility rate represents the number of children a typical woman will have during her lifetime.

Total fertility rates are similar among developed nations. In the United States in 2000 the total fertility rate was 2.0, that is, a typical woman is expected to produce 2.0 children by age 50. In Britain, the rate was 1.7. The fertility rate is much higher in develop-

ing nations. In 2000 it was 5.5 in eastern and middle African countries, 3.2 in northern Africa, 3.6 in southern Africa, and 5.4 in western Africa. Couples in these countries tend to have bigger families because the risk of losing children is considerably greater.

The replacement level of fertility is the degree of fertility at which a group of women have, on average, just enough daughters to replace themselves in the total population. By definition, the replacement level of fertility has a value of 1.00. The replacement level of fertility may be compared with the gross

FERTILITY DRUGS

Fertility drugs have been used for more than 30 years to treat disorders of ovulation. Most of the drugs contain natural or synthetic hormones that act on the hypothalamus or pituitary gland and stimulate ovulation. Clomiphene citrate is the most commonly prescribed fertility drug. Clomiphene tablets make the hypothalamus register that a woman has lost all her estrogen (female sex hormone). The hypothalamus instructs the pituitary to produce more FSH. Clomiphene is effective in up to 90 percent of women. Around 10 percent of women who conceive as a result of treatment with clomiphene have twins.

If clomiphene fails, other drugs may be used, such as GnRH. Injections of GnRH are given periodically to urge the pituitary to release FSH and LH. After treatment for two to three months, 80 percent of women can become pregnant.

Bromocriptine stops the production of the hormone prolactin. Most women whose failure to ovulate is due to high levels of prolactin begin ovulating after taking bromocriptine tablets for about three weeks.

A CLOSER LOOK

People in developing countries tend to decide to have large families. One reason is that the risk of losing children to disease at an early age is high in these countries.

IN VITRO FERTILIZATION TECHNIQUES

In vitro fertilization (IVF) procedures have been used by veterinarians for many years, and in 1978 the first "test-tube" baby, Louise Brown, was born in Britain. Since then, the techniques of IVF and embryo transfer have been used by tens of thousands of infertile couples.

In vitro fertilization literally means fertilization "in glass"—that is, in a test tube. The basic technique involves removing eggs from a woman, fertilizing them outside her body, and then inserting the fertilized eggs or embryo into the uterus. A single course of IVF treatment results in the birth of an infant for 9 to 14 percent of women. However, 30 percent of such births are premature.

There are two important variations of the basic IVF technique—gamete intrafallopian transfer (GIFT) and zygote intrafallopian transfer (ZIFT). GIFT, pioneered in 1984, involves removing a woman's eggs, mixing them with sperm, and inserting both eggs and sperm into the fallopian tube so that fertilization takes place in its natural setting. Birth of an infant occurs in 20 percent of women undergoing GIFT.

Like standard IVF, ZIFT involves removing a woman's eggs and fertilizing them outside the body. Instead of inserting the fertilized egg (zygote) into the uterus, the zygote is placed in the fallopian tube.

IVF has been most successful in women younger than age 35, and it has only a 9 percent success rate per treatment in older women. A new technique may improve these chances. Called assisted hatching, the procedure opens the outer layer of a fertilized egg so the embryo can emerge more easily. Once the embryo has been "hatched," it is implanted in the uterus. Initial experience with this method in older women doubled the pregnancy success rate.

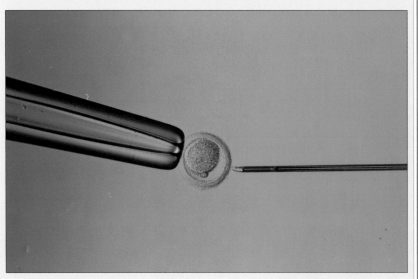

An IVF technique in which the sperm is introduced into the ovum by a needle. The ovum is being held by a micropipette.

SCIENCE AND SOCIETY

reproduction rate. The gross reproduction rate measures only female births. When multiplied by the total fertility rate for a country, the gross reproduction rate indicates whether women are producing enough female offspring to assure growth of the overall population. In the United States, the gross reproduction rate is 0.98. Because the birth rate is less than 1.0, the fertility rate is declining because not every woman will have a daughter to replace her.

Crude birth rates (the number of births in any given year divided by the total population) have been decreasing in the United States and other developed countries for decades, ever since reliable contracep-

tive measures became available. For example, the U.S. crude birth rate was 30.1 percent in 1900 but only 18.0 in 1980, 16.3 in 1990, and 14.1 in 2001. These figures indicate that a great many couples are choosing to have smaller families, to remain childless, or are living longer postreproductively.

INFERTILITY

A man or a woman is said to be infertile if he or she has a reduced or impaired ability to conceive a child. Infertility must be distinguished from sterility, which is a complete inability to produce offspring. According to the World Health Organization, there are two forms of infertility. Primary infertility applies to couples unable to conceive a child after trying for a year. Approximately 71 percent of infertile couples fall into this category. The remaining 29 percent of couples are classified as having secondary infertility: they have conceived at least one child in the past but have not been able to conceive again after trying for a year.

Between 10 and 15 percent of couples are infertile. Therefore, for example, more than three million couples in Canada and the United States, 400,000 in Britain, and 100,000 in Australia and New Zealand have been unsuccessful in their attempts to conceive.

Older couples have more problems with infertility. Only one couple in 10 is infertile when the woman is between the ages of 25 and 34. However, when the woman is between the ages of 40 and 49, nearly 8 of every 10 couples are infertile.

Infertility affects slightly more women than men. Thirty-one percent of couples are infertile because of a problem on the woman's side; in 22 percent infertility is traceable to the man, and 22 percent of cases of infertility are associated with difficulties on the part of both partners. The remaining 25 percent of cases show no clear-cut cause.

Male infertility

The most common cause of infertility in men is the quantity and quality of sperm. Some men are unable to produce any sperm because the testes (male sex glands) are not functioning properly or because the sperm enter the bladder instead of the urethra (the tube that carries sperm from the testes to the penis). This latter condition is called retrograde ejaculation. Other men have a low sperm count (fewer than 20 million sperm per ml of semen), usually accompanied by reduced sperm motility.

When doctors suspect a man is infertile, they undertake a laboratory evaluation of his semen to determine the concentration, motility, shape, and viability of the sperm. The semen is also examined for signs of infection or other problems that may affect sperm production and function.

Sexually transmitted diseases, such as gonorrhea, may cause chronic infection of the genital tract if not treated properly. Such chronic infections often produce no obvious symptoms; they are detected only when large numbers of white blood cells are found in the semen.

A normal initial semen evaluation indicates that there is no problem with the sperm. An abnormal initial evaluation is suspicious but not conclusive. However, abnormal results from repeat semen evaluations performed at two- and four-week intervals confirm that the infertility is related to the sperm.

In addition to a semen evaluation, men have a standard physical examination of the external sex organs to detect varicocele or other conditions, such as a tumor, that may be responsible for infertility. Varicocele, a condition in which the veins surrounding the testes are distended and cause swelling, is a factor in nearly 30 percent of infertile men.

Sperm count and motility improve after surgical treatment of varicocele in nearly 66 percent of men. Between 30 and 40 percent of these men go on to impregnate their partners.

Other causes of male infertility have not responded as well to treatment. Various substances, including vitamins C and E, caffeine, testosterone, and antibiotics, have been given to men to try to improve their sperm count and motility. Fertility drugs that are given to women, such as clomiphene citrate (see the box on page 709), have also been given to men in the hope they would increase GnRH or testosterone and enhance sperm production. None has improved the quantity and quality of sperm or increased the probability of conception.

When the man is infertile, there is the option of donor artificial insemination: the use of sperm obtained from another man for insertion into the woman's cervical canal. The procedure is simple and painless and can be carried out in a physician's office. It results in pregnancy in approximately 51 percent of cases within a year.

Female infertility

Disorders of ovulation and damaged fallopian tubes are the most frequent causes of infertility in women. There are five major disorders of ovulation. First, the hypothalamus may fail to release enough GnRH to stimulate the pituitary gland: without the hormones produced by the pituitary, there is no stimulus to the ovaries to initiate ovulation. Second, the pituitary gland may fail to respond to GnRH, or it may release large quantities of the hormone prolactin, which inhibits ovarian function. Third, the ovaries may not respond to the pituitary hormones. This situation is normal after menopause, but during the child-bearing years, it is called premature ovarian failure. Fourth, the ovarian follicle may develop abnormally and interrupt the chain of hormone production needed to prepare the uterus to accept the fertilized egg. Fifth, the ovarian follicle may fail to release the egg.

The diagnosis of a disorder of ovulation is made on the basis of a thorough medical history, physical examination, and radiologic and laboratory tests. The physician explores in particular a woman's pattern of menstruation, use of contraceptives, and eating and exercise habits to identify a behavioral cause of lack of ovulation, such as an eating

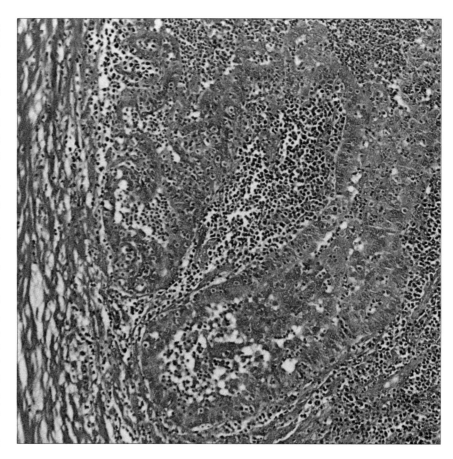

disorder or a physiological cause, for example, long-term strenuous exercise or a delayed return to ovulation, following use of the contraceptive pill.

The physical examination reviews the woman's overall health and the health of her reproductive organs. Ultrasound is often used to assess the condition of the ovaries, and a computerized tomography (CT) or a magnetic resonance imaging (MRI) scan of the skull is performed to screen for the presence of a pituitary tumor (which would interrupt the natural sequence of hormone production).

Female infertility is often caused by damaged fallopian tubes. This is a section from an infected fallopian tube. The walls of the tube are inflamed, and there is pus in the center.

EMBRYO TRANSPLANTATION

The embryo transfers that occur with in vitro fertilization must be distinguished from embryo transplantation, in which a donor is artificially inseminated with the sperm of the husband of an infertile couple. When pregnancy results, the embryo is washed out of the donor's uterus and transplanted into the uterus of the wife.

Many argue that embryo transplantation is the only option for some involuntarily childless women, such as those who have no ovaries or nonfunctional ones and postmenopausal women. However, there are many ethical and legal problems associated with the procedure. First, the washing out process may endanger the embryo. The procedure also may pose risks for the donor. As with any pregnancy, the fertilized egg may implant in the fallopian tube and thus result in a potentially life-threatening ectopic pregnancy, in which the egg implants elsewhere than in the uterus.

Because of these risks, critics of embryo transplantation contend that it may be unethical for infertile couples to endanger the lives of others in their bid to produce offspring. Also, payment for acting as a donor—reportedly available at some clinics—may be construed as baby selling, with legal and ethical implications not only for the donor but for the clinics and physicians involved.

SCIENCE AND SOCIETY

SURROGATE MOTHERHOOD

Women who cannot sustain a pregnancy, such as those who have no uterus, who have a genetic disease, or who have other health problems that preclude pregnancy, may seek the services of a surrogate mother. Surrogate mothers are inseminated with the sperm of the husband of an infertile woman, having agreed to carry the fetus and then turn over the baby to the couple after birth.

Surrogate mothers usually receive substantial payment, which, some critics argue, makes the practice a form of baby selling. However, the husband may claim that payments to the surrogate mother are made merely to support a woman he has impregnated or to secure adoption rights to the child.

U.S. laws do not recognize surrogacy arrangements. Nevertheless, many couples still make such arrangements, which raise several questions. Who takes responsibility for a deformed or mentally disabled infant? Who should pay for emergency medical treatment during the surrogacy period and after birth? What should happen if the surrogate mother endangers the life of the fetus? These complicated issues remain unresolved.

FSH and prolactin hormone levels are measured in the blood. Reduction of high prolactin levels using the drug bromocriptine may restore ovulation (see the box on page 709). A normal level of FSH suggests the need for the progesterone challenge test, which determines whether the uterus will respond to female sex hormones. During the test, a woman takes a synthetic progesterone tablet twice a day for five days. If she begins menstruating within four days after the test, her ovulation disorder will likely respond to treatment with a fertility drug.

A high level of FSH in several repeat blood tests points to premature ovarian failure, the most effective solution being in vitro fertilization (IVF), using the semen of the woman's partner and ova from a donor (see the box on page 710). IVF techniques have helped approximately 50 percent of women with ovarian failure to become pregnant.

Damage to the fallopian tubes is usually the result of infection in the reproductive organs, such as pelvic inflammatory disease, a leading cause of infertility. Infection may injure the interior of the fallopian tube to such an extent that the tube becomes completely blocked. Infection may attack the cells that line the interior of the tube and inhibit their normal function, or it may produce fibrous growths on the exterior surface of the tube that pinch or close the interior channel.

Dysfunction of the fallopian tubes usually cannot be detected during physical examination. The diagnosis requires X-ray pictures or direct examination of the tubes through an instrument inserted into the abdomen. Surgical procedures to correct tube damage have varying degrees of success. Removing the fibrous growths from the exterior of the tube allows 40 percent of women to achieve pregnancy within three years. Surgery to replace a blocked section of tube leads to pregnancy in only 15 to 20 percent within three years.

In vitro fertilization gives women a better chance to become pregnant, ranging from 9 percent to 19 percent per treatment. However, treatment for infertility can be expensive and emotionally taxing. Some couples may spend as long as two years repeatedly trying to conceive, without success.

K. SANDRICK

See also: ADOLESCENCE; MENSTRUAL CYCLE; PREGNANCY AND BIRTH; REPRODUCTION; REPRODUCTIVE SYSTEMS; SELECTIVE BREEDING.

Further reading:
Aronson, D., D. Clapp, and M. Hollister. 2001. *Resolving Infertility*. New York: Harper Resource.
McGuirk, J., and M. Elizabeth. 1991. *For Want of a Child. A Psychologist and His Wife Explore the Emotional Effects and Challenges of Infertility*. New York: Continuum Publishing Company.
Peoples, D., and H. Ferguson. 2000. *Experiencing Infertility*. New York: W. W. Norton
Steidle, C., and J. Mulcahy. 1999. *Impotence Sourcebook*. New York: McGraw Hill.

ANIMAL INFERTILITY

As in people, infertility in animals may have behavioral and physiological causes. Female pandas kept in zoos, for example, may reject the advances of male pandas, and males may be inept at courting females. In addition, estrus occurs only once a year in pandas, and the female may be fertile for only 12 hours, yet the male can take 24 hours to recover his sperm count following a mating attempt; the timing of mating is obviously crucial.

Such infertility problems in captive animals are often tackled by using artificial insemination. In most species, the sperm must be preserved until needed, usually by freezing, and it is essential to ensure that the female is ovulating when the semen is introduced. In vitro fertilization avoids this problem, and sometimes surrogate mothers (of a related but different species) are also used.

Przewalski's horse (Equus przewalski) became extinct in the wild, but conservationists preserved the species using techniques such as artificial insemination and other techniques in a captive breeding program.

FERTILIZATION

Fertilization, in both animals and plants, is the sexual union of a male sperm with a female egg

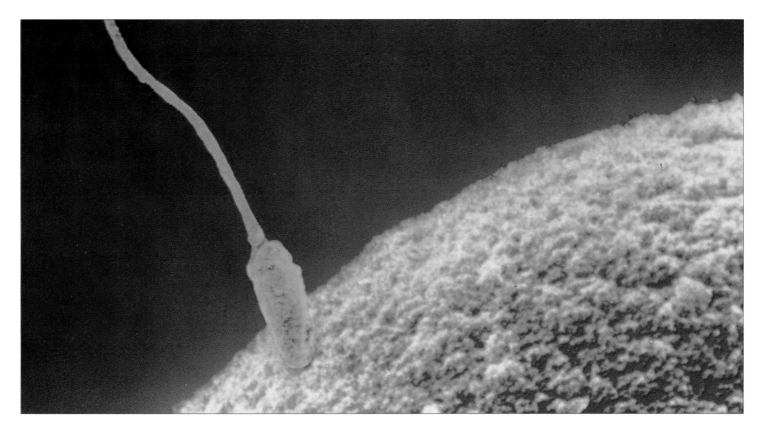

The most complex living organisms are produced by sexual reproduction. The key moment of sexual reproduction is fertilization, the meeting of the reproductive cells of two different parents. Sexual reproduction combines hereditary characteristics (genes) contributed by both parents.

Fertilization in heterogamous organisms (those having unlike gametes) involves two interconnected stages: activation of a female reproductive cell (gamete, or germ cell) called the ovum, or egg, and fusion of the female gamete with a male gamete (a spermatozoon, or sperm). Each gamete is haploid (containing half the normal number of chromosomes) and fusion results in a zygote, which is diploid (with a full complement of chromosomes).

ANIMAL FERTILIZATION

All animal sexual reproductive systems require the male sperm to swim to the female egg, and therefore

---

CORE FACTS

- Fertilization is the fusion of male and female gametes (reproductive cells) in both animals and plants.
- In animals the sperm is the male gamete and the egg is the female gamete.
- Animal fertilization may be internal or external.
- Plant fertilization may involve freely moving male and female gametes, a stationary female gamete and a motile male gamete, or stationary male and female gametes.

---

fluid must be available. Aquatic animals, such as sea urchins and most fish, shed their sperm and eggs directly into water. An egg that is ready for fertilization releases chemicals to attract sperm.

Among terrestrial animals, structural and chemical processes of fertilization vary as much as the forms of the animals themselves. However, they are generally designed to protect gametes by means of internal fertilization. The sperm travel in a fluid manufactured by the male reproductive organs, and secretions in the female tract provide further fluid.

In internal fertilization, sperm are introduced into the female reproductive tract by an organ specially adapted for insertion. This organ may be a penis—or even a modified arm, as in marine animals such as squid and octopuses (cephalopods). The egg is generally large and immobile, containing stores (the yolk) to sustain the early embryo, as well as genetic information from the mother (in the nucleus). The sperm is smaller and mobile. It contributes genes from the father and gives the signal to the egg to start development.

When the sperm reaches the egg, its approach is barred by a thick, elastic, gel-like coat called the zona pellucida. Contact with this gel causes a small bladderlike structure (called the acrosome) in the sperm head to rupture. The burst acrosome releases lysins (enzymes) that digest a hole through the outer layers of the egg. When the sperm head is about halfway through the outer layers, tiny projections called microvilli form at the base of the acrosome

A colored scanning electron microscope photograph of a human sperm (colored blue) penetrating the much larger human egg (colored pink) during fertilization.

CONNECTIONS

● The alternative to sexual **REPRODUCTION** is asexual reproduction, in which an exact replica of the parent is produced, with an identical **GENETIC** makeup.

● The transfer of male pollen from an anther to the stigma in **ANGIOSPERMS** or from the micro-sporangium to the micropyle in **GYMNOSPERMS** is called **POLLINATION**.

in the sperm. The sperm and egg microvilli fuse, and the sperm and egg plasma membranes become continuous. In many animals, including humans, the egg has not completed the final stage of meiosis before contacting the sperm. Sperm then triggers the egg to complete meiosis before the fusion of male and female nuclei (see CELL BIOLOGY).

In most animal species, penetration of an egg by more than one sperm would be fatal to an embryo. The egg prevents penetration by additional sperm in two ways. First, the egg's plasma membrane changes its electrical charge. Usually the egg has a negative charge compared with the surrounding fluid, but after fertilization it becomes positively charged. This change prevents other sperm cells from fusing with the already-fertilized egg. Granules called cortical granules, which lie just under the egg's vitelline layer (a second protective layer), release enzymes. The enzymes toughen the jelly coat and lift it away from the egg membrane.

After the sperm and egg plasma membranes have fused, the sperm nucleus loses its membrane. Proteins holding the sperm chromosomes are exchanged for proteins from the egg, and a new nuclear membrane forms around the sperm chromosomes. The new formation rotates 180 degrees and migrates toward the interior of the egg. When the sperm and the egg nuclei meet, the membranes fuse to form a new diploid nucleus. In sea urchins this process takes about an hour. In mammals the nuclear membranes break down rather than fuse, and this process takes up to 12 hours.

Fertilization cannot take place unless reproductive activities precede it. The readiness of female mammals to mate (with the exception of humans and some primates) is dictated by what is called the estrus cycle. Most female mammals will mate with males only at the time of estrus, when ovulation occurs. Depending on the mammal, estrus may last anywhere from a few hours to several days. It may occur once or several times during a breeding period. Most females ovulate (shed their one or more ova, or eggs, from the ovary) close to the end of estrus in a process controlled by hormones. If fertilization takes place and is successful, pregnancy occurs.

Human fertilization

Human male sperm is manufactured in the testes at a rate of 50,000 per minute every day until the male reaches his 70s or beyond. The process begins with growth and then division of a spermatogonium, a primitive male germ cell. Male germ cells are present in the testes and are the biological ancestors of sperm cells. This mitotic division results in two primary spermatocytes, which then

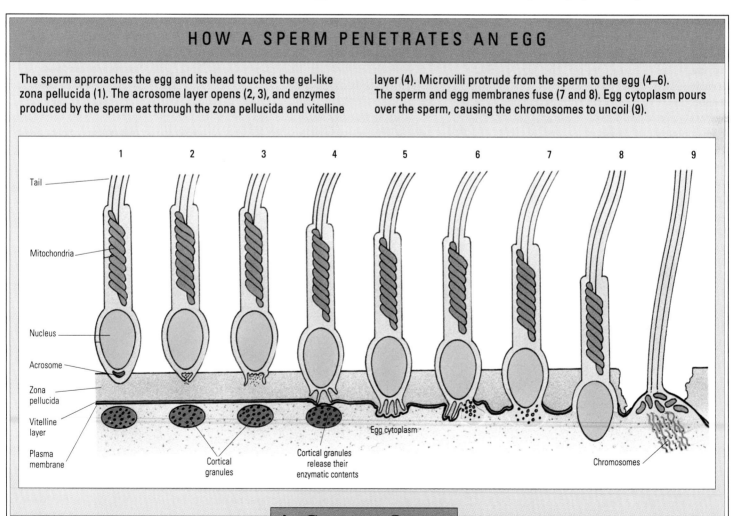

HOW A SPERM PENETRATES AN EGG

The sperm approaches the egg and its head touches the gel-like zona pellucida (1). The acrosome layer opens (2, 3), and enzymes produced by the sperm eat through the zona pellucida and vitelline layer (4). Microvilli protrude from the sperm to the egg (4–6). The sperm and egg membranes fuse (7 and 8). Egg cytoplasm pours over the sperm, causing the chromosomes to uncoil (9).

Tail
Mitochondria
Nucleus
Acrosome
Zona pellucida
Vitelline layer
Plasma membrane
Cortical granules
Cortical granules release their enzymatic contents
Egg cytoplasm
Chromosomes

A CLOSER LOOK

undergo meiosis I to become two secondary spermatocytes, which give rise to sperm cells (see CELL BIOLOGY; REPRODUCTION).

When the secondary spermatocytes become spermatids, in the second meiotic division (meiosis II), they halve the number of chromosomes that would normally be found in somatic (body) cells. Each spermatid has 23 chromosomes instead of the full complement of 46 (23 pairs). These spermatids mature into sperm, capable of fertilizing an ovum. Both the ovum and sperm must be haploid, so fertilization and subsequent fusion of the nuclei produces a zygote with the full set of 46 chromosomes.

A human female is born with between 700,000 and 2 million egg cells in her ovaries. Only 200 to 300 of these eggs will ever reach maturity. The pituitary gland at the base of the human female brain periodically releases hormones to stimulate the ovaries and other organs. In the process called ovulation, occurring about once every 28 days, an ovary usually releases a single ovum.

If the egg and the sperm do not meet quickly, they die. Although the egg can survive for 24 hours, the optimum time for fertilization after ovulation is six to eight hours. In the favorable environment of the fallopian tube, sperm can survive for about 48 hours, awaiting the arrival of an egg to fertilize.

Human fertilization is a complex event. A human female ovulates more or less regularly, except during pregnancy, for approximately 30 years, but even when no measures are taken to prevent pregnancy, few women produce anything approaching 30 babies. The female cycle's intricately timed reproductive sequence can be disrupted easily. Breastfeeding, for example, interferes with the production of ova.

In human females, one of the few clues that ovulation has taken place is a slight change in the woman's temperature. In the females of most other mammal species, the signs of estrus are much more obvious, sometimes by swellings of the sexual organs, sometimes by the secretion of scents. However, because ovulation in humans is difficult to detect, the chance of a successful fertilization from a single mating is not high, and irregular menstrual cycles make estimation of a fertile period even more difficult (see MENSTRUAL CYCLE).

PLANT FERTILIZATION

Vegetative or asexual reproduction (production of offspring from a cutting or by budding) is common in some species of plants. This process is quite different from sexual reproduction, which involves gamete fusion and nuclear fusion (fertilization). Haploid male and female plant gametes must meet, much as gametes must fuse in animals. The gamete cell membranes fuse and form a single cell. The nuclear membranes then fuse, the result being a single diploid cell with a diploid nucleus.

The male and female cells of different groups of plants are produced in a wide variety of ways, and their methods of fertilization are equally

diverse. They reflect three periods of plant evolution. It is thought that the first period, over 400 million years ago, began with the adaptation to land of a species of green algae. Two groups of plants then evolved, nonvascular plants, or bryophytes (appearing in the fossil record about 350 million years ago), and the vascular plants, which developed a little earlier. Bryophytes, such as mosses, differ from vascular plants in that they do not have tubes, called the xylem and the phloem (the vascular system), to distribute water and nutrients around the plant.

A second major period of plant evolution, about 360 million years ago, began with the development of the seed in vascular plants. Seed production allows the young plant to remain dormant and protected until conditions are favorable for growth: seed-bearing plants dominate today's flora. The third period, about 130 million years ago, saw the emergence of flowering plants.

Among plants that are more primitive, fertilization takes place between freely moving male and female cells. In somewhat more advanced plants, the female gamete remains stationary and partly enclosed by cells, while the male gamete is motile (capable of motion). In highly evolved plants, fertilization takes place between nonmotile gametes in the female's organ of reproduction.

Algae and bryophytes

Algae are a large group of photosynthetic organisms, in six groups. Three groups are almost entirely multicellular, while the others are almost all

A pair of common frogs (Rana temporaria) mating. The male clasps the female with his forelegs, and the sperm is deposited as the eggs are laid. This is an example of external fertilization.

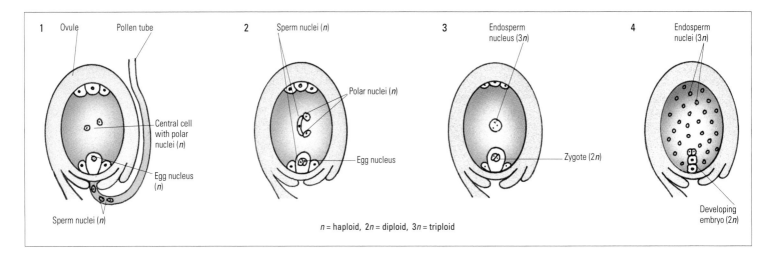

1 Ovule · Pollen tube · Central cell with polar nuclei (*n*) · Egg nucleus (*n*) · Sperm nuclei (*n*)

2 Sperm nuclei (*n*) · Polar nuclei (*n*) · Egg nucleus

3 Endosperm nucleus (3*n*) · Zygote (2*n*)

4 Endosperm nuclei (3*n*) · Developing embryo (2*n*)

n = haploid, 2*n* = diploid, 3*n* = triploid

Double fertilization in flowering plants. The pollen tube enters the micropyle, or the opening of the ovule (1). One sperm cell fuses with the egg cell to form the zygote, while the other fuses with the central cell to form the endosperm, or nutritive tissue (2 and 3). The zygote develops into the embryo, while the endosperm forms the food store (4).

unicellular. Most unicellular algae reproduce asexually. In multicellular algae that reproduce sexually, there are large differences in the gametes. In some algae, the cells of the two different mating types are identical in size and structure. These plants are termed isogamous. Other species have larger female gametes or immobile female gametes (see ALGAE).

All plants in the bryophyte group (liverworts and mosses) have a large and immobile female gamete and heteromorphic alternation of generations, in which the haploid and diploid forms of the plant look very different. In bryophytes the gametophyte is the dominant and conspicuous generation, unlike vascular plants, where the sporophyte is the dominant stage (see FERNS AND FERN ALLIES).

Seed plants

The evolution of seed is the most successful mechanism for the reproduction of plants that has evolved so far. Rather than developing in the soil as an independent generation, seed-plant gametophytes are protected inside the moist reproductive tissue of the sporophyte generation, and the zygote is packaged with a food supply into a seed coat.

The plant develops two types of spores (small reproductive bodies): the megaspore, which becomes the female gametophyte, and the microspore. The female gametophyte develops within a structure called the ovule, which eventually matures to form the seed. The male gametophyte develops in the anther and is made up of the microspore and a pollen tube. When the male gametophyte produces sperm, they travel through the tube, and fertilization takes place.

Gymnosperms (seed ferns and conifers)

Gymnosperms do not have enclosed chambers in which seeds develop. For example, in pines the male and female sporangia are borne on different cones (see CONIFERS). A male, or microsporangiate, cone produces many haploid microspores. The microspore develops into a winged pollen grain. Released pollen grains are carried by the wind to female, or megasporangiate, cones. The grains become trapped in a droplet of sticky liquid at the micropyle (the opening to the ovule). The droplet evaporates, pulling the pollen grain into the ovule, where it produces a tube (the true male gametophyte), which grows down into and fertilizes the ovule (see GYMNOSPERMS).

Angiosperms

The word *angiosperm* comes from the Greek words *angios*, which means "capsule," and *sperma*, which means "seed." The male gametophyte consists of three cells, two sperm cells and a vegetative (related to growth or nutrition) cell. In most flowering plants, the female gametophyte is made up of seven cells embedded within the ovary of the carpel (the seed-bearing organ). The carpel includes the ovary, the stigma (the apex on which pollen—the mature gametophyte—is deposited), and the style (the slender stalk between the ovary and the stigma). When a pollen grain is deposited on the stigma of a compatible carpel, the pollen extrudes a tube, which grows down into the style.

The pollen tube grows down to the ovary. Following entry, the pollen tube deposits its contents. One sperm cell fuses with the egg cell, and the second fuses with the central cell, which has two haploid nuclei.

In flowering plants, the fusion product of the haploid egg with the haploid sperm gives rise to the embryo in the seed. The fusion of the second sperm with the two haploid nuclei of the central cell gives rise to a triploid cell (with three sets of chromosomes) that forms the nutritive tissue (or endosperm) of the seed. The endosperm develops within the embryo sac.

M. DICANIO

See also: ALGAE; CELL BIOLOGY; CONIFERS; EMBRYO; FERNS AND FERN ALLIES; FERTILITY; HERMAPHRODITES; MENSTRUAL CYCLE; PLANT KINGDOM; PREGNANCY AND BIRTH; SEEDS AND SEED DISPERSAL.

Further reading:

Gilbert, S. 2000. *Developmental Biology*. Sunderland, U.K.: Sinauer Associates.
Wolpert, L., R. Beddington, J. Brockes, T. Jessell, P. Lawrence, and E. Meyerowitz. 1998. *Principles of Development*. Oxford: Oxford University Press.

FERTILIZERS

Fertilizers are supplements for plants, providing the specific nutrients needed to keep plants healthy

Just as people would soon become sick if they did not eat properly, so plants need the right nutrients for healthy growth. Fertilizers are extra nutrients for plants, which are added, usually for agricultural purposes, to those nutrients that already exist naturally in the soil.

Each plant needs 16 vital elements to be healthy. Hydrogen, carbon, and oxygen are obtained directly from air and water. The remaining nutrients are obtained from the soil—namely, nitrogen, phosphorus, potassium (the primary macronutrients); calcium, magnesium, sulfur (the secondary macronutrients); boron, chlorine, copper, iron, manganese, molybdenum, and zinc (the micronutrients, or trace elements).

The elements nitrogen, phosphorus, and potassium are needed in large quantities by all plants. They are the base of most fertilizers because they are the most critical nutrients, and vital for plant life but are often at relatively low levels in the soil. By adding these minerals in the form of fertilizers, any soil deficiency is alleviated, and plant growth is therefore optimized.

Plant nutrients are returned to the soil through natural processes. Depletion occurs when these processes are interrupted by erosion, leaching (where the soil constituents dissolve and are washed away), and plant harvesting.

Historical aspects

In some areas, the mechanism of replacing nutrients lost to agriculture is natural. Flooding in river valleys, such as the Nile in Egypt and the Mississippi in the United States, used to replenish farmlands with layers of silt. However, modern dams and levees have reduced flooding, and other methods of nutrient replacement must now be used.

The use of fertilizers goes back many centuries: canals carried sewage to the olive groves and vegetable gardens in ancient Athens. However, commercial fertilizers have been available only since the mid-19th century. Production increased after

World War II (1939–1945), when more crops were needed. Several factories in the United States that had produced nitrogen compounds for war munitions switched to making nitrogen-based fertilizers.

Fertilizer manufacture

Air, which is about 80 percent nitrogen, is the primary source of raw material for nitrogen fertilizer manufacture. Most factories are powered by natural gas, a hydrogen-carbon compound that also supplies hydrogen for ammonia. Ammonia is the poisonous, gaseous, nitrogen-hydrogen compound that is the basic building block of most nitrogen fertilizers.

Phosphoric rock is the primary source of phosphorus. Deposits in Idaho, Florida, Montana, North Carolina, Tennessee, and Wyoming make up about 30 percent of the world's known reserves; about 50 percent are in North Africa. Although some potassium is obtained from natural sources of brine (such as the Great Salt Lake in Utah and the Dead Sea in Israel and Jordan), most commercial supplies come from potash ore (potassium carbonate).

The high yields of modern agriculture are possible only because of the effective use of fertilizers.

CORE FACTS

- Sixteen plant nutrients are essential for healthy plant growth.
- Three elements—nitrogen, phosphorus, and potassium (the primary macronutrients)—are needed in relatively large quantities. They are the most critical nutrients and the ones most often at agriculturally low levels in soil. Therefore, they are the basis for most fertilizers.
- Air, about 80 percent nitrogen, is the primary source of raw material for modern nitrogen fertilizer manufacture.
- Organic and inorganic fertilizers can cause environmental problems, such as destruction of the ozone layer.

CONNECTIONS

● Fertilizers are used extensively in **AGRICULTURE** to increase crop yields.

● Animal and plant pests destroy around 50 percent of the world's agricultural produce. **BIOLOGICAL CONTROL** kills such pests using natural biological methods.

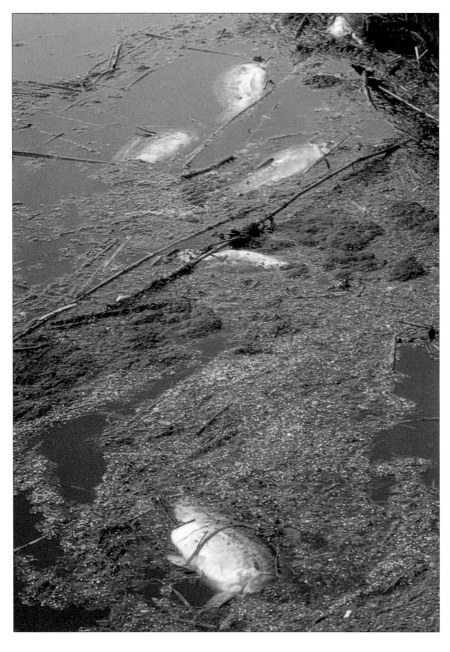

of inorganic and organic fertilizers. Emissions of nitric acid and sulfur dioxide from industrial plants where fertilizers are made cause acid rain, while nitrous oxide, an ozone-depleting gas, can be produced when ammonia-based nitrogen fertilizers are applied to the soil. Nitrogen and phosphorus are the elements most often linked to environmental problems from agricultural fertilizers. Soluble nitrogen can reach the water supply when it washes out of the soil. Fertilizer nitrogen is often in the form of nitrates, which can be a health hazard when highly concentrated in water. In people nitrates are transformed into nitrites, which reduce the capacity of hemoglobin in the blood to carry oxygen. Nitrites are also carcinogenic.

Organic fertilizers (of plant or animal origin) can also create problems. Animal waste produces less than 20 percent of the nitrogen fertilizer used in the United States and yet accounts for a larger percentage of nitrogen released into the environment. Replacing other nitrogen fertilizers with animal waste would increase the number of animals and the acreage of forage crops and reduce the amount of land available for food production. Animal waste is also harder to store and transport, loses nitrogen faster than inorganic fertilizer, and poses health risks because of the bacteria it contains.

Ancient techniques and modern science

Agricultural researchers combine the most ancient techniques of returning nutrients to the soil with the most modern of scientific methods. These studies focus on: increasing the use of animal waste and sewage sludge; planting a wider variety of crops; using cultivation, planting time, and labor as substitutes for pesticides; and increasing use of green manure. Green manure is a cover crop tilled back into the soil to increase the soil's organic component and nutrients. Legumes (family Leguminosae or Fabaceae) such as alfalfa (*Medicago sativa*) are particularly valuable because they can "fix," or utilize, atmospheric nitrogen. Bacteria growing in nodules on the roots of legumes convert nitrogen in the air to a form usable by the plant.

Organic fertilizers and farming methods, including crop rotation, biological diversity, and the use of beneficial insects (see BIOLOGICAL CONTROL), are intended to reduce the use of petroleum-based chemical fertilizers, pesticides, and herbicides. Farmers have already reduced their use of fertilizers because of environmental and economic concerns.

J. RHODES

See also: NITROGEN CYCLE; PESTICIDES.

Dead fish in a polluted river. Fertilizers (especially those consisting of nitrogen or phosphorus compounds) can leach from the land and enter nearby water sources. If they are allowed to build up, fertilizers can have disastrous consequences for the aquatic ecosystems.

Preventing food shortages

Led by the U.S. Department of Agriculture and the United Nations Food and Agriculture Organization (FAO), the Green Revolution was a global effort in the late 1960s to avoid food shortages. New, high-yielding, genetically improved varieties of wheat (*Triticum* spp.), corn (*Zea mays*), sorghum (*Sorghum bicolor*), and rice (*Oryza sativa*) adapted to growing in developing countries, combined with better farming techniques and increased use of machinery, pesticides, herbicides, and fertilizers, dramatically increased agricultural production. According to the FAO, fertilizer was probably the single most important factor in increasing yields.

This revolution has barely kept pace with population growth, however. Nearly 90 million people are added to the world's population every year, most in the developing countries.

Fertilizers and the environment

Whenever people intervene in nature, things can go wrong. Such is the case with agriculture and the use

Further reading:
Benjamin, Joan. 2000. *Great Garden Formulas: The Ultimate Book of Mix-It-Yourself Concoctions for Your Garden*. Emmaus, Pa.: Rodale Press.
Laegreid, M., et al. 2000. *Agriculture, Fertilizers, and the Environment*. New York: Oxford University Press.

INDEX

Headings and page numbers in **bold** refer to main articles. Page numbers in *italics* refer to photographs and illustrations or their captions.